PENGUIN HANDBOOKS

YOUR WEDDING

Yetta Fisher Gruen works for the *Washington Post* at the Bridal Desk. The Bridal page, which appears each Wednesday in the Style section and has a large reader interest, prompted the public to telephone questions to her about wedding etiquette. Fascinated by the types of queries, Mrs. Gruen realized that some questions were a lot more serious or deeper than they appeared to be on the surface and that a book was needed on the subject. Her expertise comes from research, from talking to people about their experiences, and from her instinct about voices on the telephone. Born and educated in England, Mrs. Gruen lives in Rockville, Maryland, with her husband. They have two sons and a daughter-in-law.

Your Wedding

Making It Perfect

Yetta Fisher Gruen

PENGUIN BOOKS

PENGUIN BOOKS
Viking Penguin Inc., 40 West 23rd Street,
New York, New York 10010, U.S.A.
Penguin Books Ltd, Harmondsworth,
Middlesex, England
Penguin Books Australia Ltd, Ringwood,
Victoria, Australia
Penguin Books Canada Limited, 2801 John Street,
Markham, Ontario, Canada L3R 1B4
Penguin Books (N.Z.) Ltd, 182–190 Wairau Road,
Auckland 10, New Zealand

First published in Penguin Books 1986
Published simultaneously in Canada

Copyright © Yetta Fisher Gruen, 1986
Illustrations copyright © Viking Penguin Inc., 1986
All rights reserved

LIBRARY OF CONGRESS CATALOGING IN PUBLICATION DATA
Gruen, Yetta Fisher.
Your wedding.
Includes index.
1. Weddings—United States—Planning.   2. Marriage
service—United States.   I. Title.
HQ745.G78   1986   395'.22   86-9475
ISBN 0 14 046.755 6

Illustrations by Mena Dolobowsky
Design by Ann Gold

Printed in the United States of America by
R. R. Donnelley & Sons Company, Harrisonburg, Virginia
Set in Sabon

TO MY HUSBAND, BERTRAM

AUTHOR'S NOTE

For a short period in the late 1960s and early 1970s, etiquette and tradition were supposedly being tossed in a "new wave" of doing your own thing. Since friends and relatives didn't hurry from the premises, it seemed everything was all right. Ah, free at last! But to most people freedom still meant a responsibility to tradition and good taste.

Questions on wedding etiquette began to increase over my fourteen years at the Bridal Desk of the *Washington Post* and have been coming in on a steady basis. My research on old and new books in this field was of immeasurable help. What a comfort to be able to read Amy Vanderbilt, Emily Post, and Oretha D. Swartz's *Service Etiquette,* along with numerous magazines and wedding advice books, and to find most in agreement. I am glad to have had these sources to draw on and adapt to the particular questions, not only from those planning a wedding but from those going to a wedding and from musicians and photographers, that came across the Bridal Desk.

ACKNOWLEDGMENTS

To my husband, Bertram, for confidence in my ability to write this book, and for his extensive research and his patience in reading the manuscript so many times; to my son Mark Howard Gruen, for teaching me the word processor, being my early editor, and giving me the input I needed in his specialty—music; to my son Dr. Richard Alan Gruen—a physician and history buff— whose suggestions were invaluable, and to his wife, Ruth Jakubowski, for her loving support.

To Kathryn Court, editor in chief, and Dawn Seferian, editor, at Viking Penguin Inc., and to Mr. Ronald Goldfarb, lawyer and literary agent.

How does one value friendship and what does one say in appreciation? To Scotte Manns, Director of Advertising at the *Washington Post,* for her encouragement over the years; to Elsie Selman, for her interest and suggestions; and to other friends, whose support was beyond the call of duty and common sense.

To Richard Harwood, Deputy Managing Editor at the *Washington Post,* for accepting my first short stories to be published, which appeared in the *Washington Post* magazine section; Mrs. Jane Irvin of the Washington Cathedral, Episcopal, in Washington, D.C.; the Reverend Doctor Arnold F. Keller of the Church of the Reformation, Lutheran, on Capitol Hill in Washington, D.C.; Mr. William Samuel of the Adelphi Friends Meeting, Quaker, in Adelphi, Maryland; Beverly Campbell of the Church of Jesus Christ of Latter-day Saints, Mormon; Mrs. Aileen Sox, assistant editor of the *Adventist Review,* the publication of the Seventh-day Adventist Church; the Reverend Father Hughes of St. Mary's Catholic Church in Rockville, Maryland; Father George of St. George's Eastern Orthodox Church in Bethesda, Maryland; Rabbi Tzvi H. Porath, Rabbi Emeritus of Ohr Kodesh Congregation,

Conservative, in Chevy Chase, Maryland; and Rabbi Joshua Haberman of the Washington Hebrew Congregation, Reform, in Washington, D.C.

Among other countless books, source material was found in the *Encyclopaedia Britannica;* and in the Library of Congress (where I studied while trying not to spend most of my time admiring its magnificent architecture).

I also wish to acknowledge a debt of gratitude to all those who asked me all those questions all those years.

Contents

Introduction

"Feelings, feelings, nothing but feelings" can turn into questions, questions, nothing but questions when planning a wedding. Knowing how traditions are passed from one generation to another is one thing; puzzling out the intricacies of getting together two families who have nothing in common except that their children are in love often needs a great deal of understanding on both sides, even though there is no objection to the match.

Some questions combine those of protocol and of human relationships; other queries concern straightforward wedding etiquette. To successfully navigate the maze, one must separate protocol and etiquette from tangled family situations. The answers can insure a happy wedding day as well as a strong family foundation on both sides.

Your Wedding evolved from the many questions asked of me from the inception of the *Washington Post*'s Bridal Desk. It became apparent that the public needed a book that takes an in-depth look at the whole wedding process from all sides: the bride's point of view; the bridegroom's; both of their families'; guests'; and services'. Because wedding etiquette is not set in concrete and these "rules" change as society evolves, discussing questions can help the reader to make decisions to suit his or her particular needs.

Knowing what is generally done helps us make choices based on knowledge rather than desperation. Knowing what others have experienced helps us understand the process of decision-making. After all, how many weddings does a family sponsor in a lifetime? How many functions larger than a dinner or a cocktail party have any of us planned . . . to say nothing of the emotional aspect—the actions, reactions, and counterreactions within families?

What is relatively easy is the gathering of the services, such as those of a caterer, photographer, and engraver, needed for a successful event. What is more difficult is the complexity of human relations, which can be hard to fathom. Even families who have known each other for years can become sensitive about decisions regarding their children's marriage. The bride's family may be waiting for his parents to offer to pay part of the wedding expenses but the bridegroom's parents do not see it that way. Perhaps the expenses are being split down the middle, giving both sides the chance to have an equal say.

There are times when I have been asked a question and I sense there is more to the story than the query indicates. I cite the simple etiquette question below—though it is used elsewhere in this book in a simpler context—as an example of etiquette's more complicated aspects:

Q: *Is it obligatory to attend a church ceremony when invited only to the church and not to the wedding reception?*

Accepting or declining an invitation to attend any event is up to the individual. Who asks if he *has* to go to any function? The phrasing of this query suggested to me that it was a surface one. An invitation to the church ceremony carries no pressure; not even a reply is expected. The answer to that question is found in various wedding books. But the second layer revealed a dilemma.

Suppose it is asked by an employer? The bridegroom has worked for him for the past fifteen years, and apparently the employer finds the young man an asset. Mr. and Mrs. Employer have even entertained the young couple in their home. Yet when the invitation arrived they were surprised to find they were only invited to the ceremony. They were in a quandary and really did not want to attend.

Careful thought should have gone into the decision to invite Mr. and Mrs. Employer to the ceremony only. Though it sometimes can't be helped, I have uncomfortable feelings about inviting some guests to the ceremony only and not to the reception—which I discuss elsewhere in this book. What bothers me most about this situation, however, is that the bridegroom did not question a decision that would more than likely hurt his employer's feelings. When he was asked about it the bridegroom responded, "I have nothing to do with it. 'They' are arranging the whole thing." By disclaiming any involvement he sets a bad precedent, which doesn't augur well for the health of his relationship with his wife. What is he saying? She'll make the mistakes in this family; he will have nothing to do with it so it will be her fault if plans go awry! It was *his* employer and wife who were put in an awkward position. Not only does the young man make a living working for that firm but perhaps his employer was keeping him in mind for promotion.

Someone should have pointed out to the young man that an inaction is an action in itself and that silence is taken as acquiescence. He didn't say to his bride that it was not a good idea to invite Mr. and Mrs. Employer to the ceremony but not to the reception. It would have been different if there had been no reception, which was not the case. There must have been another alternative.

Perhaps the reception site was too small to accommodate the guest list, which suggests poor planning. I doubt the reason given to me would have mollified anyone. It had been suggested to Mr. Employer that the bride, in order to reap lots of gifts, invited a church full of guests but only the bridal party and the couple's family were invited to the reception.

The way decisions are carried out is the key to good relationships. Some parents are take-charge types; they evaluate what they can or can't do and go on from that point. Others agonize that they simply can't meet the needs or expectations of others. They feel the happiness of their child hinges on the upcoming events and cannot forget that they are dealing with strangers—their child's future in-laws.

As for the wedding itself, when one is considering a change in a traditional wedding ceremony, the determining factors should be: does the change have to do with religious rites? If it does, permission has to be obtained from the clergy. The next question is: will the change offend? In other words, is the procedure just a mite different from what is generally done, and is it in good taste?

However, there is broad leeway when arrranging the other elements. In today's world it is needed. To tell a divorcée she cannot be married in the manner of a bride is one thing, but advising that she should not overdo the wedding bit is another. Though it may not be intended, the feeling conveyed by some of the do's and don'ts of wedding etiquette seems unfair to widows and divorcées—a leftover attitude of history toward such women. In Western society the attitude mainly took the form of mild disdain toward divorcées while widows were expected to behave quietly, but in some sects in India, for example, a widow was expected to throw herself on her deceased husband's funeral pyre. Now the first-time bridegroom is told that he cannot have a wedding celebrating his first and only marriage because his bride has been married before. But that is also changing.

To me these changes are minor. The major, time-honored conventions of weddings remain the same. Most cultures recognize that marriage is the most important step a man and a woman can take and that society benefits from the solid structure that the union brings: the umbrella of protection it brings to children and the continuity it has with the past. Nothing I have read convinces me that there has been a successful substitute.

Whether the marriage is conducted by a justice of the peace or by a clergyman, the components are the same: the hopeful promises, the company in attendance, and the feting that follows. The world may not celebrate the event but the immediate circle of the bride and bridegroom does. From that group comes a sense of security that most couples experience when they decide to marry.

Engagement

The Promise

The engagement period is a special time. Everything seems so right. The impermanence of dating and the uncertainty that one or the other may have felt before making the commitment have been overcome. The engaged couple feel the excitement and see their friends' and familys' happiness when they learn the news. Even if the couple have been living together, the prospect of exchanging vows still generates a special kind of excitement.

This delicate time is a balance of pleasure and pressure. Family, friends, and acquaintances can be nonchalant about the couple while they're dating but when the words "We're going to be married" are announced, everyone takes their place in the formalities—like chess pieces at the start of the game.

Though people sometimes marry their first love, the choices are their own and freely made, which was not so in the past in Europe. Apparently, parental choice is still the system in Eastern cultures. The phrase "Love comes later" has been echoed for centuries from one generation to another. In India the selection of a mate is made not by the young couple but by both sets of parents. Preferably the choice is from the same sect and even from the same region. Children, in some cases, might not have seen each other until the betrothal party or at the gathering where the girl's parents negotiated the dowry to satisfy the young man's family—a commitment that might take her people years to pay.

Couples here expect to live under their own roof and build lives independently of parents, but in the land of the Taj Mahal the bride knows that she will more than likely live with her in-laws and be obedient to them, which can present difficulties.

I invite readers to compare ancient societies around the globe with America just entering its third century—so very, very young. Other cultures may raise their eyebrows at our outwardly freewheeling attitudes, just as we raise ours over their different or more rigid customs.

As a charming Indian woman, a professor at one of our Ivy League universities, told me: "Our system of marrying off our children works. Unlike in America, where the focus is on the individual, the whole family is of central importance to us, as well as the sect from which the family stems—all are reliant one on the other. When the bride comes to live with her in-laws, to whom her dowry belongs, she will find her husband's brothers, wives, and children under one roof. Our children," she added, "are not financially independent of their parents."

The professor asked if we were happier marrying for romantic love. How could I make comparisons, not knowing how successful arranged marriages were in India? Brought up in Western society I could not imagine being unable to choose whom I would marry. At the time of this discussion the divorce rate in this country was not encouraging, but what was hopeful was the increase in both first and second marriages.

Does love come later? I wondered. We both decided that the human condition was the same all over the world—it depended on how well one adjusted to the other. Romantic love, one hopes, deepens with maturity and combines with friendship; the greatest compliment one spouse can give another is to call him or her one's best friend.

How does this romantic love deepen with maturity?

From the moment the betrothal is announced the engaged couple start building their future. Now understanding each other truly begins. Not only do they plan the wedding but they have to decide where they will live and how they wish to spend their money. If both are established in their chosen professions and own homes, does one rent out and live in the other's house? Do they sell? Will it be necessary to draw up a premarital contract if either or both have children from a previous marriage?

A couple in their twenties, just starting out, have to select living quarters, decide how they will support themselves, and learn how to manage their incomes. The type of wedding, however, is generally a decision based on what parents can afford. In any case, the likelihood of families being acquainted before meeting their child's future in-laws is remote.

If we were in India, all this would be prescribed by custom and I would not be writing this book. Most of us do not realize that we have mixed marriages in America, not just on racial or religious grounds but in the cultural sense. For example, Catholics may marry Catholics but the ethnicity is different; a person of Italian descent might marry someone from an Irish, Polish, Spanish, or French background. An American and an Asian might be surprised, to the point of culture shock, at the extent to which they have to adjust not only to each other's foibles—as do most couples—but to the other's mores.

Most children in America no longer stay within family and neighborhood circles but travel all over the country to colleges or job opportunities. Unlike older societies, we are a conglomerate of backgrounds looking for guidelines, and nothing reveals this more clearly than courtship and the planning stages of a wedding.

When my son and his now wife decided to get married, they were young professionals. At that time she lived in Baltimore; he lived in Florida; her parents were in Syracuse and we were in the Washington, D.C., area. Her parents were on holiday in Florida when Ruth and my son flew down to visit them. Richard approached Ruth's father by saying: "I would like to be a member of your family." The warmth of the statement was touching. What was really happening was an attempt to establish a bond of respect.

Now the chess pieces are beginning to move . . . The newly betrothed and their parents telephone grandparents and close relatives to share the news with them directly since no one wants to hear it through the family rumor mill.

Before the bride's mother calls the newspaper to arrange for an announcement she waits for the young man's mother to get in touch with her; but suppose nothing happens. Her daughter assures her that all is well: his folks are delighted with the news. Her mother waits, since everyone knows that the bridegroom's mother contacts the bride's family to express her pleasure over the turn of events. After a while, the bride's mother telephones and finds a thrilled and excited future mother-in-law on the other end of the line saying how pleased she and her husband are and what a lovely daughter they have. Then the bride's mother suggests they all meet at her house next Friday. Now both families can think about future plans.

Could it be that the bridegroom's mother just wasn't sure how to proceed? That the difficulty was not lack of warmth but merely shyness? Or it might have seemed natural to her that she would hear from the bride's mother since it is customary for the bride's parents to handle all the arrangements.

Suppose, however, the mother of the bride decided that it was not her place to call her future son-in-law's parents—never mind the state of his mother's psyche. That could be the beginning of a precarious relationship. Being socially correct is not always the right thing. The first question below is a good case in point.

Q: *My son is engaged to a girl whose parents are divorced. Since it is up to the groom's family to get in touch with hers, which parent do I contact?*

The parent with whom the young lady lives. If your future daughter-in-law is not living with either, contact her mother first. Later, arrange to meet her father.

Q: *My husband is very hurt. A daughter from his first marriage has become engaged to a fine young man whom we have met many times. We hear that his family and the bride's mother have gotten together. Because the future groom's people have not made a move to contact us, I have debated whether to say something to my stepdaughter. What do you think?*

When you think enough time has gone by, tell your step-daughter how pleased you and her father would be to meet her future in-laws. Suggest that you would like them to come to dinner. Then pick up the telephone or write a note to them. You can't go wrong with a warm gesture of welcome, even though the meeting may not have happened the way you and your husband thought it would.

The relationship the bride has with her mother shouldn't prevent the loving one you and your husband have established with the engaged couple from continuing. There's plenty of room in their lives for all. But remember, everyone needs a little breathing space because touchy questions will pop up.

LADIES AND GENTLEMEN, even though divorce is not unusual, there are those who either haven't had much experience with broken marriages or have had too much. Whichever category they fall into, they may be unsure of the relationship between divorced partners and more than a little wary with a couple who might disagree with each other over these plans or with a couple who find it hard to agree on anything.

Q: *Who hosts the engagement party?*

Anyone who feels like it. It is generally given by the bride's parents and is a great way for the bridegoom's family to meet their future daughter-in-law's family. Often, if the bridegroom's family lives out of town, they give a separate welcoming celebration there for family and friends in honor of the betrothed. The bride's family should also be invited.

Q: *My daughter and her fiancé live far away. His parents reside equally far away but in the opposite direction. The logistics of getting together make it next to impossible for me to entertain them. I don't want to seem inhospitable but it is likely that we won't be meeting his parents until the wedding. Have you heard of such a situation?*

Don't be upset; you can always entertain them at a future date. It is not so unusual these days. Like a triangle stretched over the length of America, the children might be working or at college in the northwest, the bride's family on the eastern seaboard, and the bridegroom's family in the southwest.

LADIES AND GENTLEMEN, many people have told me that the first time they met their child's in-laws was at the wedding. On general principles they would have liked to meet the family into which their child was marrying before the wedding.

Q: *I'm not enthusiastic about formal entertaining or large crowds. My daughter's future in-laws have already hosted a lavish party for the engaged couple and my daughter wants me to reciprocate in kind. Do I have to match their efforts? Both my husband and I come from small families and have no experience in the niceties of "his family, her family."*

As in other decisions you make in life, you do what suits your needs and taste. Because his parents like to entertain on that level does not mean you have to follow suit. If it is possible to invite them to meet your small social circle, do it simply in a way that will show you to your best advantage. Explain to your daughter that the reciprocal event doesn't have to be a minor wedding and that you just don't want to compete.

Future in-laws entertain each other in various ways. Sometimes informal entertaining is done between the two families with a small guest list. Other introductions to friends and family take place in a more casual manner on occasions that may not be specifically in honor of the soon-to-be-marrieds. Those friends and relations keep the couple busy with invitations to dinner or in other ways.

Q: *As future in-laws, we are invited to the home of the bride's parents for lunch after church on Sunday. We are not exactly ill at ease but we would like the meeting to go well since this will be the first time we meet. Do I take a gift?*

Judge the occasion the way you would when invited to someone's home for the first time. If it is the custom in your part of the country to take a gift of some kind, then do so in this case. A present is always appreciated. Flowers express goodwill, as does a favorite cookbook, and they make charming gifts for your hostess. How about a bottle of champagne to toast the lovers? A note of thanks afterward saying how much you enjoyed meeting them and complimenting your hostess on her gracious hospitality is a thoughtful and warm gesture.

Q: *Though my future in-laws are warm people, I feel self-conscious when addressing them by name. My parents are the only ones I can sincerely call Mom and Dad, so right now I use Mr. and Mrs., but what do I do after the wedding?*

Until your marriage it is fine to call them by their surnames, though some young ladies find it easy even before their marriage to refer to their future in-laws as Mom and Dad. In time you will feel like a member of your husband's family and addressing them in more affectionate terms will come naturally.

You could ask your future in-laws what their preferences

are, or you could say something like "Do you mind if I call you Mrs. Smith?" But you might receive a response such as "Fine, but do you mind if I call *you* Mrs. Smith?"

Q: *I would like some information on the purchase of an engagement ring. Does a man buy the ring before "popping the question"? Who chooses the wedding bands and when? Etiquette books seem to be written for women. What about the groom's role?*

The best way of becoming engaged is to find out how the lady of your choice feels. Naturally, you must be fairly sure of your standing so now you should do some research on the cost of rings. Will it be a diamond and mounted in platinum or gold? A diamond set in platinum is the top of the line; set in gold is a little less expensive. That is just the first phase of buying a ring, so go to the library and read about what to look for in quality. Other choices are a ring set with the bride's birthstone or a pearl.

If you want to ask her to marry you with the ring in your pocket, then do so—but make sure the ring can be exchanged. The ring will probably have to be adjusted to the size of her finger. Personally, I think that after you know what is on the market and how much jewelry costs, both of you should go together and make a selection. An engagement ring is worn above the wedding band so it might be that your fiancée would like a matching set. It is all a matter of taste and cost.

In your letter you don't mention whether you have parents. The engagement period is an important time when both sets of parents are brought together. Unlike in times past, your role is to be part of the decision-making, so join your bride and her family in discussions and don't be reluctant to voice your opinion. But you should also remember that the financial burden may be wholly on the bride and her parents so temper your point of view. There are many unpredictable problems that arise; all you can do is to meet each step as it comes along.

Large weddings may be a little harder to arrange than smaller ones but either way there is a certain amount of delicious pressure and anxiety you and your fiancée will feel. It is your job to keep things on an even keel.

YOUNG LOVERS

First, before you read further. Though you must have a wedding ring for the ceremony, you do not need an engagement ring to be engaged to be married. A remembrance of the time you decided to marry need not be a ring but something the bride will cherish nevertheless. If this is not the right time for such an expenditure, just let it go for now. There are always occasions to gather those other trappings.

If you do decide to buy a ring, however, start researching information on diamonds and other gems. According to my husband, who had a courtship with the jewelry industry as a young man, you will find that diamonds in particular have had an illustrious history. The first diamond was discovered in Golconda in India in 800 B.C. Though its recorded history starts in the fourteenth century, legend has it that the famous 186-carat Koh-i-noor (meaning "mountain of life") was found there some four thousand years ago and has two superstitions attached to it: its owner would become a ruler, but unless that owner was a woman, possession of the diamond placed him in mortal danger. It now rests in the crown worn by Elizabeth, England's Queen Mother.

In the 1400s, Agnès Sorel, a beauty with an eye on the French king, Charles VII, wore a diamond necklace at court. The court held its breath as the king (the Dauphin whom Joan of Arc helped put on the throne) stared at the damsel, smiled, and promptly fell in love. She became his mistress and his gift to her was the Beauté-sur-Marne castle, not a bad return on an investment.

Another diamond necklace had a less happy result. Marie Antoinette, the Austrian noblewoman who married Louis XVI, was the recipient of a magnificent necklace at a time when the French government was having a dispute with Austria and the French people were starving. Marie claimed the necklace was bought without her knowledge. There was a public scandal and some connected with it suffered prison and disgrace. Historians believe that the affair contributed to the people's growing animosity toward the Crown and eventually to the Revolution.

In the mid-1800s, a black woman found the 128-carat Star of the South in a mine in Brazil.

Prince Orloff, a former lover of Catherine the Great of Russia (a lady very fond of gems), bought what is now known as the

Orloff diamond. He presented it to his Empress hoping to be restored to favor but to no avail . . . though she graciously accepted the gift.

The handsome Hope diamond is exhibited at the Smithsonian Institution in Washington, D.C. And if you happen to be in New York, walk into Tiffany's to see the stunning 128-carat Tiffany gem.

The Jonker diamond was found in South Africa in the 1930s and weighed approximately 726 carats. Mr. Winston of Harry Winston, Inc., in New York, purchased the magnificent uncut gem and had his cutters study its structure for a full year before cutting it into twelve stones worth over $2.5 million—each gem of the finest brilliance.

A diamond is pure crystalline carbon. Tempered by volcanic heat and pressure, its crystals are the hardest material on earth. Only a diamond can cut another diamond. When faceted properly its prisms have an iridescent beauty.

The value of a diamond depends on a number of factors. Shop for a diamond with the seven Cs in mind.

CLARITY: Most diamonds have natural flaws but these imperfections should not hamper the flow of light through the stone.

CARAT: A unit weight for measuring precious gems. There are a hundred points to one carat, which is considered large—the size of a plump pea. If the size of a carat doesn't sound too impressive, just price it.

COLOR: Most diamonds are a transparent white with a touch of color—blue, yellow, pink.

CUT: There are six popular solitaire shapes: round, square, heart, pear, marquis, and oval. Cut also means the way the diamond cutter fashions the uncut gem; one wrong stroke can destroy the value of the stone.

COST: According to the Diamond Information Center, the average couple spend at least two months' salary on a diamond engagement ring.

COVERAGE: Precious gems should be insured separately, not just under an overall homeowner's policy. Ask the jeweler for an appraisal for insurance purposes.

CARE: Be careful not to bang the stone; it can chip. Also remove the ring when washing hands or dishes because the gem can become loose in its setting. When you take your ring off always put it in the same place at home. There's always the danger of forgetting where you left it, so you must be aware of what you are doing.

Your jeweler can advise how to keep the diamond sparklingly clean.

Like gold, diamonds can be used as international barter and always retain *a* value. When I say "retain *a* value," I mean that the value may go up or down on the market. The traditional solitaire is still the most popular choice and the best investment since nearly all its value is in one diamond. So, like marriage, these brilliant prisms represent love and stability.

MY BETROTHED, MY FIANCÉ(E)

Q: *What is the correct pronunciation for the words "fiancé" (male) and "fiancée" (female)? I was corrected the other day when I referred to my future husband as my "fiance," which rhymes with "dance." I maintained that only the woman is known as a "fiance-SAY."*

The word is sounded the same for both genders: "fee-on-SAY." This French word is the only one I can think of which perfectly fits the state of being engaged to be married. "My boyfriend" sounds juvenile to me. Though I am particularly fond of the word "betrothed," it does not flow as smoothly in everyday conversation. It is the sort of word better read than said.

Q: *I do not recall ever having received printed engagement announcements. Are they out of style? I am a working mother, and it would save a lot of time from the cumbersome task of having to write notes to so many out-of-town people.*

I don't think engraved engagement announcements were ever in style, though they are not unheard of, especially in the New York City area. Books on wedding-related etiquette seem to prefer telephoning close relatives, writing personal notes to those out-of-town, and sharing the news through local newspapers.

However, if you are interested, why not discuss it with the stationers. The example I like best is:

Jill Candace Ode
Frederick Eldon Hampenstance

Engaged   January 1985

STOP THE PRESSES— WE'RE GETTING MARRIED!

But before you do, ladies and gentlemen, I caution you to check the facts thoroughly. Nothing annoys someone more than seeing his or her name incorrectly spelled in the newspaper. It is better to get the information in writing from in-laws. If pertinent facts are taken over the telephone, don't take anything for granted, but code each name: GRANT—G as in George; R as in Richard, etc. Schools and organizations are given their legal designation and are not abbreviated: U of M in place of the University of Maryland just won't do. Few establishments can be as easily recognized by initials as the CIA or IRS. Don't leave the reader puzzling over your story—it is not a classified ad.

Confessions from the Wedding Desk remembers I'll Never Forget What's-his-name. A woman sent a notice to the Bridal Desk spelling her future son-in-law's name incorrectly. Even when I checked it over the telephone she didn't realize the error. After publication she called to say how upsetting it was, especially to the bridegroom, that a newspaper should make such a serious mistake. When I went over the copy she had sent, she blithely cooed, "Oh, I'll tell him you did it, anyway!" Wasn't that sporting of her?

I was amused by one young woman who complained that the town in which she lived was spelled wrong in the newspaper. Anyone can make a mistake, as those experienced in proofreading know, but I remembered proofing very carefully. Then I looked at her notepaper; she was unaware of the printer's mistake although she had been using the stationery for some time.

Q: *How do we announce our daughter's engagement in the newspaper and how do we word it?*

Call or write the publications of your choice about their policy on printing announcements. They will explain their guidelines: whether you need to fill out a newspaper form, or supply the information typed, double spaced, and in duplicate. Your signature, along with your address and both daytime (business) and home telephone numbers, is required for verification purposes.

WORDING OF ENGAGEMENT ANNOUNCEMENT

Mr. and Mrs. James Person Ode of Washington, D.C., are pleased to announce the engagement of their daughter, Jill Candace, to Frederick Eldon Hampenstance, son of Mr. and Mrs. Harold Dean Hampenstance of Darien, Ct. A June wedding is planned.

You might want to add schools and place of employment:

Miss Ode is a graduate of the College of William and Mary and is currently studying for a master's degree in business administration at the Wharton School of Business and Finance of the University of Pennsylvania, from which Mr. Hampenstance received both bachelor's and master's degrees. He is now with the management consulting firm of Smart, Smart and Certane Lee Smarter in New York City.

Since the article in the newspaper is supposed to give identifying information about the families, facts can be included such as names of grandparents, parents' business connections, and the organizations to which the engaged couple belong. Don't be reluctant to give as much information as possible, including being presented to society. Newspapers will edit if they do not have space for the entire article.

DON'T BE SHY...

A word to those who might feel self-conscious about not having a list of clubs or ancestors going back to the Ice Age. Not only is your announcement interesting and happy news to those you know, it also makes the page interesting to readers. You are part of the building blocks of society.

FORGOTTEN PARENTS

Q: *My son is engaged. The announcement appeared in the bride's hometown paper without mention of our names in the article. I felt terrible. Is this the proper procedure?*

I can't tell you how many times the bridegroom's parents fail to be included in the copy sent to me at the Bridal Desk. It is even more hurtful if both families live in the same city and the article is published that way. But let me assure you that in most cases it is an oversight, not a slight. This often happens because the wording on most wedding invitations does not include the bridegroom's parents, so when the bride's family sends the story to the newspapers they think in terms of a formal statement rather than an item that identifies the principals. Should the omission of his parents be discovered in time, and copies have been given to more than one newspaper, send the corrected version to them as soon as possible.

LADIES AND GENTLEMEN, I do, occasionally, encounter a reluctant person who feels that the others will not see the release in the paper. They have to be convinced that the chances are much greater than not, even if the family lives out of town. 'Tis a small world, and I could fill these pages with coincidences!

- Deceased in-laws should be identified in the announcement and the copy should make clear that they are no longer living.
- A widowed mother announcing her daughter's engagement should mention her deceased husband in the story:

  Mrs. James Person Ode of Washington, D.C., is pleased to announce the engagement of her daughter, Jill Candace. . . . Miss Ode is the daughter also of the late Mr. Ode . . .

- A remarried mother uses her current husband's name and can announce alone or with her husband. Be sure to use the future bride's full name and include the bride's deceased father's full name.

Mrs. William Williams

or

Mr. and Mrs. William Williams of Vienna, Va., announce the engagement of her daughter, Jill Candace Ode . . . Miss Ode is the daughter also of the late Mr. James Person Ode . . .

If the bride's mother and stepfather have been married for many years and the relationship is close, then the words "their" can be substituted for "her daughter."

• A widowed father makes an announcement that includes his deceased wife's given, maiden, and married names but omits the "Mrs."

Mr. James Person Ode of Washington, D.C., announces the engagement of his daughter . . . Miss Ode is the daughter also of the late Sarah Manning Ode . . .

or

Miss Ode is the daughter also of the late Mrs. Ode . . .

• A remarried father announces along with his wife, especially if they have been married for some time:

Mr. and Mrs. James Person Ode of Washington, D.C., announce the engagement of his (or their) daughter . . .

Don't forget to mention the bride's deceased mother.

SEPARATED BUT NOT SEPARATE

Q: *My friend, whose parents have been separated for some time, is getting married, but the announcement in the newspaper reads as if the parents were still living together. The wedding invitation was issued the same way. Isn't that misleading?*

No, because legally they are still Mr. and Mrs. and can participate in all phases of the wedding as if they were living together.

Remember, they are not divorced. For some, the separation might be temporary; others remain in that limbo state until they take steps to end their marriage through the courts.

DIVORCED PARENTS

Q: *My divorced parents both wish to announce my engagement. How should it be worded?*

> Mrs. William Williams of Vienna, Va., and Mr. James Person Ode of Washington, D.C., announce the engagement of their daughter . . .

If it is decided that your mother should announce, since you live with her:

> Mrs. William Williams of Vienna, Va., announces the engagement of her daughter, Jill Candace Ode . . .

Add somewhere in the announcement:

> Miss Ode is the daughter also of Mr. James Person Ode of Washington, D.C.

Or, if the bride's father is doing the honors, her mother's name is mentioned:

> Miss Ode is the daughter also of Mrs. William Williams of Vienna, Va.

LADIES AND GENTLEMEN, several years ago a woman came to place the announcement of her daughter's engagement. She made a telephone call to her ex-husband to clarify his exact business title. His secretary asked who was calling and she answered, "Mrs. James Current." When he found out that the person on the other line was his former wife, he actually shouted at her over the phone that he was married to a woman who is rightfully known as Mrs. James Current. Mrs. Ex dissolved into tears. She had continued to use her ex-husband's name despite the fact that most divorcées now are anxious to divest themselves of their married names.

Q: *Yes, I am divorced, but why do you say I should not use the name I have used for over twenty-seven years?*

I am not saying you can't but I think it is confusing to use your ex-husband's full name, especially if he has remarried. At one time a divorced woman kept her ex-husband's name, but today most prefer to use their first name with maiden and married surnames, preceded by either Mrs. or Ms. It is not uncommon, though, for a divorced woman to take back her maiden name, dropping her ex-husband's name altogether, and using "Ms.," especially if her children are married.

HAPPY NEWS, SAD MOMENTS

Q: *An engagement announcement is supposed to be a happy news item. Why mention my mother, who died last year? The thought of reading "the late" in the paper would make my father and me, and everyone who knew her, very sad.*

Life is bittersweet. It is understandable that you miss your mother more than ever now that you are being married. But I strongly recommend that you include her name in the announcement. If you can picture yourself reading the clipping a few years from today, you will be so glad that, by sharing the news of her daughter's engagement, you brought her to mind once again in a special way.

Consider another point. If you do not mention one parent or the other, for whatever reason, the omission just leaves the reader wondering: has the parent died? run away? or is the omission due to a nasty divorce? Readers can come to any conclusion they like, so it is better to make the statement clear. That is why, even when there are bitter feelings between divorced parents or between parent and child, papers identify the principals.

Q: *I simply do not like the written expression "the late" when referring to a person who has passed away. Isn't there a softer way to phrase it?*

You are not the only one who feels that "the late" is a cold way of saying the person has died, especially if the loss is recent and close. I have tried many different approaches: "Miss Ode's mother, Sarah Manning Ode, is deceased," or "has passed away," but the result is the same. Someone has died. Changing a word doesn't change the hurt.

BROTHERLY LOVE— SIBLINGS WITHOUT RIVALRY

When it is not possible for parents to announce for the future bride, then her brother, sister, grandparents, or another relative or close friend can do so.

Mr. and Mrs. Jeremy Person Ode of Chevy Chase, Md., announce the engagement of his sister . . .

Whether her parents are divorced, living, or deceased they should be mentioned in the story:

Miss Ode is the daughter of Mr. and Mrs. James Person Ode of Washington, D.C., now living in Bangkok, Thailand . . .

MARRIED BUT OTHERWISE ENGAGED

Q: *My mother won't announce my engagement publicly because my fiancé's divorce is not going to be final until the end of June. But this is my first marriage and I've read that it's the bride's status that counts, not the bridegroom's. She says that it is not so in this case. Isn't she wrong?*

According to tradition, it is true that the bride's status determines what type of wedding is planned and that it does not matter how many times the bridegroom has walked the path to matrimony. But your mother is right. A public announcement before the divorce is final is tasteless.

You can plan a wedding wearing the frothiest wedding dress imaginable; your veil can have yards and yards of bridal illusion and your walk down the aisle can be flanked by ten maids and ten ushers, *but* the news item read by countless people affects more than just the two of you and has nothing to do with whether you have been previously married or not. Aside from the legal ramifications, what do you think his associates, his family, and his acquaintances will make of a news story that says he is marrying again when the divorce has not yet been finalized? I understand how you feel but don't be impetuous. Waiting for the appropriate time might save you and your family embarrassing questions and possible snickering behind your backs.

DISAPPROVING PARENTS

Q: *My fiancée's parents disapprove of our upcoming marriage because they say their daughter is too young. They will not participate in or attend the wedding and have forbidden us to use their names in the engagement or marriage announcements for the newspaper.*

Though my parents are willing to announce for us, don't you think it will look strange that her parents are not mentioned? Also, why can't we name them without their permission since all we will be doing is stating the truth—she is the daughter of Mr. and Mrs. James Person Ode?

I recommend that you wait until after you are married to have an announcement published but I have a sneaking suspicion you are thinking that when her parents see the news in the paper they will realize just how serious you both are about each other.

You should not use her parents' names against their will, even though the announcement would not be worded as coming from them. Her parents might soften by the wedding day, but to make that possible you must not antagonize them further. Your parents should be mentioned discreetly since they are in a very difficult position. I suggest the following:

The engagement of Jill Candace Ode to Frederick Eldon Hampenstance has been announced. The future bride is a recent graduate of Hilton High School. Mr. Hampenstance, son of Mr. and Mrs. Harold Dean Hampenstance of Darien, Ct., is a graduate of the Stone Academy and a first-year student at the University of Virginia. A June wedding is planned.

After you are married and if her parents still have not accepted the event:

> Jill Candace Ode and Frederick Eldon Hampenstance were married on June 6 in the Chapel of the University of Virginia. Mr. Hampenstance is the son of Mr. and Mrs. Harold Dean Hampenstance of Darien, Ct. The couple will live in Charlottesville, Va.

TIMING OF THE ENGAGEMENT ANNOUNCEMENT

Q: *My mother says we should wait three months before the wedding (which is nine months away) to announce my engagement in the newspaper; my aunt is sure a year ahead of the wedding is acceptable. I'm engaged to a great guy who is as anxious as I am to tell the world about it; after all, I am wearing his engagement ring. What is the time frame for publishing engagement announcements?*

When to announce depends on your point of view. Some people do it when the event occurs because they wish to make known that these two people are pledged to each other, even if wedding plans are more than a year away. This is in line with your aunt's opinion. Others feel that since an engagement is a statement of intent and can be broken, the announcement should be made public not more than six months before the wedding. I favor publishing the news after the wedding date has been set but not after the invitations have been mailed.

The Bridal Desk has accepted forthcoming-marriage stories for publication up to the week before the wedding:

> Mr. and Mrs. James Person Ode of Washington, D.C., announce that their daughter, Jill Candace, will marry Frederick Eldon Hampenstance, son of Mr. and Mrs. Harold Dean Hampenstance of Darien, Ct., on the sixth of June.

HONOR NOT THYSELF

Q: *Since my husband is a judge I see no reason why we cannot begin the newspaper announcement with "the Honorable and Mrs." The newspaper article is referring to him as "the honorable," we are not. Isn't that so?*

Why not use the title "judge" since that word would clearly identify your husband to readers? As you know, one never refers to one's self as "the honorable" since that term is only used when a person entitled to that respect is introduced in person or addressed by letter. I've had this discussion many times. Some people insist that it is a newspaper story. That may be so, but I feel it is done in the name of the family and reads as such.

COUPLE ANNOUNCING FOR THEMSELVES

Q: *My fiancé and I plan to announce our own engagement. My parents seem a little hurt by our decision. Am I wrong to feel a bit self-conscious about having my parents announce for me? I am in my thirties and I have lived away from home for some time. This is my first marriage.*

Many independent adults announce for themselves. But, since there is no age limit on having one's parents announce, you should not feel awkward in having them do so.

Analyze it. Even though most of the arrangements will be done by you and your fiancé, getting married is the most important step you can take and neither age nor living away from home interferes with the traditions and customs of the betrothal and marriage rites. Parents have a special place in the wedding proceedings; your father will escort you to the altar, your mother will be the last to be seated before the ceremony begins, and if rites include it, the clergyman will ask: "Who gives this woman in marriage?" and it will be your father or both parents answering. Their participation enriches the whole process.

Q: *If my fiancé and I do decide to speak for ourselves, how would you suggest that the wording read?*

The engagement of Jill Candace Ode to Frederick Eldon Hampenstance has been announced. The future bride, daughter of Mr. and Mrs. James Person Ode of Washington, D.C., holds the position of Personnel Manager of the . . .

Mr. Hampenstance is the son of Mr. and Mrs. Harold Dean Hampenstance of Darien, Ct. He is the Manager of the Division of . . .

You can add information about schools or change the start of the announcement:

Jill Candace Ode and Frederick Eldon Hampenstance plan a June wedding to take place here in . . .

Miss (Ms.) Ode, daughter of . . . etc.

COUPLE ANNOUNCING
FORTHCOMING SECOND MARRIAGE

Q: *We are established people who have been married before. My fiancé and I have a wide circle of friends and business associates. We are reluctant to announce our engagement as such, but it is important for both of us to have some statement in the newspaper. What wording should we use for an upcoming marriage announcement? Also, since we don't want to sound like a young couple, is it appropriate for my mother to announce?*

You have a choice of whether to announce yourselves or have it done in the name of your mother (or both parents, if living). If your mother announces:

Mrs. James Person Ode of Washington, D.C., announces the forthcoming marriage of her daughter . . .

Or if you wish to make your own statement:

Jill Ode Hampenstance and William Jones Westings plan to marry in June. The future bride is Director of . . . Mr. Westings is Manager of the Division . . . etc.

To identify yourselves further add information about your parents, schooling, and organizations.

MARRIAGE ANNOUNCEMENT FOR NEWSPAPER

The marriage of Jill Candace Ode to Frederick Eldon Hampenstance took place last Saturday afternoon in St. Bartholomew's Church in this city. The Reverend Marion Peaceful officiated at the double-ring ceremony. A reception followed at the Jockey Club.

The bride is the daughter of Mr. and Mrs. James Person Ode of Washington, D.C., and Mr. Hampenstance is the son of Mr. and Mrs. Harold Dean Hampenstance of Darien, Ct.

The couple will reside in Manhattan after a wedding trip to France.

For a more complete announcement the first paragraph would be the same but the following paragraphs would be descriptive and informative:

The bride wore a Bianchi creation of silk taffeta with reembroidered Alençon lace on the bodice, sleeves, and flowing cathedral train. Her attendants were [list their names but cities in which they live are optional] . . . Serving the bridegroom were . . .

Mrs. Hampenstance, who will retain her maiden name for professional purposes, took degrees from Williams College and Harvard Business School. She spent her junior year at the Sorbonne in Paris and was introduced to society at a dinner given by her parents. Her father is Vice-President of Simple, Simple and Simpler. Recently, she has joined the firm of Masters and Masters.

Mr. Hampenstance is Manager of Allied Complete Living Corporation, of which his father is President and his grandfather, the late James J. Hampenstance, the founder. The bridegroom is a direct descendant of . . . He did undergraduate work at Williams College, where he met his bride, and later took advanced degrees in finance and in economics at Stanford University.

The couple will reside in Manhattan after a wedding trip to France.

SOCIAL OR SOCIETY?

Q: *In my day, newspapers published only those wedding and engagement notices sent by people who were considered society. When my engagement made the newspapers it meant a recognition of my family's place in the city. Is that true today?*

In some cities that is still true. I have spoken to a number of newspaper people throughout the country and most, especially smaller dailies, tell me that all one has to do is mail a signed statement and the paper will use it on a space-available basis depending on their policy regarding announcements. It is hardly treated as society news.

Once, the fact that the bride and bridegroom had attended private schools and colleges was a legitimate basis for publication, an indication that the family had position. Today, when we have a strong middle class, it is difficult for newspapers to make such obvious distinctions. Only the famous or infamous, not necessarily members of "society," are covered strictly as news items.

LADIES AND GENTLEMEN, times have changed since newspapers clamored for engagement and wedding stories. During the '60s and '70s it was thought that such news belonged on the "women's page."

At the same time, the cost of producing newspapers kept climbing, forcing some dailies to stop publishing these stories. Others set limits: no engagement announcements and only short notices and photographs for marriages. Or, if an engagement story was published, there was no coverage of the wedding. Some eliminated photographs altogether. Depending on the policy of the newspaper, if the nuptial article did not arrive at the editor's desk by a specified date (which could be two to three weeks before the wedding day), the paper would not publish the news—an effective way of controlling the amount of space used for these types of stories without really refusing the public. Some papers were and still are "selective," which means the family wishing to announce must be prominent in some way.

Today, since there really is no equitable way of handling announcements—and in an effort to keep the volume from becoming overwhelming, especially in large cities—some newspapers have instituted charges for the space the article occupies. Small-town newspapers use these items as filler, which means the news will be published if they have the space.

The importance of announcing in the newspapers has increased more than ever, especially in large cities. Whether it is their first or a subsequent marriage, professional men and women need an efficient way of notifying their business associates, friends, and acquaintances, as well as the general public, of their change of status. Parents want the pleasure of telling and recording the news in such a manner.

The general public enjoys reading announcements and many a reader has been delighted to recognize the name or face of someone with whom he grew up or met in college. There can be unexpected results from such a news story . . .

LADY LUCK SMILES ON BRIDEGROOM

The bridegroom had just established a firm in an area of engineering new to the industry. A million-dollar deal came his way because his business interest was mentioned in the marriage announcement in the newspaper. A Navy man happened to read the story and telephoned the young man's firm because that specialty was exactly what the Navy needed.

One of my most treasured letters of thanks is from an engaged young lady who, at my suggestion, mentioned her deceased grandfather in the announcement, a black minister who had been a Civil Rights activist in the 1960s and had marched with Martin Luther King. He was also the first black minister to give the convocation at the Republican National Convention. The announcement made a huge splash. She received telephone calls and letters from people who had known her grandfather. They had had no idea that his granddaughter was in the area. The news in the paper widened her world and enriched her life beyond measure.

Q: *Is it true some papers charge for bridal stories and that one cannot distinguish between socially prominent people and others? Don't you think that's sad?*

Yes, some papers charge; and no, I do not think it's sad that announcements are treated that way. In England only the royal family receives engagement and wedding coverage as news. Large newspapers there have always charged the general public and a hefty fee it is. If the announcee wants to appear on the page that lists that day's activities of the members of the royal family, the charge is higher than if the announcement is printed on another page. These announcements are limited in information and no photographs are accepted.

"Society" in America still recognize one another in *Who's Who in America*. Or they scan the Social Register to see who made it this year and who was dropped. They are used to newspaper announcements and some have expressed to me their frustration with dailies that refuse to publish these notices. Aside from the flattery of it all, it is a traditional, romantic, and efficient way of spreading the news, and those who have had this coverage in the past want it to continue.

Some people feel the egalitarian approach removes the anxiety of whether the "society" editor deems them worthy of publication and the nervousness about "where will our announcement appear on the page?" Yes, even placement told a tale; if the item was on the top of the page then that family really counted; on the bottom, well, at least they made the paper. Whew, what a relief!

While many of our young people find it hard to comprehend such artificial problems, others take the position that the news of their engagement or marriage is just that—news. The idea of a paid announcement removes the spontaneity from the statement; they feel the newspaper should print the news as a public service. Of course, they are sure that if the newspaper did not have the charge policy their announcement would have been published. That could happen, but then again, it might not.

SHORT AND TO THE POINT

Q: *We just want a short statement for the newspaper announcing that the wedding took place. Isn't it vain to state how many degrees one has and who your great-grandfather is, not to mention going into detail describing the wedding day?*

It is strictly a matter of taste. There is nothing wrong with a brief item stating that the event took place. But there is nothing wrong, either, with a more traditional one, and they are great fun for the public to read. Beats world news any day.

Q: *I am the mother of the future groom. Each week I scan the newspaper hoping to see our son's engagement notice, which was supposed to be sent by the bride-to-be's mother. I am finally calling you to ask: doesn't the bride's family handle these matters any longer?*

At one time the bride's family sent the engagement or marriage announcement, with or without a photograph, to the newspapers. The bride's mother asked the bridegroom's mother for family background information and mailed the story to publications, hoping it would be accepted. The newspapers would then publish the news on a selective or space-available basis, according to their policy—editing copy at will.

Since some newspapers charge for the space, the situation can become sensitive. Suppose the bride's parents, who live in a small town where announcements are free, send the notice to a newspaper in a large city that charges. The bride's mother may object to taking on what is, according to her, a surprising expense in a city not important to her. After all, the only connection her family has with that area is that their daughter is marrying a man who lives in that location. She is in a dilemma: if she says no to publishing the announcement in that city, she might inadvertently deny the bridegroom's family the choice of having the announcement in their hometown daily, which may be important to them. On the other hand, her family feels that the expense is a responsibility that his side should assume, and rightly so. She should be up-front about it by telling the newspaper to speak to the bridegroom's family. If the newspaper's policy is not known beforehand, the bridegroom's family should be sent the information that will appear in the bride's hometown daily, allowing them to carry on from that point.

Q: *I am the mother of the groom. The bride's parents didn't send the engagement announcement to our newspaper. Now I*

find myself wondering what to do about the marriage announce-
ment. My family traditionally sends stories for publication; pay-
ment has nothing to do with it. I don't see why we should not
have coverage. Does the information have to come from them?

No, you don't have to rely on her family even for the engagement, if you know that it appeared in the bride's hometown
paper or if you discussed the notice with the bride saying that
you would like to handle the news yourself. You can feel free to
send the information to your paper but be careful to word the
story so that her parents are announcing, as is customary.

Q: *Why does the story have to be worded so that her parents*
are announcing the engagement and does the marriage an-
nouncement have to read the same way?

In days of yore, it was necessary for the safety of an unmarried
young lady to come under the protection of parents or a guardian
since she had no legal rights. Also, parents had to have complete
control over their children, because the actions of a child or even
a grandchild could anger the Crown or the powerful. The entire
family could lose property and position. When the young woman
married, her husband became her protector and the keeper of
her fortune.

The custom has perpetuated itself in the engagement process.
Traditionally, the bride's parents do the announcing and issue
the wedding invitations in their names. There is more leeway with
the wording of the marriage announcement:

> In the Great Choir of the Washington Cathedral in Washington,
> D.C., Jill Candace Ode became the bride of Frederick Eldon
> Hampenstance with the Reverend Jonathan Jardy conducting
> the double ring ceremony. The bride is the daughter of Mr.
> and Mrs. James Person Ode of this city and Mr. Hampenstance
> is the son of Mr. and Mrs. Harold Dean Hampenstance of
> Darien, Ct. . . .

If the bride's parents would like to announce the marriage
then the wording would begin:

Mr. and Mrs. James Person Ode of Washington, D.C., announce the marriage of their daughter, Jill Candace . . .

The content of the story is up to the person sending in the information, provided the newspaper gives that latitude, but you should include:

- Full maiden name of the bride
- Full name of her parents
  Give address and home and daytime telephone numbers for verification purposes
- Full name of bridegroom
- Full name of his parents
  Give address and home and daytime telephone numbers for verification purposes.
- Date of wedding
- Where event took place
- Name of clergyman or woman
- Reception site
- Description of wedding gown
- Names of bridal party
- Grandparents
- Schools and organizations
- Employment and position, if you desire
- Honeymoon and where couple will live

Since a notice in the paper is to identify the families involved, some people like to add a line or two about both sets of parents, if they are known or if the family wishes it. The public also enjoys reading about one's ancestors.

ENGRAVED MARRIAGE ANNOUNCEMENT

Mr. and Mrs. James Person Ode
have the pleasure of announcing
the marriage of their daughter
Jill Candace
to
Frederick Eldon Hampenstance

Saturday, the sixth of June
*Nineteen hundred eighty-seven
in Washington, District of Columbia

or

Jill Candace Ode
to
Frederick Eldon Hampenstance
Saturday, the sixth of June
One thousand nineteen hundred and eighty-seven
in the City of Washington

Marriage announcements are generally ordered at the same time as the wedding invitations. They should be addressed before the wedding day and mailed as soon after the wedding as possible to friends, relations, and acquaintances who were not invited to the event.

NEWSPAPER ANNOUNCEMENT

Mr. and Mrs. James Person Ode of Washington, D.C., announce the marriage of their daughter, Jill Candace, to Frederick Eldon Hampenstance. The future bride is Director of Second Chance Inc. and Mr. Hampenstance is Vice President of the parent company . . . etc. His parents, Mr. and Mrs. Harold Dean Hampenstance, live in Darien, Ct.

PHOTOGRAPHS FOR NEWSPAPER

Q: *My mother says it is customary to have only the future bride pictured in the newspaper along with the engagement announcement. My fiancé and I would like to have a photograph taken together for publication purposes. Why isn't it considered appropriate?*

In some parts of the country picturing betrothed couples in the newspaper has not been customary. It may be that the events

*Noting the year is optional and appropriate.

from engagement to the wedding day are centered on the bride. Or that marriage is a permanent change in status and hence more newsworthy, while the engagement can be broken without legal steps.

I do know, however, that today a picture of both partners is extremely popular with many young couples, both sets of parents, and with readers. In times past, the prospective bridegroom was treated as a minor actor who hardly participated in the various aspects of this special event in his life. Now he and his fiancée want to share the spotlight and have the thrill of seeing their photograph in the newspaper and the thrill of public recognition. After all, what is happening in their lives is happening to both equally.

One young man won the point with his future mother-in-law, when she voiced a preference for only the bride in the photograph, by claiming reverse chauvinism.

An engagement announcement appeared not long ago of a couple pictured together; the man was quite handsome, the woman plump and really plain. The contrast was so striking that everyone connected with the production of the wedding column pointed out that couple to me. The reason for the alliance was speculated on from one department to the other: she's pregnant, has money, family position—you name it, they thought of it. My own thoughts were that one could not judge from appearances alone. *However,* being a weaver of tales I concocted several romantic and whimsical and then not-so-whimsical stories of my own imagination which I discreetly kept to myself . . . I will never know, I suppose.

Q: *What type of photograph is acceptable for publication?*

Most newspapers want a 5" X 7" or 8" X 10" black-and-white glossy of the bride alone. If you want a shot of the two of you together, ask the newspaper for its policy. Tape your name(s) on the bottom of the photograph or write on the back with a very light hand so that the pencil impression does not show on the print side; this will ensure that it can be identified should it become separated from your letter. Since newspapers do not guarantee the return of the photograph, enclose a stamped, self-addressed envelope.

For a successful couple shot, have your heads fairly close together so that the newspaper can "crop and scale" the print to fit their own specifications. A photo of two people standing shoulder to shoulder would be difficult to reduce to the narrow columns in some newspapers. Avoid dramatic or overly romantic poses.

Since newspapers use black ink on gray-white paper, there are no subtle shadings to soften extremes of dark and light areas of the photograph and it is hard for the engraving department to produce a balance. Your photographer should be able to give you a likeness that has clarity with facial features sharply defined while also obtaining a balance of light on both faces.

COLOR PHOTOGRAPHS

Q: *Though our wedding photographs are simply beautiful, we are sorely disappointed to find that newspapers will not accept them because they are in color. Why do they refuse color pictures and what do I do now?*

Color photos look pleasing to the eye but can lose softness during the two-step process some newspapers have to put them through before going to press. For most dailies special handling is both time-consuming and costly. There are photographic stores that can produce black-and-white glossy prints from color photographs.

I am surprised that some wedding photographers fail to mention the special requirements of news photographs when their services are first engaged by the bride. Generally, when the photographer's print is used in the paper, the daily gives a credit line under the picture, which is first-class promotion. But, most important, the photographer cannot assume that the bride and family know what type of print is required for the newspaper.

A portrait sitting can be arranged ahead of the wedding day. On the same day that she goes for a fitting of the bridal gown, the future bride can take the dress, along with her shoes and veil, to the photographer for a picture-taking session. At that time, the photographer can take a black-and-white glossy shot for the newspaper.

BROKEN ENGAGEMENT

Below is a repeat of a conversation I had with a young man which made quite an impression on me.

Q: *When I became engaged to a young lady six months ago, my friends were not particularly enthusiastic, but I would not allow them to interfere. Just between you and me, she had bouts of temper and I finally came to realize that whatever feelings I had for her lessened with every tantrum, so I broke the engagement. Somehow I did not expect to fend off inquisitive questions from friends. Why do I have to give an explanation?*

Friends should be more discreet but maybe they want to hear you say they were right. Try a little humor. My father tells this parable about a man who had a difficult wife. Every time friends would ask what the trouble was between them, he would answer: "I never talk about my wife." He lived in misery until the children were grown and had left home; then he decided to obtain a divorce. When the papers became final his friends asked him: "Now that you are no longer living with that woman, can you tell us what was wrong between you?" He answered: "I'm sorry, but I never talk about strangers."

LADIES AND GENTLEMEN, rare is the man or woman who wants to play Shakespeare's Petruchio to an ill-natured Katherine. In *The Taming of the Shrew*, Petruchio takes over the task of subduing Katherine's volatile character, recognizing that her behavior was a cry for recognition. And rare is the person who possesses the insight to a complex human being—to know the difference between a psychologically disturbed individual and someone sending a message.

By the way, I looked up the word "shrew," which, in this sense, means an ill-tempered woman. However, my fellow females, I could not find the male equivalent of the word. So, since I believe in equality of the sexes in this respect, I have designated an ill-tempered man as a "shrow." The dictionary term is "a scold, a shrew." Actually, a shrow can be likened to the Tasmanian devil, an animal about the size of a badger that growls and bares its teeth and will fight anything in sight—even a stick . . .

Now, where was I? Oh, yes, we were talking about broken engagements.

During the courtship period lovers are generally on their best behavior. Conscious of what pleases the other, they try to anticipate each other's needs. It is a time of discovery and newfound happiness. Surely there is something dreadfully wrong when there are many sudden bouts of temper and uncontrolled diatribes— a rather strange way to woo one's beloved. Don't confuse these tantrums with one nervous outburst during the planning stages of the wedding; it is hard being cool all the time when working or studying, partying, and trying to keep up with all the hundred and one things there are to do.

It is important that couples meet each other's friends as well as family, even though our unwilling Petruchio might not have agreed with me had I said this at the time of our conversation. Not all favorite friends on either side will get along as well as could be hoped but it is an important gauge of compatibility. Friends enrich life, and if one partner has always been sociable and the other almost a recluse, that will be a hard adjustment. However, if these differences aren't too extreme, that can be a good balance.

RETRACTION OF NEWS STORY

Q: *We announced our daughter's engagement in the newspaper. Now that it has been broken, do you think we ought to have a statement published to that effect?*

Books on etiquette vary on this subject. Most advise that if the engagement was announced in the newspaper(s) then send a simple statement of it to any paper in which the notice(s) appeared, e.g.:

The engagement of Jill Candace Ode and Frederick Eldon Hampenstance has been terminated by mutual consent.

or

Mr. and Mrs. James Person Ode announce that the engagement between their daughter, Jill Candace, and Frederick Eldon Hampenstance has been broken by mutual consent.

In most cases I would just let the news flow by word of mouth. The only time I feel a newspaper item would be advisable is if the couple or parents are well known. It would be an efficient way of notifying those expecting an invitation to the church, if not the reception, that there will be no wedding. Family and close friends should be notified by a note or telephone call.

There is always an "on the other hand" for wanting a retraction of this kind. Let us suppose that because you were not keen on your daughter's choice, you wish it to be known to as many people as possible that the alliance is severed. Since you cannot stand on a rooftop and yell "Yippee!" it might be hard to resist a public statement.

LADIES AND GENTLEMEN, this subject needs more comment. Since the ending of a romance that leads to engagement is not complicated by a marriage contract, most couples, on the surface at least, want to make a clean sweep. Granted the termination of a relationship which was expected to lead to marriage is terribly upsetting and may be more so for one side than the other—but there are certain "sporting" attitudes that should be assumed.

First, couples should not vilify each other; there must have been love in the beginning. All expensive presents exchanged over the engagement period should be returned, as well as intimate correspondence—though in this day and age of lazy letter writers it seems highly unlikely that many couples will have a problem in that area.

Second, if there is an established household or an apartment full of furnishings, then the dismantling and the decisions about whom this or that belongs to are more involved. Sometimes a disinterested third party can help decide ownership, but be sure that person really is impartial.

Engagement and wedding presents from family and friends should also be returned to donors.

CATHOLIC ENGAGED ENCOUNTER

Marry 'em first and change 'em later is the biggest darn fool trap of the betrothal period. Few people are manipulative or shrewd enough to play that game successfully throughout married life. For most people this is a shaky step to take toward the most important decision in one's life.

When a couple fall in love, they may make certain assumptions about their relationship. He may assume that the object of his passion thinks and reacts the same way he does. She is reluctant, however, to bring up subjects that might cause an argument. As the relationship deepens and the couple begin to talk about marriage, topics are avoided that might mar this idyllic time of courtship.

He told her that he was not interested in having children; she did not say anything. He does not realize it now, she thinks to herself, but once we have been married for a time he will change his mind. However, she missed an extremely important clue and was shocked to find, after a few years, that he really meant it. She may have married him anyway, but had they discussed the topic before marriage she would have known what a chance she was taking.

Other couples do not give careful thought to marriage or what it entails; they discover life as they live it.

After a few years of marriage, a couple had their first child. Suddenly, the fact that she was Catholic and he was not became very important. When they married in a Catholic ceremony, the Church expected her to raise their children as Catholics. It was not a signed agreement with the parish church but an obligation on her part, though not on his. Previously, when a Catholic married a person of another faith, the non-Catholic had to agree in writing that their children would be brought up in the Catholic faith.

From the moment he saw his child, the father experienced a reawakening of his religious heritage and was not willing to allow his wife complete control of their child's religious education. "The child should know about both his parents' beliefs," he stated, "so that when he's grown up he can decide for himself." "You knew the implications when we had a Catholic ceremony. It didn't seem to matter to you," she protested. "I just didn't realize it," he responded. Both admitted that it had never occurred to them that their attitudes might change. They really did expect to marry and be eternally happy without ever having to come to terms with their different religious beliefs.

Recognizing the high rate of unhappy unions, and analyzing troubled areas in marriage, the Catholic Church has initiated an Engaged Encounter program, which is a weekend retreat, and the Pre-Cana meeting, an afternoon meeting with similar aims. The couple must attend one of these programs before being married in a Catholic ceremony.

At the Catholic Engaged Encounter, two lay volunteer couples, one of which has been married much longer than the other, run the encounter program, which takes place from Friday evening to Sunday afternoon at a retreat or hotel. The men and women have separate quarters.

The format is outlined by the archdiocese and the sessions deal with all aspects of marriage: its meaning; what one can reasonably expect from the other; sex and birth control; and finances. The couples learn, among other things, that when Catholics marry in a Catholic ceremony marriage vows are made not only to each other but to God, making the union not just a contract between two people but also a sacrament.

Everyone is given a list of statements asking for "I agree/don't agree" answers. The betrothed exchange lists and answers are compared. By Sunday afternoon the couples are brought face to face with what they can expect from each other in the future; they have an understanding of whether or not they agree on vital questions. In spite of their strong physical attraction they may discover there is much to separate them. Some find their love so strong that they are willing to adjust and compromise. Others knew all along that they were well suited and had no difficulty discussing the sensitive subjects others so adeptly sidestepped. Their relationship deepened.

There are other encounter groups, marriage counselors, and members of the clergy of all faiths who advise and guide couples in achieving some understanding of the important step they are taking.

Gifts

To Give or Not to Give . . .

T hat is the question. Would you believe that some people actually want to put the words "No gifts, please" somewhere on the wedding invitations? They feel self-conscious about accepting gifts or appearing as if they expect them. Gift giving is customary and reaches back into mankind's beginnings.

Og, walking through the woods near his cave after a day of hunting, has picked a few flowers for the dining-room table. His new bride would be so pleased at this civilized gesture. Iggle was kidnapped from her tribe by the indelicate hair-dragging method of the day, the way sturdy young cavemen obtained brides. She constantly talks about her people from the north country, who are infinitely more cultured than his people; they are even into two-syllable words.

Suddenly Og hears a sound; he swings about. Standing before him is a stranger holding a club. Instinctively, he hands the flowers to the stranger, who eagerly accepts them, along with an invitation to supper. Our cave-dweller returns to Iggle, who graciously accepts the bouquet from the traveler. She throws Og a triumphant look designed to show him that the stranger's behavior was the ultimate in the new-wave etiquette that has now resulted in a beautiful friendship.

And so we learn from our venerable ancestors that presents are tokens of goodwill, of affection, of commitment, and are fun to give and fun to receive.

Conversely, if some are embarrassed to accept presents, there are others who are confused about the when, what, and how of gift giving. Some interpret every function to which they are invited as a way for people to pry a present from them. That is a different question from whether it is appropriate to give one or what type of gift is suitable for the occasion.

Does a lavish wedding entail a correspondingly expensive wedding present? Nonsense. What seems more likely is that the

41

amount of money spent is determined by the giver, who is generally in economic circumstances similar to the host's. It is assumed that those giving the wedding can afford the cost of the function they arrange. Presents, as well as weddings, should be given within one's means.

A late-nineteenth-century book on general etiquette has a very strange suggestion. Everyone who sends a present should be invited to the wedding but not all who are asked to the wedding are expected to send presents! I reread the entire book looking for a clue to the reasoning behind that statement.

One tongue-in-cheek book written in the 1920s gave excellent advice on etiquette. It suggests that bridal showers should be "informal" affairs; only the "dearest or wealthiest" should be invited and the bride should give back 10 percent of the gross to the hostess.

WHO SENT WHAT AND WHEN?

To keep her sanity intact, the bride should maintain a strict record of presents as they arrive at her home. She may think she will remember who gave what but few brides, no matter how clear-headed, can avoid a slip-up now and again. Record the name of the sender, what they gave, the date the present arrived, and the date the thank-you note was posted.

If some guests bring presents to the reception, a cloth-covered gift table should be set up and a friend or relative assigned to note the items in the bride's book.

Q: *I am invited to an engagement party and have no idea whether a gift is in order.*

Though it is not incorrect to do so, there is no obligation to give an engagement present, whether there is a party or not. The thought behind this suggestion is sensible, since people invited to the engagement party are supposed to be only those who will also be invited to the wedding and prewedding parties, such as showers, which do involve gifts.

I agree with this view because a betrothal is a statement of intent and doesn't always lead to marriage. In days gone by, though, an impending marriage represented a very serious vow. Breach-of-promise suits were not uncommon and were somewhat like today's palimony cases—without the sex involved.

Some people tell me they take a present to an engagement party. They don't, however, give one if the engagement is announced informally. In this case, those close to the future bride and bridegroom can give presents if they like.

Years ago surprise engagement parties were all the rage. Naturally, a guest could not take a gift to the party if the engagement was a secret. Today we are much more open about betrothals and so an engagement party is called an engagement party. But people do worry about this question, since they do not want to be the only ones with a present or the only ones without it.

Someone once told me that she was unsure of what to do. It was an occasion in which it was particularly important to her to do "the right thing" or, more realistically, to do what others were going to do. So she took a present along and sat in her car until she could observe that others were carrying packages. What if everyone did that, we joked.

Another, more confident, woman once told me, however, that "her set" always gives engagement presents no matter what the books say. So if it is a custom in your area to indulge in this practice, why fight it?

At the party, if some people bring presents and some don't, the hostess should direct that they be placed in another room. To prevent embarrassment, open the gifts in private, since the occasion, unlike a shower, does not call for concentration on presents.

Q: *I am debating whether the engagement gift I take to the party celebrating the news should be a joint one for the bridal couple or for the bride-elect alone.*

The future bride's parents generally give the party to announce their daughter's engagement to the young suitor, so often presents are geared to her taste. You have a wide choice from lingerie, jewelry, table or bed linen, towels, or household items.

Though it is unusual for the future married couple to receive joint engagement presents it is not unheard of, especially today when both are so much a part of the proceedings. In years gone by, all presents were considered given to the bride whether for the engagement or the wedding.

Q: *What is today's attitude toward giving money as wedding presents? At one time it was not considered proper.*

Considered not proper? By whom? We are a nation of different backgrounds so the question has to be examined from that perspective. Presents should be thoughtfully suited to the recipient's as well as to the giver's philosophy. That is why so much attention is focused on the subject. If you think that the feelings of the person receiving cash will be hurt by its implication then find something else.

I would agree that the question of whether to present a check or a gift depends a lot on your closeness to the family, your outlook, and on the circumstances of the bridal couple. The choice is still made on the intimacy of the relationship, whether friend or family.

There are those who feel that giving a monetary wedding present is not appropriate . . . only the nearest of relatives, such as grandparents and aunts and uncles, would do so. But the contrary view held by some is that they would not consider giving a cash gift for any other occasion *but* a wedding.

I find that middle-aged people have no misgivings about sending a bond or check to a young couple who are either still in school or have not yet landed decent jobs. They would not, however, think of it for a mature or established couple. It's a good idea for younger people to choose something within their means, from the bridal registry perhaps, so they don't have to worry whether a monetary amount is an adequate showing.

Groups culturally tied to their origins have never been embarrassed by receiving or giving money. In eastern Europe it was not uncommon for guests to put cash gifts into the bride's wedding apron, worn for that purpose, or to pay to dance with the bride and the bridegroom.

Q: *What is the average amount people spend on wedding presents?*

I have spoken to salespeople in department stores and the answers vary. One gift-registry specialist told me about two hundred dollars, but when I checked this figure with my acquaintances, they thought it inflated. My observations from just hanging about purchasers don't tell me much either. It has a lot to do with the closeness of the individuals and the spending customs of the donor. I happened to talk to one young woman who was buying a single crystal wine goblet, which at that time cost about forty dollars. The occasion was a shower for the bride. "What will you give as a wedding gift?" I asked. She hadn't decided whether she would add a place setting to the couple's silver flatware or the formal dinner set. Another woman, shopping for a wedding present, bought a pretty crystal pitcher for about ninety dollars and was pleased with her find.

Q: *I have been invited to the ceremony only and not to the wedding reception. Do I have to give a present whether or not I attend?*

The consensus seems to be that it is optional to give a present if you do not attend the ceremony. It would be appropriate if you do attend but in no way is it obligatory. I have been asked this question many times and the sound of the voice over the telephone can be quite fretful. Others merely want to know what is customary. Some souls interpret that limited invitation as a way for the family to reap twice as many presents without the expense of entertaining. (See p. 76.)

The resentful feel that way because they are being told, so they think, that the relationship they have with the families is not close enough to warrant being received at the celebration after the exchange of vows. They realize, of course, that it is impossible to ask everyone to the reception but they do not see themselves in the "not as close to us" category. According to those who set the standards in the past, you should not feel slighted, because a ceremony-only invitation carries no obligation—neither a present nor a written acceptance or regret is expected.

I do not think it is that easy. Guide yourself on the basis of your relationship or closeness to the bride, the bridegroom, or their families. Analyze the situation: if you are a neighbor and you are asked in a casual way to attend the ceremony, a wedding present is optional, though you might decide to send a less expensive gift anyway. But if you are a co-worker—one who works closely with the bride or bridegroom on a daily basis—then a present might be in order. I would feel more comfortable giving something if I had decided to attend the ceremony.

Q: *I am a single person and was asked by my friends, two married couples, to buy a joint wedding present for a mutual friend. I thought it a good idea but they divided the cost by three, making my part of the obligation the same as theirs. I do not think that equitable. Now I have had to spend more than I intended or could afford. Am I right?*

In a subtle way you are right, since a wedding is counted in terms of the number of people invited. A married couple costs the host twice as much as a single person and, whether or not you agree with that way of thinking, many people choose a present on that basis.

I have spoken to singles. Some agree with you that the cost should have been split into fifths, reasoning that if you were dining together in a restaurant you would not be expected to pay one third of the check but only your part of the total.

However, you should have asked beforehand how much they intended to spend and how the cost would be divided. Though your friends could have been more sensitive to your situation, it probably did not occur to them that they might be being unfair. They think of their money as coming from one source.

Other unmarrieds, who have larger incomes and do not have to think twice about money, say it would never have occurred to them not to split it into thirds since they would have spent about the same amount anyway. Besides, the advantage of a joint present is to give something of greater value.

Q: *I am in the store ordering a gift to be sent to my future daughter-in-law. I'm phoning you to ask how I sign my name? Mom? Mrs. Doe?*

Since the subject has not yet been dealt with, just sign your name, Sonia Hampenstance, but use a term such as "affectionately" to indicate a feeling of warmth.

Q: *What is a suitable present to give my son's fiancée? They have just become engaged.*

A piece of jewelry or a cut-glass bowl, not necessarily new or just purchased. Something you feel would be unique as a remembrance of the first present you gave to welcome her into your family. In addition, your future daughter-in-law might be amused by your son's lock of baby hair, the bronze baby shoe, or his bear-rug bare baby photo—that'll please *him* no end.

Q: *What would you consider parents of the bridegroom should give as a wedding present? For the engagement I gave my future daughter-in-law an heirloom strand of pearls, and had them restrung and placed in a box especially made for them. I also had them appraised.*
Now the wedding is close and I am thinking of giving them $5,000 for the honeymoon, since my son expressed a desire to go somewhere special, and then $5,000 to get them started. Do you think that adequate?

I have had many questions on the when, what, and if of present giving but I have never been asked what parents think fit to give one's own children. How can anyone tell you that? There are so many factors involved. Though some parents are wealthy they might give much less than others who spend much more than they should, given their circumstances. Attitudes toward gift giving are selective, and a lifetime of raising a child leads him or her to certain expectations, whether reasonable or not.

A wedding present of ten thousand dollars might be a fortune to some but a pittance to others. Your son and his bride are just beginning life together. You will have many opportunities in the future to make life easier for them on birthdays, anniversaries, and when grandchildren are born. You might be approached for a down payment on a home when they are ready to buy one.

Q: *We want to give a check to the bridal couple. In whose name is it drafted—that of the bride-to-be or both hers and her fiancé's?*

Checks can be drafted in the bride's name before the wedding and sent to her home address. Some engaged couples open a joint account, so you could make it out in both their names: Jill Ode and/or Frederick Hampenstance. This enables either person to deposit the check or draw on the account. After the wedding, of course, it is made out to Mr. and Mrs., or, if the bride has retained her maiden name, both names are used.

FUN AND THE BRIDAL REGISTRY

One great memory the engaged couple will recall in future years is choosing the setup of their household. For those whose funds are limited the choices will be more practical. Do not let the advice on what constitutes a fine set of silver flatware be daunting; it is good to know how to evaluate these things, for you never know what fortune has in store for you. Often it is not what you have that counts but how you use it. Bone china, crystal, and silver implements will not do it for you if you are not gracious and relaxed hosts. Learning to set a table, the art of listening and of good conversation, and serving even the simplest though well-prepared food in an inviting manner are the ingredients that will build a reputation of refinement and cordial hospitality. If you are at ease, your company will be also.

List choices with the bridal registry and buy the best within the limits of the budget—stainless-steel flatware has handsome patterns and there are bountiful selections of dinner sets that look lovely on a well-laid table.

It might be a good idea to do some "window shopping" before registering. When you both know what you like call the bridal registry to make an appointment so that the person can spend time with you.

The bridal registry is a good idea because you can spend time examining what is on the market that suits your tastes, pocketbooks, and life style. There is no charge for the registry, since it is to the store's benefit, and it is also a convenience to all who take advantage of it. Registering does not mean that people have to buy only what is listed; they have the option of purchasing what they wish.

A young couple should think about everyday flatware, glasses, and dishes as well as fine china, silver pieces, and crystal, along with practical household goods. This gives people a great range of choices for wedding presents, and the pleasure of knowing that they have a hand in putting the couple's home together.

If either, or both, is marrying for the second time, a couple may be reluctant to register even though they are having a wedding followed by a reception. Please do so. It is just as important as for the first marriage, especially since both probably have established households. The problem of what to get would be solved if guests knew a serving spoon or a gravy boat would be a great addition to the couple's silver, silver-plate, or pewter collection. Remember, registering does not ask for presents; it is there for practicality's sake and is used as a guide.

RELUCTANT BRIDES
AND THE BRIDAL REGISTRY

The hesitation some brides and their families have toward registering their preferences comes from the "no gifts" syndrome, which says if you let it be known that you like enamel cookware more than stainless steel you are hinting at what people should spend. It just is not so and I cannot reiterate this often enough. All you are doing is giving an idea of your taste, but this does not obligate givers to go beyond what they think is sensible. Registering makes life easier for the betrothed and for others. One cannot worry about the unsophisticated.

CHOOSING STERLING-SILVER FLATWARE

There are major items that take some thought because of their cost and potential investment value, such as diamonds, Oriental rugs, and sterling-silver flatware. Granted, the value fluctuates with the world market, but, as I mentioned elsewhere in this book, diamonds always retain *some* value and so it is with sterling silver.

Sterling silver is, of course, the most expensive flatware and the most handsome. There is a look to solid sterling that cannot be duplicated; the way it gleams and enhances a dining-room table, it *almost* does not matter what is being served.

Some couples start out with complete sets of fine china, crystal stemware, and sterling-silver flatware given to them as wedding presents by close members of their families. Others gather them as the years go by, using special occasions to fill in when they are able with either a single piece or a place setting.

When shopping for crystal, china, or flatware, call your favorite store and ask when their most knowledgeable salesperson will be on duty. It happens, at times, that department stores will assign a salesperson from another area who knows next to nothing about the product he or she is selling, let alone what constitutes a place setting. Don't waste your time. Just pick up the various brochures and window-shop. Return when the expert is there.

Some department stores do not carry sterling-silver flatware, so it might be better to register with a small store that carries fine china and crystal as well as silver. Such stores are bound to have specialists who can advise on style and design.

The ideal number of place settings is twelve, since most dinner parties are made up of eight, ten, or twelve people. An eight-piece place setting is the next choice, but more than one young couple has begun with what is called a starter set of four, though six is more useful.

Reed & Barton tells me that in recent years people are choosing a slightly smaller standard-size *place* knife and fork. Europeans are accustomed to using a continental *dinner* knife and fork, which are 15 to 20 percent larger than the American place size. At one time flat silver was made up of an array of implements for every type of food one could think of, from oyster forks to grapefruit spoons, orange spoons, berry spoons, cream-soup spoons, and iced-beverage spoons. But now a utensil has more than one purpose.

A basic place setting consists of four to six pieces—five being the most popular:

Place fork
Place knife

Salad or dessert fork
Place spoon for soup, dessert, or cereal
Teaspoon

Some experts advise that butter spreaders should be the choice for a five-place grouping, adding for a six-place setting teaspoons used mainly for stirring coffee or tea and for scooping sections from grapefruit halves. I suggest, as most people do, ordering teaspoons as the fifth piece and buying a single butter knife as part of the serving pieces.

If the betrothed are lucky enough to have the traditional place settings, they might want to gather other additional matching pieces to the set, such as meat-serving forks and vegetable spoons, larger serving spoons, fruit knives and forks, sauce ladles, cake knife, pie server—the list goes on and on. Include them on the bridal registry list. One person might give you the soup ladle and another the pie server.

The decision on what is a good grouping is important but so is the advice given to evaluate sterling (solid) silver:

- Choose a reputable store that stands behind its merchandise and carries brand names. Be sure there is a guarantee or warranty.
- It is wise to have as many place settings in flatware as you have for china and crystal.
- The implement should be heavy yet balanced.
- Forks and spoons are well balanced if, when you place the curved part of the implement (where the stem meets the bowl) horizontally across your index finger, it rocks gently back and forth like a beam bar on a doctor's scale. It will fall if it is not weighted properly. Compare brand names by this method and you will begin to realize the difference.
- Look at the silver fork; the tines should be smooth and even.
- The knife handle is of silver and the blade of stainless steel.
- American silver has the name of the manufacturer and the word "sterling" on the back of the flatware.
- Old World pieces have a hallmark giving the country of origin, the date of manufacture, and the quality of the silver.
- Sterling is pure silver with a small amount of alloy added

for strength and toughness. Each piece has to have the proper percentage of silver and alloy to qualify to be called sterling.

• Style means classical, contemporary, or modern; the shape of the handle determines the shape of the bowl of the spoons and of the fork tines.

• Design is the pattern on the flatware. Some patterns have clean, simple lines, while others have intricate and ornately carved designs that are said by some to hide scratches that gather over years of use, but which are harder to clean.

• Ask the store about an airtight, tarnish-preventing silver chest lined with felt to hold your flatware; it keeps the sulfur in the air from reaching the silver. Silverware-keeper kits are available to build into a silverware drawer to keep the silver tarnish-free.

• Reed & Barton recommends that new silver or silver plate should be hand-washed with soap and warm-to-hot water after using the first few times, to season the silver and to rid it of the alloy that leaches out of the surface. The silver is then pure and reaches its full beauty. Keep a jar of cleaner above the sink. If there is a sign of tarnish on a piece of silver just touch it with the polish and sponge and rinse with hot water.

• Reed & Barton assures me that silver flatware can be safely washed in the dishwasher, provided that it is washed with no other metal present.

• It is not necessary to clean silver more than twice a year, especially if you use it often. Use a product like Hagerty polish and a nonabrasive natural ocean sponge. Rubbing with a soft cloth to prevent scratches should keep its lovely shine.

If you have the four- or five-piece table setting and your uncle from France sent a set of teaspoons, use them. Silver flat pieces do not have to match. If you have teaspoons instead of soup or dessert spoons because you did not know what constituted a basic setting, you can always add another pattern, whether its design is as ornate as yours or not.

MONOGRAMMING OR INITIALING

Whether on silver or silver plate, monogramming is not a simple decision as it once was. Years ago, if silver was part of the bride's trousseau, bought before she knew who her husband would be, her maiden surname initial was etched on each implement. Given as a wedding present by a favorite aunt, her married surname initial(s) was used as the monogram

H

or

J O
*
H

*(the sur-initial can be placed
above or below the J O)*

Other choices would be hers and her husband's given name initials along with his surname initial:

J   F
H

Looks lovely, doesn't it?

Today some women retain their maiden names after marriage. If the silver comes to the woman from her family, and not as a collection of presents from relatives and friends on both sides, then her initials could stand alone. However, if the silver was bought by the couple, both sets of initials should be used.

When both sets of initials are used:

J   O

*

F   H

Before the wedding, presents are sent to the bride-to-be's home so that they will be in a central place and lessen confusion. The idea that all wedding presents belong to the bride is not realistic. It does not seem sporting or very promising for the future if the thought is that there might be a divorce later. But if that is the case, do not have the silver engraved and reserve the grand fight for possession when there are trade-offs.

SILVER-PLATED FLATWARE

Silver-plated flatware is next in beauty but not nearly as expensive. The designs and patterns often are the same as those in sterling. Like sterling, silver plate is evaluated according to weight, balance, and the content of silver used. A well-made piece has a convex back or seam that gives the utensil more strength and can be monogrammed. Carefully examine the finish and the detail.

STAINLESS STEEL

There are people who prefer stainless steel even though they can well afford to own the most expensive sterling-silver flatware. Stainless-steel flatware is less costly by far. It has an appealing silvery-gray patina with designs ranging from modern to classic, even elaborately engraved. Be sure to use a dishwashing detergent that does not spot.

DINNERWARE

Like flatware, dinner sets should be bought by the place setting, which has:

- Dinner plate
- Rimmed soup plate
- Dessert or salad plate
- Cup and saucer
- Bread-and-butter plate

The rimmed soup plate is versatile. Aside from the obvious, it can be used as a salad plate when the salad plate is being used for dessert.

Additions are luncheon plates, serving platters, vegetable and covered serving dishes, a soup tureen, demitasse cups and saucers, a teapot, a coffeepot, creamer and sugar bowl, and fruit or dessert bowls.

It is best to start with two sets. Basic everyday dishes should be worry-free and not too fragile. Your dinner set for entertaining can be a style following that of your crystal and flatware, since you might like the same classic look in all three, or one can be more ornate than the others.

It is tempting to use the prettiest dishes often but they should be brought out mainly on special occasions. You will enjoy setting a holiday table or having a dinner party knowing you have a complete dinner service.

In England, a dinner service and a tea set are separate. Dinnerware does not include cups, saucers, or cake plates, teapot or coffeepot, creamer or sugar bowl, and is generally a completely different design from a tea set. Americans seem to prefer a complete matching set.

Check what the words "open stock" means. To most reputable stores it means that the manufacturer will produce that pattern for many years, allowing for future purchase of additional place settings or for the replacement of broken dishes that can be bought by the piece. It may be that a particular pattern is attractive but is a closeout, leaving the chances of hunting down replacements an exercise in futility. It would be wise to resist such bargains.

When deciding on the shape of the cup, whether part of your dinner set or not, you should both lift it to your lips to see if the shape of the rim and the bowl of the cup make it as graceful to use as it is to look at. Men do not seem comfortable drinking coffee or tea from a narrow-rimmed cup.

Bone china, translucent and delicate looking, is the most expensive. Another choice is ovenware—oven-to-table dishes. Informal earthenware has a rich range of colors and is often made individually, so that each piece has a slightly different look. No matter what your taste, dishes should be dishwasher safe.

CRYSTAL AND GLASSWARE

The range of sizes considered necessary for a complete set of crystal differs. A basic starter setting has:

- Water goblet
- Goblet for red wine

A goblet is a long-stemmed glass. When the choice is a two-piece set, the red-wine goblet is used because it is larger than that for white wine and looks better balanced next to the water goblet. And, yes, white wine will taste as good in a goblet for red wine.

Champagne in tall, narrow-rimmed champagne goblets holds its sparkle longer. Wide-rimmed goblets, though, are more versatile, since they can be used for custard or ice-cream desserts as well as for champagne.

Other additions to a set of crystal are the smaller V-shaped goblets for sherry and the short-stemmed brandy glass with its wide bowl and narrower rim. (Connoisseurs of brandy hold the goblet in cupped hands to warm the liquid, while inhaling the aroma and sipping slowly. Some purists go as far as having a holder for the glass with a candle under it to bring the spirits to the right temperature.) The smallest-size liqueur glasses, holding but two tablespoons of the sweeter, thicker aromatic spirits, are used for after-dinner drinks.

Larger, stemless glasses have many uses, including holding mixed drinks and nonalcoholic beverages. The smaller size is for straight liquor and fruit juice.

Life in the United States has been simplified to such a degree that some women who have fine china and crystal tell me that unless the occasion is a formal one they do not use them for entertaining as much as they once did because they have to be hand-washed. They use a dishwasher-safe middle set for company.

BRIDAL REGISTRY
AND A TALE OF TWO CITIES

An excellent suggestion from a mother of the bride planning her daughter's wedding is to register at a store that has a branch in the bridegroom's hometown. Since his folks lived in Chicago and hers in the Washington, D.C., area, it was not difficult to do and made buying presents much easier for everyone.

If some towns do not have the same department-store branches, it might be feasible to divide the list to avoid duplicates. Also, some stores will get in touch with an out-of-town one, even though they have no direct business contact with it, to ask for bridal registry information. This is good public relations; the stores increase their sales, the bridal couple receives useful presents, and the shopper is satisfied that the gift will be well thought of.

Q: *I have just come from the bridal registry at the local department store. Surely the bridal couple do not expect me, a single self-supporting individual, to buy sterling-silver flatware or a place setting of bone china as a wedding present?*

No, of course not. If you can afford it, a single piece will do. If not, find something else within your budget you think your friends might like. Or buy a gift certificate so they can add to the amount and choose for themselves.

LADIES AND GENTLEMEN, just a word about gift certificates vs. money gifts. Some people tell me that gift certificates limit the bridal couple to one store, and that they would prefer to bank or spend the check where and whenever they please. Others say they dislike giving money because it shows no imagination or thought to gift giving; a gift certificate is in the same class as money. I do not agree that it shows no thought, especially if a close member of the family had been "sounded out" and the giver had been led to believe that that type of present would be appreciated. Since it is supposed that presents are voluntarily given, people should be allowed to choose the type of present that they feel comfortable offering. In most cases they want to give the best they can afford.

EXCHANGING PRESENTS

Q: *It is not supposed to be polite to exchange wedding presents, but what if there are duplicates or completely useless items for one's life style? We have received a few gifts we cannot possibly use and, since we are starting from scratch and living on a tight budget, I feel like taking them back to the store and choosing something else.*

Exchanging duplicates is easy since no one need know whose present was exchanged. In researching the experts I find there are some who say that *only* duplicate presents can be exchanged. But most people want the couple to have items that can be of use and do not mind them being taken back to the store. However, one has to use judgment. Ask yourself if the person would be offended if you did not keep what was sent. If the answer is yes and you might be entertaining the donor in your home, then don't return it. However, if you have a number of presents you would like to exchange from people with whom you are not closely associated, I see no reason why you should not do so.

But think about it a moment. Sometimes a present is appreciated more and more over the years. A cut-glass bowl may not be the most practical present for your immediate needs, but it might be the start of the extra-fine serving pieces you will enjoy collecting for use in the future.

LOST PRESENT
OR LATE ACKNOWLEDGMENT

Q: *Seven months ago, just before the event, I sent a wedding present through the department-store bridal registry. I carefully watched the salesperson write the address so I felt confident the gift would arrive before the wedding. Though I have paid the bill I have not received a thank-you note. If the bride doesn't get around to acknowledgments how do I know that it was ever received or that the store sent the correct item?*

Call the department store to ascertain that the package was delivered to the correct address. They keep excellent records since, unfortunately, they receive many inquiries such as yours. At least you will know that a present was received. Had you sent it by insured parcel post, at your request the post office could have put a tracer on it. If the present was received, relax; the recipients are tardy in sending their thanks. Should it be determined that the package was not delivered and possibly lost, then write to the newlyweds and explain.

LADIES AND GENTLEMEN, some sources say that the bride has a year to write thank-yous. In most cases, unless the couple is on a desert island for 365 days or lost in the wilds of Alaska, one year is too much time to accomplish the task. That great suggestion is for the lucky rich on a year's honeymoon trip around the world who neglected to take writing equipment because of their deep absorption in each other. Wouldn't it be nice if the not-so-newly-wedded couple, when writing thank yous, could hold on to that feeling of pleasure that they first felt when they opened the gifts.

Don't blame mothers for their children's tardiness. The most devoted of progenitors have some uncomfortable moments when they are asked if presents were received. All they can do is answer that the couple was delighted with them.

The bridal couple can seek help with the many things they have to do, but there are certain niceties that give a sense of caring and appreciation. One of those is the short hand-written letter from either the bride or the bridegroom (yes, men can and do take pen in hand) saying how pleased they were with the gift. Note the item received, especially if it was sent through a store, so that the giver knows that the correct present arrived.

Thank yous but no thanks were showered on a busy career woman who bemoaned the fix in which she found herself when she hired someone to write thank-you notes. Well, she said the impact of these epistles on those who knew her handwriting was the equal to audit notices from the IRS. I asked her to put the situation in perspective and tell me how many people died of surprise when they did not recognize her penmanship—many fewer than would have been offended wondering whether presents were received in the first place.

Past gurus of etiquette look with as much displeasure at those pseudo thank-you notes as they do when cards with the words THANK YOU are printed on the front, as if the sender had a mental block about writing those words. Though I too question the good taste of saying thanks that way, I felt sympathetic toward that young woman. She had the added pressure of moving and traveling on business both before and right after her marriage. I was also surprised at the to-do over a faux pas committed out of sheer pressure. Most of us are too polite to make a fuss. As well-brought-up people, we might think it was an awkward thing to do but would be too delicate to say anything. The woman's solution backfired and she was bewildered by the lack of understanding shown her.

Ah, had she only spoken to me! It would have been better if she had had her original "thank-you scribe" write that the present had been received but due to work pressures the bride and bridegroom had been unable to write and would do so in the near future. Later, she and her husband could have divided the chore by doing a few every evening, she handling her side and he his.

THANK-YOU NOTES BEFORE THE WEDDING

If the letter is to someone with whom you are not on a first-name basis, I suggest signing your name in full so that he or she will recognize the writer:

Dear Mr. and Mrs. Homer,
   Frederick and I thank you for the salad-bowl set. It is just what we wanted.
   We are so looking forward to seeing you at the wedding.
                                                        Sincerely,
                                                        Jill Candace Ode

Apart from "sincerely," other phrases are suitable depending on the relationship, such as "affectionately," "as ever," "with love," "very," or "most sincerely."

When writing to relatives and friends close to you, picture them in your mind's eye and the words will come with warmth.

Dear Aggie and Johnnie,
   Fred and I can't wait to become hosts after our wedding so we can use the beautiful fruit bowl you sent us. As soon as we are back from Bermuda we'll make a date.
   Meantime, see you two weeks from Saturday.
   Thanks from us both.
                                                        Love,
                                                        Jill

BETTER-LATE-THAN-NEVER NOTES

Q: *My husband and I have been married almost a year but haven't had time to send thank-you notes. I know I have up to a year to do so. Besides, we ordered a photo of both of us to include as part of the thank-you card that was ready only recently. Now I don't know how to word the note. Should I write an excuse? Also, is it all right to put the date we were married under the photo?*

Just write your letter. Don't make any excuses, and I would not include the date of your marriage under the photograph. It would be a reminder that the thank-yous are late. I suggest:

Dear Sally and John,
    Frederick and I think of you every time we use the lovely crystal pitcher you sent us. It reminds us of our wedding and that you were there to share the day with us.
    Thank you very much.

With affection,
Jill

If you do not know the sender well:

Dear Mr. and Mrs. Homer,
    My husband, Frederick, and I think of you every time we use the lovely crystal pitcher you sent us. It reminds us of our wedding day and that you were there to share it with us.
    Thank you so much.

Sincerely,
Jill Ode Hampenstance

REITERATIONS

I know I have written this elsewhere, but on the subject of letters of appreciation I think it worth repeating. The bride should always send a note of thanks to those who have entertained her and her beau. The graciousness of a hostess is a gesture worth more than money can buy.

MARRIAGE ANNOUNCEMENT

Q: *We've received a marriage announcement from an acquaint-ance. My husband says they are asking for a gift. I sent a note expressing our good wishes. Was I right?*

Yes, you were. No gift is requested or expected. Marriage announcements are sent after the wedding to people who are not close enough to be invited or to those living at a great distance away who were not able to attend. Again, a present is optional.

ELOPEMENT

Elopement is not as common a happening as it once was, but occasionally I am asked if a present is due a couple who marry without notifying anyone. Why not, I say, especially if they are in the family or close friends. If you had been invited to the wedding a gift might have been sent. Besides, there might be a good reason for the elopement even if the reason is not shared with most of their acquaintances.

Q: *Just before the ceremony was to begin, my stepdaughter decided that she could not go through with the proceedings. The clergyman spoke to the bridal couple privately and recommended a postponement. Her father and I had prepared a reception for 150 people.*
  Now we want to return the presents, but she says they will marry in six months' time, though when I asked if they had reset the date she said no. From our point of view they will have to marry quietly as we will not go to the effort and expense of another wedding. We feel awkward about not sending back the gifts. Do you agree?

If the wedding is postponed for a short time and the reason for the delay is not a serious difference between the betrothed, then the presents do not have to be returned. But unless the date has been reset, even in the distant future, six months is too long, so it is best to send them back sooner. Try to convince your stepdaughter that she has enough on her mind and if too much time elapses people will begin to wonder whether the marriage is to take place. Also, stores have a time limit on the return of items. Close relatives and friends, whether or not they have an understanding of the postponement, will leave the decision to the reluctant couple. I am confident that others will be patient, realizing that this is a difficult time for all involved and that the recipients of their gifts do not wish to keep them but might be finding the situation confusing.

Q: *My next question: how does one go about returning wedding presents? Should I ask people who live in the vicinity to tea or cocktails to pick up their gifts?*

It is a monumental and expensive task, but the most direct way of returning presents is to wrap and mail them, enclosing a note that your daughter and her fiancé hope to be married later on but since they have not set the date you are returning the gift. That will give people the option of sending their gift back to the shops or of holding it should the couple decide to marry.

If you invite people to tea you may be leaving yourself open to unwanted questions, and you must decide if you are ready to reply to or fend off people's inquisitiveness. How do you feel about delivering packages in person, matter of factly and without fanfare, to those who live nearby?

Q: *I was engaged to a young lady who decided that she did not want to get married. I am not only upset by her decision but she has made no move to return the many presents I bought her. Isn't she supposed to return all presents?*

Yes, you both should give back the more expensive presents you gave to each other. Most people have no intention of keeping these offerings and the delay might be the emotional result of the breakup—even though it was her doing. If you don't hear from her, write saying you wish to return the things she gave you and request the valuables you gave her. Later, if the letter brings no results, and if the expense is warranted, you might be able to sue.

THE ENGAGEMENT BANDIT
STRIKES AGAIN

This young woman has quite a hobby. She dates during the summer, promises to marry in the spring, and wants to become engaged on Christmas Day or on her birthday, at which point she is presented with a diamond ring. A month later she realizes the whole thing is a mistake and breaks the engagement but keeps the diamond because it was a Christmas or birthday present. At last count our collector has been engaged three times.

If only our innocent young gentlemen could have proved the gems were heirlooms given by mothers or family members they could have outsmarted the gal with the glittering tastes.

And so, my young gallants and damsels, I am as surprised as you are to find that some avaricious people are shabby enough to keep the symbol of your shattered love to have and to hold forever. I warn you to think twice about combining your engagement presents with so worthy an event as your avowed's birthday.

Did you know that *Your Wedding* is a tricky game? . . . And you thought becoming betrothed was hazardous. I am, at times, tested by queries as unanswerable as the old lawyer's trick, "Answer yes or no . . . Do you still beat your wife?" Or a question can be so artfully put that it tries to elicit an answer designed to make the questioner seem correct or feel better about him- or herself. Practiced by all ages, below are two perfect examples of telephone calls—both from young women:

Q: *My co-worker is extremely cold to me because I couldn't go to her wedding. I think she is unreasonable. Should I send her a present anyway? My cousin says I don't have to since I did not attend.*

Surely the bride would not be annoyed that you could not attend. There is always a percentage of guests who have to decline the invitation for one reason or another. Since presents arrive over a period of time after the wedding, I cannot imagine that that would bother her, either. Were you invited to the complete affair and did you accept?

Q: *I was invited to both and I said I would come.*

When did you tell her you could not attend?

Q: *When she returned to work after the honeymoon.*

What reason did you offer?

Q: *A friend came over unexpectedly.*

If you told her that then I am afraid she must feel that you treated her special day very lightly and is hurt. She is probably annoyed because she not only paid the caterer for your place at the reception—a day or two before the wedding the bride has to pay for the amount of guests she guaranteed whether they show up or not—but most families have a limited amount of people they can invite to the wedding and they could have chosen someone in your place. She might have been more understanding if the reason had been less frivolous.

I think a present is in order since the general guidelines are that a gift is appropriate if you are invited to both the ceremony and the reception whether you show up or not, and, after all, you had accepted. However, I do not know if a present will improve your relationship with the bride. I hope so.

GIFT TIMING

"When," asked a young voice over the telephone, "is it okay to give my friend a wedding present?"

"Preferably," I answered, "gifts should be sent soon after receiving the invitation to the wedding, but the time span is liberal since some people send presents even six months after the event. When," I continued, as an afterthought, "is the wedding?"

"I don't know," was the answer, "I haven't received the invitation yet."

"In that case," I cautioned, "you ought to wait for the invitation before you send a present because you would not want to put yourself in the awkward position of assuming an invitation is forthcoming. Even the family might not know now how many guests they will be able to include. Not that receiving a wedding present obligates the bridal couple to invite more guests than they are able."

It may have been a coincidence but I received the following question around the same time:

Q: *We have a limited guest list and I find myself in the embarrassing position of receiving a wedding present from a person I had no intention of inviting to the wedding. Am I obligated to invite her?*

Even though you might feel uncomfortable about it, no, a wedding present does not ensure a wedding invitation. Just send a thank-you note soon.

SECOND-TIME-AROUND PRESENTS

Q: *There is a sudden rash of second-time marriages that we will be attending soon. I have read somewhere that two-timers are not entitled to wedding presents.*

Two-timers? Are you sure you want to use that term? As a little girl in England I learned from American films that the slang expression meant a person was double-crossing someone, or being unfaithful. The Chicago gangster, cigar hanging from his lips, rasped: "That two-timer! Rub her out!"

Oh, well, back to your query. I have read that some people take the stand that one present is sufficient, others not. But I have been to a few second-go-rounders' weddings that I thought a joy to attend, and sent a present. It is my way of celebrating friends' newfound happiness after probably unhappy experiences with more than a little bit of loneliness thrown in. Since I don't know anyone like Tommy Manville, the marrying millionaire, I expect most of my friends will stop at two tries, and if some hardy soul wants to try for a third time I shall decide how generous I feel at the time.

OPENING PRESENTS

Q: *Since we are being married in church and the reception is to take place at our club, we are not going to have a display table for presents. How do I let people know that we would prefer not to have them bring presents to the wedding and, if they do, we will not be opening them?*

There is no direct way you can mention your preference other than handling it the way one would the bridal registry—through a third party. Ideally, presents should be sent to the bride's home before the wedding. It would be better for guests to mail their presents to the couple's home after the wedding if they were unable to do so beforehand.

You are under no obligation to open presents at the reception and it would be most unusual to do so at that time. In some areas of the country it is not considered proper. The wedding day is centered around the ceremony and the celebration afterward. It would be embarrassing to most guests to put the emphasis on wedding presents.

DISPLAYING PRESENTS

Displaying presents has been a cause of discussion. Aside from the sensitive aspects of who gave what, some brides feel it's a private matter between them and donors.

But since starting on what seemed a simple look into the "helpful answers" game, I find that there is always an on-the-other-hand. Some families feel that displaying gifts shows their thanks for their guests' generosity.

If it is done at all it should be only when the reception takes place at home. A table covered with a tablecloth, which is sometimes decorated with ribbons and scattered with flowers, is arranged in a room by itself so guests can wander in to ooh and aah. It is best not to have cards identifying the giver if you have many duplicates or if you feel that some people will be a little self-conscious that their contributions do not compete with the more expensive presents. Since it is also inconsiderate to have checks displayed with the amount seen, the sum is covered with a strip of paper allowing only the signature to show; a piece of plastic is taped over the checks so that "nosey parkers" can't peek.

That whole scene is not *Your Wedding*'s style. I agree with the supposition that presents received and given are privileged information.

Imagine having a display table full of gifts at a reception taking place in a club or hotel. A display table would have to be set up in an open area, the presents unwrapped and tastefully arranged ahead of time, with those of like value and taste grouped together so all the offerings look appealing. A reliable person would have to be assigned to look after the display. Then, when the festivities were over, someone would have to repack the presents and transport them home. No wonder this custom is unpopular with town people, who also, by the way, frown on bringing presents to the reception. I read somewhere that the country practice of bringing presents to the wedding was necessitated by poor post-office delivery in outlying areas, which has improved in recent years.

The British royal family displays all wedding presents and sometime after the wedding the public is invited to the viewing, as they were after Prince Charles and Diana, Princess of Wales, were married. The story is told that at the time Queen Elizabeth II was married to Prince Philip, an impoverished noblewoman sent an antique chess piece as a wedding present to the royal couple that looked insignificant compared to the gifts of nations and tycoons. The royal family exhibited it along with the thousands of other offerings by encasing it in glass with the legend: "This long-lost chess piece, given by ——, completes an antique chess set and is now one of the royal family's prized possessions."

SHOWER PRESENTS

Q: *At a bridal shower I gave a book on etiquette. I thought it was a practical and thoughtful present—a delightful up-to-date reference book. It was received coolly by the recipient—and guests, for that matter. It never occurred to me beforehand, but could they have interpreted it to mean that I thought the bride was lacking in manners?*

Are you sure that you are not being too sensitive? If you don't think so, then my reaction to this question is to say their response justified your choice of present and that you should have marked the page on how to practice the gracious art of acceptance.

Would anyone deliberately give a present to be insulting? I think not, but I wonder why it would be looked upon that way. Like cookbooks, reference books such as these are treasures, and there always is room for more than one in a home library because it is fun to read what different experts think. When you go into a used-book store—as I have done many times for my collection—you will find that books on etiquette are seldom discarded by their owners and are hard to come by.

OFFICE COLLECTIONS

Q: *I work in a medium-sized office. The only time our department sees some co-workers is when they take up a collection for something or other, especially wedding presents. What is your opinion on having to contribute to gifts for people one doesn't know?*

Are you sure that you *have* to contribute to every manila envelope that comes your way? The decision should be made on the basis of whether you feel it appropriate to do so and you should not feel self-conscious about refusing. Some find it hard to say no, but *no* it should be—especially if the recipient is unknown to that particular office. Other employees, no matter what is going on even in their immediate office, have a general philosophy of not joining in. I have no quarrel with that since no one would want a present not willingly given.

Most offices, unless the affair involves someone who is well known in all departments, keep collections within their areas and on a voluntary basis. If it is thought that others might wish to join, a note should be posted on bulletin boards in the various departments. If the pressure is too strong, write a note for the suggestion box; management may not be aware that the gift giving is being overdone.

It used to be a rule of etiquette strictly adhered to by management and employees alike: presents were not to be given to or accepted by supervisors or those in management. These people earn a good deal more than those under them. Even more undesirable is the appearance of currying favor. At the very least, it can make people beholden in subtle ways.

PRESENTS FOR ATTENDANTS

Two of the most frequently asked questions are what are suitable presents for bridesmaids and groomsmen and when are they given.

In Great Britain it is customary for the bridegroom to pay for presents for the bridesmaids, as it once was in the United States. (How the change came about here I do not know.)

In this country the bride pays for her maids' presents and the bridegroom for those who serve him. A gracious way of expressing appreciation, these presents are generally keepsakes—something that will remind them of the happy day they shared with the bride and bridegroom. I hesitate to list items other than to suggest those in the general area of jewelry, brass library embossers engraved with the person's name, or something used for the wedding and treasured afterward.

It is best to choose presents that are identical or almost identical. However, maids and matrons of honor receive a slightly more expensive present, as does the best man, since their functions demand much more of their time than do the bridesmaids' and ushers'.

The amount of money spent is up to you. As with other decisions in this area it depends on your budget. Some people have a wonderful eye for unusual presents that look much more expensive than they really are. Other brides are uncomfortable unless they spend a certain sum on each present.

PRESENTS FROM ATTENDANTS

Q: *Is it proper for the attendants, male and female, to buy a joint present for the bridal couple? Some of us feel that if a collective present is decided upon, the bridesmaids should give separately from the ushers. But others say that the more money, the more valuable a present can be given.*

It is a great idea for all to contribute; I see nothing wrong with it. Remember, part of the fun of receiving presents is the uniqueness of choices. One solid gift is more useful than several smaller ones, and less strain on each budget—especially since most of you gave gifts at prewedding parties, not to mention the cost of wedding-party clothing.

PRESENTS BETWEEN BRIDE AND BRIDEGROOM

It is a private matter between the bride and the bridegroom whether they wish to give each other special presents on their wedding day. It depends on their financial footing at the moment of marriage. To pay for a wedding and furnish a home many a young couple have to put off buying luxuries they can later afford. It is traditional in some families for the bridegroom to present his bride with a piece of jewelry, such as a string of pearls, on their wedding day, as it is for the husband to give his wife something when a child is born.

PRESENTS FOR PARENTS

To show their appreciation for past nurturing, some couples send both sets of parents tokens of love. At this point in the budget, it might be better for them to wait until they reach their honeymoon destination and find something special for them.

GUIDELINES

- Send wedding presents when possible after the invitation has been received.
- A wedding present should be sent if an invitation is received and accepted to both the ceremony and reception.
- It is optional to send a present if the invitation has to be declined, but appropriate if one is family or a close friend.

- For ceremony-only invitations giving a present is optional.
- It is also optional to send a gift when receiving a wedding announcement. There is no obligation.
- Address wedding presents sent before the event to the future bride. After the wedding they would be sent to "Mr. and Mrs."
- Prompt, hand-written letters of thanks should be sent by the bride or the bridegroom.
- Engagement presents exchanged between the betrothed should be returned if the engagement is broken.
- When an engagement is broken or a wedding is canceled, presents are returned to the givers.
- After a divorce, even soon after the wedding, presents are not returned but are divided between the couple.

Guests

Who and How Many

Ladies and gentlemen, I have a confession to make. I've been avoiding the subject of the guest list. For a while I was tempted to work on a fictional story that had nothing to do with weddings, but that would have been the coward's way out. Anyone who can, in the most delicate way, tell a stepmom to "butt out" and Mrs. Ex-wife to give everyone breathing space is no coward—foolhardy, maybe, but not timorous. What is more, I now know why past books on weddings have adroitly avoided addressing the subject.

Deciding on the number of guests is the first step. Then, if the bride's family is hosting the entire event, the next step is whether the guest list is to be divided equally between both families. At one time, the bride's family allotted themselves more invitations than they did the bridegroom's and some still hold to that policy. I am told there is now a more balanced approach and most often the list is split evenly. Again, it depends on the circumstances.

A potential trouble area might arise if the bridegroom's family wishes to invite more guests than they have been allotted. That's only appropriate if there is enough space to accommodate more people and if the bridegroom's family understands that they will have to pay for their overflow of guests.

Some handle the guest list unemotionally and stick to it. With the expectation that 10 percent of invited guests have to decline for one reason or another, the bride's family allows a certain number of people for both sides of the family. When regrets are received, neither the bride's nor the bridegroom's family is allowed to invite others in their stead. That way the figure stays within the original budget, yet more have been invited than are able to attend. I am assured that this works.

All who are expected to attend the wedding receive wedding invitations; yes, even the bridegroom's parents, sisters, brothers, along with all members of the bridal party. If the clergyman or woman is to be invited to the reception, an invitation should be sent that includes his or her spouse.

A bereaved person should be invited to the wedding if he or she would have been anyway, and should try to attend if at all possible. Sometimes celebrants feel guilty because they are so happy while others are full of grief, but I think it hurtful not to send an invitation.

An old quip says: rich or poor, it is good to have money. When money is no object and the wedding planned is large enough to satisfy both families' requirements, putting the guest list together demands concentration and attention to detail.

But when the guest list is limited and one's acquaintance is large, the problem of keeping within the established number is difficult. Most of us find these decisions tough to face; who wants to be in the position of having to omit friends or relatives whom we are fond of, or, if not that, who at least have a place in our lives?

When only a limited number can be invited to the reception, some people solve the problem by asking a larger group to the ceremony only. This is an accustomed route and, it seems, an accepted practice.

Ceremony-only invitations are a subject of discussion, both pro and con. One's reaction on receiving one depends on oneself and whether one understands the nature of such an invitation. Some people are not surprised by ceremony-only invitations. They did not expect to be invited to the celebration afterward but would have been hurt if they had not been asked to the ceremony. Those who receive a limited invitation can decide to attend if they have time and send a present or not as they wish. But others are hurt. Their reaction is often awkward: ought I to attend, and, if I do, must I take a present? Less kind souls assume that the family has devised a diabolical way of accumulating presents without the obligation of entertaining.

Some communities have what is called "Open Church"— everyone in the community is welcome and there is a simple repast of some sort in the fellowship hall after the ceremony.

While I understand the sometimes unavoidable necessity of a dual guest list, personally I would try to avoid ceremony-only invitations. My style is to have an affair that combines both the ceremony and reception with a guest list that fits the budget. There might be explanations due some people, but if an up-front declaration is made, most understand. I remember a conversation with a woman who said she was put out when told that as much as her friends would miss her, they had a limited wedding-guest list. It was only when her son was being married and she found herself faced with the unenviable job of paring names that she realized those decisions were no fun.

Invitations to the ceremony only are engraved and mailed without an R.S.V.P., conveying to the recipients that they are either not invited to the reception or that there will not be a celebration afterward. Sometimes the ceremony takes place in the morning and festivities are held in the evening.

Another way of issuing ceremony-only invitations is to write a note or telephone each person individually. The note might say that the guest list had to be limited but that the couple would be honored if Mr. and Mrs. Ceremony Only would come to the house of worship to witness the ceremony. However, I would not invite anyone only to the ceremony if the reception were taking place immediately afterward on the premises. That would be too obvious.

Ideally, the guest list should include relatives, friends, and parents' business associates on both sides of the family, along with the bridal couple's friends and business associates.

Now, when the word "relative" arises, where does the cutoff come—cousins? their children? one's sister's brothers- and sisters-in-law? It is probably best to start paring the list with the most distant relatives, such as the children of cousins, or it might be decided that no one's children will be invited except those in the bride's and bridegroom's immediate families.

Now, this is no hard-and-fast rule, because it may be that second cousins, or cousins once removed, are friends as well as relatives. Does one chance omitting that second cousin's brothers or sisters, who are hardly known to the family but who would suppose that because a second cousin was invited all should have been? My friend invited everyone to her first son's wedding but the relationships remained the same; the second cousins of whom she was so fond were as attentive as ever and the others just disappeared after the wedding When her second son was married she cut the guest list to the friendly second cousins.

The choice might be between relatives who have had very little contact with the family and friends who have enriched the celebrants' adult lives. Who can make that decision for anyone? There are some who will say without hesitation that they would invite friends over some relatives, friends who stood by them during difficult times—those times that couldn't be shared with family members, who are now expecting an invitation. Others would not think of omitting any member of their family.

Whether fellow employees or business associates are invited also depends on the type of function planned. I would advise caution on how to approach this part of the guest list. A lot depends on diplomacy and on working relationships. Remember the employer and his wife who were vexed because they received an invitation to the ceremony but not to the reception? That's a perfect example of what an employee should not do.

Depending on the size of the wedding, and whether or not a person works in a small business where there is a measure of friendliness, an invitation to the wedding can be appropriate. But there are difficulties if the organization is large. A person who works for a large organization doesn't generally invite its president to his or her wedding unless he or she is also in an extremely high position. Inviting the manager of a large department might be feasible if the celebrant is a supervisor, but it is not even debatable if the office atmosphere is strictly business and the hierarchy clearly defined. Inviting a person in a supervisory position along with close fellow workers might be a good decision. Only the person working in that particular area can decide whether it is a good idea to include all or part of the office or department.

It is hard for some to separate business and social circles but there are people who manage to combine both. There are career professionals whose lives are so structured that they have little contact with people outside business anyway. Using the invitation for political reasons does not always work but it might cement a developing relationship.

To put it simply, decide the importance of each individual or couple and make a personal determination. The cutoff is based on the practicality of the situation and the closeness of family members.

When the bridegroom has never been married before but the bride has, and the traditional custom of a small, limited wedding is followed, many people close to the bridegroom's family may be sorely disappointed. A bit of rethinking should go into the guest list, taking care to notice the bridegroom's point of view. The step into matrimony is as important to him and his circle as it is to the bride and hers. I advise having a "to meet the newlyweds" party after the honeymoon, though it is not the same as being present at the exchange of vows.

Q: *When is the latest that wedding invitations can be issued? We have a few refusals and would dearly love to invite some people we couldn't include on the first list. It would make us so happy if we could do it now.*

According to guidelines, you have up to three weeks to mail wedding invitations. If you are approaching the third week, send them immediately. I hesitate to give an answer about an alternative guest list because those invitations should be handled with great care.

When planning a formal wedding, some families decide to send invitations six weeks early. They also select a three-and-a-half-week deadline for replies, and recipients are supposed to respond immediately. Should early regrets be received, alternatives can then be invited. Now there is one problem: if response cards are used and have a requested time limit printed on them, they cannot be sent as is because the recipients will realize they were not first choice. However, a few answer cards can be printed without mention of time.

Though some suggest allowing two and a half weeks to respond, I think that's too close to the wedding. It depends on the attitude of the people you wish to invite. You must be very careful to appraise the situation sensitively. Some people might not take kindly to a late invitation. Others might not mind, understanding the difficulty of a limited guest list.

I know someone who agonized over a limited guest list. When she received a refusal she telephoned a friend saying that she would be deliriously happy if the late invitation being mailed would be accepted in the spirit in which it was sent. Her friend assured her that she and her husband understood and would be delighted to attend. Could you make such a telephone call? With some it works but with others it might be best to forget it, no matter how much you would like to have them attend.

Q: *As parents of the bridegroom, we have offered to pay for extra invitations because our family is so much larger and closer knit than that of the bride's. The other side agreed. However, every time I make a suggestion regarding the wedding arrangements, I am politely ignored and feel slighted. My son says forget it. Am I wrong? After all, we are contributing.*

You are contributing only for those over the amount you were originally allotted and that fact does not invite you to make unsolicited suggestions.

LADIES AND GENTLEMEN, the involvement of the bridegroom's family in the wedding arrangements touches a sensitive area. Technically speaking, if the arrangements and the major portion of all the expenses are assumed by the bride's family, the bridegroom's family attends as honored guests. At times, this is a bit chilling to his family; after all, it is their child who is being married and their relations and friends who are going to be attending.

The bride's family, on the other hand, should not be overbearing about wedding plans. It seems surprising to have to stress such a point, but the bride's family should at least inform the bridegroom's family about the wedding plans. Though most of the arrangements are made by her family, the bridegroom's side still has to have time to make their own plans. They need to know how many guests they are allotted, what type of wedding it will be, the formality of dress, and all those things that make a wedding a successful, smoothly run event.

Q: *Our daughter's wedding is taking place next month. We allotted the groom's family sixty guests. They gave us eighty names, saying twenty of those would certainly not attend. Well, the "yes" responses are coming in. My wife is so upset that she cannot sleep because even with sixty on our side and sixty on theirs the budget was stretched. What is more, we also overstepped the sixty limit. What shall we do?*

Caterers advise that up to 10 percent of invited guests will not be able to accept the invitation and a lesser percentage may not attend at the last minute due to family or business emergencies. But I know of some affairs that received 100 percent acceptance, with only four or five people unable to show up on the day.

Analyze the situation. You cannot change the fact that you now have a guest list approaching 160 people. If 10 percent decline you will have sixteen less on your list. That leaves twenty-four extras, twelve extra guests each. The original figure was supposed to be 120, which means you are one fifth over your budget. I doubt that you could hope for one fifth no-shows. Maybe you can work something out with the bridegroom's family.

If you decide to approach them, and I know it will not be an easy thing to do, just take it for granted that a portion of the overflow is their responsibility. Remind them, without rancor, of your original limit of sixty. It might be that they expect to pay for the overflow and that you and your wife are worrying needlessly. Do not be ashamed to say frankly that you simply cannot go over the budget.

The bridegroom's family should not have added the extra twenty guests without offering to pay for them should those unexpecteds accept. When they said they would invite eighty on the assumption only sixty would accept, your immediate response should have been that you were sorry but the limit was sixty, even if you had more people on your list. They would have had to make a decision then, and it would have been a perfect opening for them to make the offer. Now you are faced with an added expense—unless you can say that you are holding them to the sixty. Also, are you sure that the reception hall can hold the overflow?

LADIES AND GENTLEMEN, as you do honor to persons by issuing invitations, they do you honor in accepting.

If ever there was a never in planning a wedding it is with the guest list. *Never* invite 10 percent more than you can handle without asking the advice of those with whom you are dealing, such as the management of the reception site or the caterer. When contracting for the place ask what is the usual percentage of regrets and determine the maximum guest limit for the room. It is hard to have a successful event if you crowd people into a small area anyway. There are also fire-code restrictions to be considered.

It is risky to invite people thinking that they will be unable to attend. The local person who you are sure will not come because he works weekends and couldn't possibly lose a day's pay found someone to exchange a working day. You certainly didn't expect your wife's aunt and uncle from Washington State to make the trip, especially since the aunt doesn't speak to most of her family. Suddenly, nothing will keep her from attending her beloved niece's wedding. After all, you invited her, and perhaps she sees it as an opportunity to make peace with her family.

People view a wedding, and rightly so, as a special event. A birthday party can take place again next year and one can visit a new homeowner another time, but a wedding is usually a once-only occasion.

Q: *We have a much larger family and wider acquaintance than does the bride's family, so we offered to pay the difference to enable us to invite as many people as we feel necessary. They, however, insist on a small wedding. What am I to tell everyone? My husband and I are very annoyed but my son tells us that there is nothing he can do about it.*

What you tell people on your side is that the bride is planning a very small wedding for whatever reason her side of the family has given you.

Money does not always have a bearing on whether a wedding is small or large. Some people plan a wedding they can ill afford; others can manage a lavish affair but it is just not their style.

If her family is small, they may want a balanced guest list. Let's face it, if they have only fifty and you have a hundred and fifty people, it would be overwhelmingly one-sided. Other families could care less; if the bridegroom's side wants to invite everyone they know and are willing to pay for it, great.

Why not plan a reception later? Those relatives, friends, and business associates you were unable to invite will be happy to attend. You can honor the newlyweds at a fantastic party and have complete control over the guest list, even including your daughter-in-law's immediate family.

Meanwhile, accept the decision in good grace.

WELL-MEANING OFFER

LADIES AND GENTLEMEN, sometimes an offer is made out of affection but just does not work out. Someone told me that a relative of hers was being married at a wedding to which only she and her husband were invited. Their grown, unattached children remarked that they would love to attend the event because of fond memories of the bride and her family.

Mrs. Invited Guest thought and thought about it; the more she dwelt on the subject the more she could picture her children seeing that side of the family gathered together for the first time in years. She also envisioned the pleasure she would receive from her children's presence at the wedding.

Well, she made an unusual offer and put her cousin in an awkward position. She telephoned to say how much her children would like to attend the wedding and offered to pay for their places at the reception.

Her cousin sounded mortified and Mrs. Invited Guest was surprised. What she had not considered were the complicated decisions involved in forming the guest list. Her children were probably not the only first cousins once removed who were not invited to the wedding. Even if the mother of the bride would consider accepting the proposal, she could not take the risk of offending others by inviting Mrs. Invited Guest's children. What would she say? That they were not really guests?

Invitations

The Honour and the Pleasure

$\backsim\!\!A$fter we have wrestled and juggled with the guest list the invitations now come to the fore. To cut down on the number of people invited the family had to eliminate second cousins, which made no one happy but had to be done.

There are a million other questions that keep cropping up. Doesn't it seem ridiculous to address the bride's favorite aunt and uncle as Mr. and Mrs. Simpson on the inner envelope when they have been Aunt Sara and Uncle John all her life? Also, is it "Jr." or "junior" or "2nd" on the invitation . . . ?

The style of wedding invitations is determined by the type of wedding. Elegant-looking paper enhanced by engraved lettering is generally used for a very formal wedding. The result is beautiful. It is assumed, of course, that if such a wedding is planned the family can stand the expense.

There are copperplate engraving and raised-letter printing as well as flat printing. Engraving is done by etching an inked copperplate that is then pressed into the paper. The lettering has fine lines and any style of typeface can be chosen. One can tell an engraved invitation by the impression of the print on the back from the pressure of the copperplating. The copperplate is one of the reasons engraved invitations are more expensive than raised-letter ones. By the way, the plate belongs to the customer after the invitations have been made, and makes a beautiful wall hanging or desk ornament.

Raised-letter printing—in some quarters known as thermography—is done by mixing a powder with the ink, applying it to the paper, and then drying under heat. I am told that if it is done well, on good-quality paper, most people will be unable to tell the difference between raised lettering and engraving, though the former is usually sans serif—meaning that the typeface has no decorative strokes. It is comparable to machine engraving on jewelry; only an expert can tell the difference. Some people find handsome paper and the raised-lettering process an acceptable substitute for more expensive engraving.

The least costly method is flat printing. One specialist told me that some customers choose flat instead of raised lettering because they do not want to appear to be paying the price for engraving when they did not. To me, flat printing has no charm. Run your fingers over the flat print: the letters cannot be felt, as with the raised text. Though engraving is the most beautiful, raised lettering is a handsome process on its own, so why not have the best-looking invitation you can afford? No matter what the choice is, before final printing ask for a sample proof; read the text, check the paper and the font (typeface). Have more than one person proofread to catch typographical errors.

Though tastes differ and today engravers or printers have examples of various styles and wording, the main components in choosing an invitation are good-quality stock, the style of the printing, and the ink. For a formal wedding, most people want both traditional wording and traditional black ink on white or cream-colored paper. If preferences are conservative, traditional is the key to formal invitations.

TRADITIONAL WEDDING INVITATION

Mr. and Mrs. James Person Ode
request the honour of your presence
at the marriage of their daughter
Jill Candace
to
Mr. Frederick Eldon Hampenstance
Saturday, the sixth of June
One thousand nine hundred and eighty-seven
at half after four o'clock
Trinity Church
New York City

Some people state the year since the invitation is a keepsake for later generations to read. If the reception is to follow and all are invited to both the ceremony and the reception, add:

and afterward at
The Montpelier

R.S.V.P
[*or*]
Please respond
[*or*]
The favour of a reply is requested.

There is a question about whether to state on the invitation or reception card the type of reception being hosted when the time scheduled for the wedding is in the morning or at four o'clock. Some families feel it is important for guests to know a reception and dinner are to follow a late-afternoon wedding or that a wedding breakfast is to be given after a morning wedding. It is acceptable to state on the invitation or reception card:

to be followed by a
wedding breakfast

or

Reception and dinner to follow
at The Montpelier

If there is more than one sponsor or host on the invitation list the name and address of the party assigned to be the keeper of acceptances and regrets under the R.S.V.P.:

The favour of a reply is requested
Mr. and Mrs. James Ode
[Address]

BLACK TIE

Traditionalists say that guests should know that when they are invited to an evening wedding and the invitation is formally worded, then it is a black tie affair—tuxedo or dinner jacket is expected. Today, however, many people do not necessarily know that fact, so, if you wish your guests to wear formal clothes, I suggest using the words "Black Tie" on the right side of the invitation. If you want to give people an option, then "Black Tie Optional" is in order.

RECEPTION CARD

When some people are invited to the ceremony only and others to both, a separate reception card is enclosed:

Reception

or

Reception and dinner
immediately following the ceremony
Carriage Room of the Hotel Pierre
Alexandria

R.S.V.P.
[Address]

WHO IS THE SPONSOR?

Traditionally, the bride's parents are her sponsors, for she is being married to Mr. Somebody—no matter who is paying for the wedding. Therefore, their names head the invitation. That formal custom has not changed and is a correct statement.

But some attitudes are changing. Modern marrying couples are more involved in the whole process and take the position that the bride and bridegroom marry each other as equal partners; a divorced father might not be as willing to allow his ex-wife to sponsor his daughter without mention of his name on the invitation; or there are those who wish to list the bridegroom's parents—which is a custom some groups follow.

DIVORCED PARENTS' JOINT INVITATION

Mrs. Sarah Manning Ode
and
Mr. James Person Ode
request the honour, etc. . . .

or

*Mrs. Sarah Ode

or

Ms. Sarah Manning
[*if bride's mother has taken back maiden name*]

BRIDEGROOM'S PARENTS' NAMES
ON INVITATION

When both the bride's parents and the bridegroom's parents share responsibilities for the wedding, the wording should be:

Mr. and Mr. James Ode
Mr. and Mrs. Harold Dean Hampenstance
request the honour of your presence
at the marriage of
Jill Candace Ode
to
Frederick Eldon Hampenstance
[etc.]

or

at the marriage of their children
Jill Candace
and
Frederick Eldon
[etc.]

The wording below is suggested when the bridegroom's name is different from his parents', which would make it difficult for guests to identify to whose wedding they have been invited. If the bridegroom's name stands alone they might think the invitation was sent by mistake, not knowing the bride's family.

Mr. and Mrs. Marlon Chester Cameron
request the honour of your presence
at the marriage of their daughter
Rebecca Anne
to
John Eric Hamilton
son of
Mr. and Mrs. Bartlett Samuel Silver

I also think it appropriate and a genial gesture to include the bridegroom's parents on all wedding invitations:

Mr. and Mrs. James Person Ode
request the honour of your presence
at the marriage of their daughter
Jill Candace
to
Frederick Eldon Hampenstance
son of
Mr. and Mrs. Harold Dean Hampenstance
[etc.]

OH, FOR THE SIMPLE LIFE!

Q: *To be gracious I asked the groom's parents if they would like their names on the invitation. Well, I now regret the gesture. His mother wants both her husband's and her name printed separately because she has a Ph.D., a hyphenated long name, and insists no one will know her by Mrs. Whatshername. I told her that it was a formal invitation and that it would not be correct. Besides, her name is too long to fit alongside her husband's name. Am I right?*

Traditionally correct, yes, but I am afraid this question seems to get more and more complicated. There are some women who have never taken their husband's name. To avoid confusion, I would not list his parents' names under your names for two reasons: first it makes it seem as if they are co-sponsoring the wedding; secondly, there will be too many names. You will have to use an extra line, which is fine. Under the groom's name add:

son of
Mr. Harold Dean Hampenstance
Dr. Sonia Eldon-Hampenstance

or

son of
Mr. and Mrs. Harold Dean Hampenstance
(Dr. Sonia Eldon-Hampenstance)

The first statement might give the impression that the bride-groom's parents are divorced, though I imagine if they were, the hyphen would be dropped from the woman's name; if she feels comfortable about it, the second version meets the traditional custom and still recognizes his mother's identity.

STEPFATHER

Q: *My father is deceased and my stepfather is the only father I have known, though for reasons I do not wish to state, I have my natural father's surname. How do we word the wedding invitation?*

Mr. and Mrs. Harold Holdern
request the honour of your presence
at the marriage
of their daughter
Jessica Miles Troth

The word "their" is most appropriate because it indicates the closeness of the relationship.

If, however, your mother has been married only a year or two, the word "her" or "Mrs. Holdern's daughter" could be substituted, not forgetting, of course, that the bride's full name is given, since it will be different from her mother's.

DOUBLE WEDDING

When parents host a double wedding for their daughters, the older daughter's name is first:

Mr. and Mrs. James Person Ode
request the honour of your presence
at the marriage of their daughters
Jill Candace
to
Mr. Frederick Eldon Hampenstance
and
Jocelyn Courtney
to
Mr. Seth Bertram Southall
Saturday, the sixth of June
[etc.]

Wording for cousins or friends would include both brides'
parents:

Mr. and Mrs. James Person Ode
and
Mr. and Mrs. Wallace Tyne Guild
request the honour of your presence
at the marriage of their daughters
Jill Candace Ode
to
Mr. Frederick Eldon Hampenstance
and
Imogene Wallace Guild
to
Mr. Jonathan Wilde Hopewell
[etc.]

JOINT INVITATIONS

Q: *We are about to order invitations to our wedding but are
not sure just how to word them since three couples are involved
in the arrangements—my parents, his, and the two of us are
sharing the expenses.*

I prefer:

Jill Candace Ode
and
Frederick Eldon Hampenstance
along with their parents
request the honour of your presence

or

request the pleasure of your company

SINGLE PARENT

Traditionally, a widow uses her deceased husband's name:

Mrs. James Person Ode
requests the honour of your presence
[etc.]

Don't forget to change the verb on the second line when a single name heads the invitation.

Q: *As a widow, I know I should use my husband's name on my daughter's wedding invitation, to which I have no objection. However, I am known by my maiden name in the business world. When I suggested to my daughter that I use my professional name, since family and friends know my history, she laughed and said that it would look to those who don't know us as if she were illegitimate or that I was remarried. I am beginning to rue the day I started on this large formal wedding routine—my personal and business life are suddenly overlapping. How do I write the invitation and yet be immediately recognized by all?*

I suggest that you use both names:

Mrs. James Person Ode
(Millicent Fantastic)
requests the honour of your presence
at the marriage of her daughter
Jill Candace
[etc.]

LADIES AND GENTLEMEN, the remark about seeming illegitimate has been made to me before by young brides. When
the bride's divorced mother has taken back her maiden name,
her daughter generally has no objection—nor should she. However, when her mother's surname is the only one on the invitation
and it is different from her own, she feels somewhat uneasy upon
seeing the invitation for the first time in print. Maybe that is why
women sometimes wait until their children are married to take
back their maiden names.

If the bride is an actress or a professional person who uses a
name other than the name she was born with and is known by
both, list both names:

> Mr. and Mrs. James Person Ode
> request the honour of your presence
> at the marriage of their daughter
> Jill Candace Ode
> (Sandra Makebelieve)
> to
> [etc.]

DIVORCÉE

Today divorcées do not retain their ex-husband's full name:
Mrs. James Person Ode. Most use their given name (optional),
their maiden name, and ex-husband's surname. Some take back
their maiden name, prefacing it with Ms. There is an ongoing
debate whether divorcées, when they revert to their maiden name,
should use Mrs. or Miss. "Mrs. Maiden Name" is not a true
statement and neither is "Miss."

BRIDEGROOM'S PARENTS AS SPONSORS

There are times when the bridegroom's parents are sponsors
of the wedding. This generally happens when the bride's parents
are deceased or there is serious difficulty between the bride and
her parents. The invitations are sent in the name of his parents:

> Mr. and Mrs. Harold Dean Hampenstance
> request the honour of your presence
> at the marriage of
> Jill Candace Ode
> to their son
> Mr. Frederick Eldon Hampenstance
> [etc.]

OTHER RELATIONSHIPS

Note the relationship to the bride when those other than the parents are sponsors with words such as "their sister," "grand-daughter," or "niece." If friends act as sponsors, then, of course, the phrase "their friend" would look awkward. Just use:

> Mr. and Mrs. Gracious Friend
> request the honour of your presence
> at the marriage of
> Jill Candace Ode
> [etc.]

Q: *How do I tell who is really doing the inviting to the wedding?*

The people whose names are at the top of the invitation are the sponsors and generally the hosts.

OWN SPONSORS

Q: *My fiancé and I have established careers and are paying for our own formal wedding. I have lived in a different city from that of my parents for many years. Do they issue the invitations or do we?*

You have the choice of issuing your own invitations or having your parents do so. Though purists scoff at the notion, it is generally assumed that the names heading the invitation are paying the cost of the event. Just be sure the R.S.V.P. address is yours if you are handling those details.

COUPLE ISSUING OWN INVITATIONS

The honour of your presence
is requested at the marriage of
Jill Candace Ode
to
Frederick Eldon Hampenstance
Saturday, the first of June
at noon
Trinity Church
New York, New York

or

Jill Candace Ode
and
Frederick Eldon Hampenstance
invite you to their wedding
Saturday, the sixth of June
at twelve o'clock
The Boyhood Home of Robert E. Lee
Alexandria, Virginia

Please respond
1111 Simeon Road
Arlington, Virginia 22222

Note that the couple doing the inviting has not used "Miss," "Ms.," or "Mr." This suggestion works well if the bride happens to have a Ph.D. and is unsure about whether she should use her title.

A young widow's or young divorcée's parents can sponsor their daughter but in both cases the bride should use her given name, maiden name, and her deceased or ex-husband's surname:

Jill Ode Hampenstance

The above style is the same if a young widow or a divorcée issues her own invitations. A mature widow, who is known by her late husband's name, issues her own invitations:

Mrs. Frederick Eldon Hampenstance

PRIVATE CEREMONY—RECEPTION ONLY

It is rare, but sometimes a private ceremony is preferred and a large reception follows. The reception invitation in that case would be standard size and the ceremony only would be approximately 5 inches by 3¾ inches in size.

*Note the change of wording, indicating a social event:

Mr. and Mrs. James Person Ode
*request the pleasure of your company
at the wedding reception
of their daughter
Jill Candace
and
Mr. Frederick Eldon Hampenstance
Saturday, the sixth of June
at half after four o'clock
at 1111 Reception Way
Alexandria, Virginia
Please respond

The address is needed under the response request if the hosts are not at the one listed on the invitation.

One would expect that only the closest of people are invited to the ceremony, making engraved invitations unnecessary. They would be asked in person, by letter, or telephone.

DELAYED OR LATE RECEPTION INVITATIONS

If the couple have eloped or married elsewhere both sets of parents might want to host a reception at a later date:

In honour of
Mr. and Mrs. Frederick Eldon Hampenstance,
Mr. and Mrs. James Person Ode
and
Mr. and Mrs. Harold Dean Hampenstance
request the pleasure of your company

Saturday, the sixth of June
at half after seven o'clock
Hotel Pierre
Alexandria

R.S.V.P.
1111 Reception Way
Alexandria, Virginia

INFORMAL INVITATIONS

An informal invitation should look tasteful and be worded clearly so that the recipients understand what they are invited to and respond in kind.

Mr. and Mrs. James Person Ode
invite you to witness
the exchange of marriage vows
between their daughter
Jill Candace
and
Mr. Frederick Eldon Hampenstance
on Saturday, the sixth of June
at noon
[etc.]

Recently I saw a wedding invitation that was a combination of a road map and the soon-to-be-marrieds' résumé. It was a folded pamphlet on thin paper, similar to that of a church program. On the outer cover was a formally worded invitation issued by the bride's parents. The inside left fold recited hers and the bridegroom's history: where they were born, educated, present employment, future plans, and that they would use both their surnames hyphenated. Under that were directions to the church. Telephone numbers of both mothers were listed, for "though gifts are not expected, if you want to send a love gift please call our mothers," because logistically it would be easier to have them sent to "our home in _____." Below that were directions to the reception. On the back page was a *Doonesbury* cartoon of a couple in casual clothes standing before a clergyman.

The couple must have been young and had arranged everything on their own. They apparently wanted their invitation to be a warm, friendly statement—it was touching, and yet . . .

BILINGUAL INVITATION

Q: *My fiancé is living in this country but was born in France where a number of his relatives are. He would like the wedding invitations to be written in French on the left side and in English on the right-hand side. My mother feels that it is an unnecessary expense. Is it such an unusual thing to do?*

It is not unusual but gracious and sensible to have the invitations written in both languages when there will be many invited from a foreign country. Imagine having to engage an interpreter not only to read the invitation but to respond to it.

THE HONOUR OR THE PLEASURE:

Q: *I am checking with you to verify phrasing on our wedding invitations. The wedding will be a formal one even though it is being held at home. Because it is a home wedding we were instructed that the wording has to read "the pleasure of your company" and not "request the honour of your presence." I want to say "the honour" but which is correct?*

There is a difference of opinion among the experts. Some state that only when vows are exchanged in a house of worship and all the aspects of the wedding are formal does "the honour of your presence" appear on the invitations. Semiformal and informal weddings require "the pleasure of your company," a phrase used for social invitations indicating that the event still has a degree of formality and is a celebration. Engravers now offer more informal types of invitations, or couples sometimes opt for their own wording.

However, some people feel that whether the ceremony takes place under the open sky or in an enclosure, it is a religious rite when a person of the cloth recites the words sanctifying the union of two people. I agree with this interpretation. Therefore, "the honour of your presence" is perfectly acceptable, since those words imply that a religious ceremony is going to be performed. You must decide what best reflects your view.

Apparently in this instance the British are less formal than

Americans, for the accepted form whether in a house of worship or elsewhere is "request the pleasure of your company." An alternate choice is "request the pleasure of the company of" and then the name of the guest is handwritten on the next line.

ECUMENICAL WEDDING INVITATION

The pitfalls presented by wedding invitations are not only whether your wedding is going to be formal or informal but the subtle or not-so-subtle story that the wording reveals.

The future bride wants to include the priest's name as the officiating minister on the invitation. Her reason for doing so is that she is a Catholic marrying a Presbyterian. The prospective bridegroom would not consent to be married in a Catholic church. They compromised; the bride agreed to have the ceremony take place in his church with the priest co-officiating in the nuptial rites. When the time came to think about the invitations, she realized that the wording made it seem as if the entire wedding ceremony would be Presbyterian, held in the "Presbyterian Church . . ." with no mention of her denomination in the invitation.

CEREMONY TIME

Q: *We are puzzled about how to state the time that the wedding ceremony is to take place in church. On the invitation do we put the exact time the ceremony is to start or give guests fifteen minutes to a half hour to arrive?*

State the exact time the ceremony is to start. To do otherwise could cause confusion—sometimes with the wedding party itself. Guests generally start arriving about a half hour to fifteen minutes before the scheduled time.

I can't emphasize enough checking the time and date with the person representing the church or house of worship. You should have it in writing and verify it again before ordering the invitations.

MISPRINT DILEMMA

Q: *What shall I do? The invitations were ordered by my daughter in the town in which she lives. She brought them home this weekend to be addressed and mailed. It is four weeks before the wedding. My daughter did not know that the Old English spelling of the word "honour" should have been used instead of the modern "honor." There is no time to have them reprinted.*

You cannot do anything about it. Just address and mail the invitations and do not give it another thought. Most people will not notice and the occasional person who does will not say anything. If someone suffering from "verbal dribulations"* is unfortunate enough to point a finger at the offending word, just stare silently, then look up and leave your observant companion to wonder if it has just come to your attention.

Generally, stationers should advise and show examples of the customary wording and spelling on various styles of invitations. It is their business to know these nuances. But I am told that it is not necessarily true that stationers know the precise phrasing because that is not a major part of their business; they sell invitations along with many other items.

It might not have been the stationer's fault. As one mother told me, her daughter thought it ridiculous to spell "honor" the Old English way and regretted her flippant attitude afterward.

Q: *I received a telephone call from the bride's mother asking how I, a widow and the groom's mother, wish to have my name printed on the wedding invitation. It is going to be a "white tie" affair but she wants both her husband's and her first names on the formal invitations.*

I have two objections. The first is that given names of the hosts should not appear on a formal invitation. Also, since my husband passed away not long ago, I would like the traditional name a widow uses and my deceased husband's name:

"son of
Mrs. Adam Silver and the late Mr. Silver"

---

*"Verbal dribulations" will not be found in any dictionary but is an expression I coined to describe a person who cannot control his or her tongue; only the mouth works, not the brain.

I agree that the use of the hosts' given names on a formal invitation looks awkward and is incorrect. However, if they decide to use "David and Dorothy Martin" instead of the traditional "Mr. and Mrs." and you want the traditional "Mrs. Adam Silver," then the invitation would not look uniform and would exaggerate the different styles. Nor should you use a deceased person's name on the invitation.

Tell her parents your preference but if they go ahead with their original plan there isn't anything you can do about it but allow them to use your given name along with your surname.

JUNIOR

Q: *When does a person drop "Junior" from a name?*

Generally after the senior and his wife have passed away.

Q: *My husband, who was quite well known, died before his father, and I have kept the designation of Mrs. Hamilton Merriman Jones, Jr. But now my son is being married and formal invitations have been printed without the junior. I am concerned on several levels: I really do not want to drop the junior since my husband was a highly respected man and my father-in-law was the family black sheep; also, my mother-in-law and her family, who are invited to the wedding, might be sensitive about it. What do you suggest?*

Since your mother-in-law is still living, you should use the junior. If there is time to have the invitations reprinted and you are willing to go to the expense yourself, then ask your future daughter-in-law to allow you to do so. She should have no reason to object if the invitations are delivered on time. The envelopes are addressed way before the invitations are ready, so that should be no problem.

ENTITLED TO TITLES

Q: *My future son-in-law is a fourth-year medical student who is graduating a few days before the wedding. Can we refer to him as doctor on the invitations we are ordering now?*

Yes, because he will have earned the right to the title by his wedding day. This holds true for any professional designation.

MY DAUGHTER THE DOCTOR

Q: *We are planning a formal wedding for my daughter, who is a doctor marrying a doctor. It does not seem fair not to be able to use her title on the invitations.*
Military women use their rank and branch of service on formal wedding invitations, so why can't women doctors? Why don't you experts change the custom?

If you wish to use your daughter's title, it is your prerogative. In a recent example, a young woman doctor objected to her mother's hesitation about using her title on the invitations. Her fiancé is a doctor and she felt offended by the lack of her designation, so both had their titles and names in full. You are not breaking any religious tenets, but please read the full explanation below.

Even though parents issue the invitations, military women are required to use their rank and branch of service on formal wedding invitations. When in the service they always represent the organization in which they serve and military etiquette is specifically spelled out.

Mr. and Mrs. James Person Ode
request the honour of your presence
at the marriage of their daughter
Jill Candace Ode
Lieutenant, United States Army

However, the bride in civilian life represents herself and is sponsored by her parents during the whole process of the wedding. The invitation tells people that you and your husband, "Mr. and Mrs. James Person Ode," request the honour of their presence at your daughter's, "Jill Candace," marriage to "Dr. [or] Mr. Like Able Fellow." When talking or writing of her to others you would not say "Dr. Jill Candace Ode" but rather "Jill," or "Jill Candace." The bridegroom's name generally stands alone on the invitation, so he has his full name and title. That is the thinking behind the formal invitation, and correctly so, I think. The marriage of one's child is an occasion not matched by any other event, except his or her birth and the births of their children.

Experts offer guidelines and tell us what is generally done in a given situation. Changes come about when people are willing to say, "This is the way I wish to do it," whether it is the accepted practice or not, or when they don't really know the correct procedure and somehow others follow. As time goes by it becomes the accepted thing to do. Other customs fade because they no longer make sense and are impractical.

When one is considering changes in traditional parts of a wedding ceremony, the determining question should be: does it have to do with the religious rites of the place of worship? Then it would need the permission of the clergy. If it is a matter of custom or style, the decision is yours. It is up to you if you wish to become a trendsetter, but at least you should know the why of the traditionally accepted practice.

ESQUIRE

Q: *Lawyers can use the title "Esquire" for business purposes. Since my future husband is a lawyer, on the wedding invitations I would like to omit "Mr." and after his name use "Esquire." Doctors use their title all the time. Is that all right?*

I know you wish to indicate that your fiancé is a professional, but in this country "Esquire" is used only occasionally by lawyers when conducting their business affairs. Unlike in Great Britain, the word is not considered a social one nor an earned title such as "doctor," "judge," or "justice." Even a professor with a doctorate in a given subject does not generally use the designation of "doctor" socially.

My research indicated that Ph.D.s use the title in the context of their work but not in private matters . . . unless one is a Dr. Kissinger or Dr. Einstein. If a Ph.D. is the president of a university, that person becomes universally known as "doctor" because the professional and social lives overlap. So the decision rests with the titleholder to determine if one's doctorate obtained in a particular subject of study, rather than by position, should be used in private life.

The guideline is: do you use your title all the time? If you do then you are obliged to use it on the invitations merely for identification purposes.

The premise is that a medical doctor is supposed to be available in a medical emergency. No one stands up in the middle of a performance in the theater to ask: "Is there a Ph.D., a lawyer, accountant, or actuary in the house?"

Addressing an envelope to a Ph.D., you would use "Dr." if you knew the person by that designation. You can ask if you are not sure. However, should you not want to pursue it any further, you can comfortably address the envelope with Mr. or Ms.

Judges and justices use their titles, as medical doctors do.

CLERGY

Although each denomination has its own designation, the correct written terminology is "the Reverend."

- Episcopal
    The Reverend; with doctorate—The Reverend Doctor
    Presiding Bishop of Episcopal Church—The Right Reverend
    Bishop of Episcopal Church—The Right Reverend
    Dean—The Very Reverend
    Archdeacon—The Venerable
    Canon—The Reverend Canon
- Lutheran
    Pastor

- Catholic
  Cardinal—His Eminence, John, Cardinal Doe
  Bishop and Archbishop—The Most Reverend
  Abbot—The Right Reverend
  Monsignor—The Right Reverend
  Priest—The Reverend Father
- Eastern Orthodox
  Archbishop—The Most Reverend
  Bishop—The Right Reverend
  Archimandrite or Priest—The Very Reverend
- Jewish
  Rabbi—Doctor or Rabbi after obtaining the doctor of philosophy
- Mormon (Church of Jesus Christ of Latter-day Saints)
  Elder
  Bishop
- Seventh-day Adventist Church
  Pastor
- Christian Scientists: Church of Christ, Scientist, is a lay church. They do not have ordained ministers; therefore, their members are married in other Christian denominations.

DR. WHO?

Q: *I work for a scientific organization. Some women here have their doctoral degrees and others are medical doctors. Recently I sent invitations to the whole department and their spouses. To those who were married I addressed the envelope to Mr. and Mrs., or, if the women were married to doctors, Dr. and Mrs. Well, I received many complaints from the women who said I should have used their titles. Was I right or are they?*

It is traditional on social occasions that a woman is known as Mrs. Husband's Name, even though she has a title of her own.

LADIES AND GENTLEMEN, though I did not say it at the time, have you ever heard of the expression "Even if you're right, you're wrong"? And in the eyes of some female doctors and holders of doctorates the traditional or socially correct custom is not to their liking. So it is becoming acceptable for a married couple with titles to have their names on separate lines:

Dr. Wilson Stephens
Dr. Millicent Stephens

or

Drs. Wilson and Millicent Stephens

The traditional would be:

Dr. and Mrs. Wilson Stephens

If she has retained her own name:

Dr. Wilson Stephens
Dr. Millicent Wiltons

The next question invariably is: "Whose name comes first?"
Alphabetical order, of course.
Could King Solomon have done better? At least I didn't suggest cutting them in half.
P.S. If you are not sure how to address the envelope, a telephone call to his or her office will solve your dilemma.

OFFICIAL LANGUAGE

There are organizations such as the diplomatic corps and the armed forces in which protocol and etiquette are strictly adhered to. Any deviation might be offensive, misread, or misunderstood.

MILITARY WOMEN

Women in the armed forces have a hard time with particular points of military protocol and etiquette. For *official* occasions in service life when a woman with the rank of major is married to a captain, which is a lower rank, the outer envelope has her name and rank first, then his name and rank below. She will be listed first on the inner envelope also.

On *social* occasions the correct form is:

Captain and Mrs. Wilson Stephens

. . . and that designation has been a sore point. Where is Major Millicent Stephens? And so the rules have been relaxed to allow the major her true place above her husband's name but only if she fusses about it.

A woman in the service who has retained her own name has the same leeway as a woman in civilian life.

LADIES AND GENTLEMEN, please, whether you are in military or civilian life, when you receive invitations in the traditional form, do not rant and rave at senders for not doing the right thing—they lost their heads.

No sooner had I unraveled this tangle than a new twist came up. A woman doctor called to ask whether she should use her title on the wedding invitations she and her future husband, who is a "Mr.," are issuing. It is perfectly acceptable if she chooses to.

Women have conflicts that they seem to overcome as the years go by.

MILITARY AND NAVAL SERVICES

The word "military" refers to the United States Army and Air Force. However, though the Marines are part of naval services, officer ranks are the same as in the Army and Air Force. The Navy has slightly different forms. The *armed forces* encompasses all services; I think of it as an umbrella word.

Q: *I must confess that I know nothing about military etiquette. My daughter is marrying a second lieutenant and I need to know how he should be titled on the invitation.*

If he is in the United States Air Force or Marine Corps then his full rank would appear under his name:

Frank Joseph Marlington
Second Lieutenant, United States Air Force

The United States Army does not require the designation of "First" or "Second" before the word "Lieutenant."

Q: *My husband is a retired regular United States Army major. Two questions: can we still use his title on the invitations? And if so, must we indicate that he is retired?*

Retired military officers with the rank of lieutenant-colonel or commander and above can use their titles and do not need to indicate that they are retired from the service on the invitation. However, a widower announcing alone would indicate whether he was retired or not. Those with lower ranks would use "Mr."

Q: *My husband is very proud of his reserve-officer status. Can he use his rank on the wedding invitations?*

A reserve officer can use his rank on the invitations only if he is on active duty. If he is not active, then his designation is "Mr."

DOCTOR OR RANK

Q: *The use of rank in the branches of the armed forces seems to vary. How is a medical doctor addressed, by his rank or by his profession?*

In the Navy a medical doctor uses his rank rather than "doctor" when his designation is commander or over; a lieutenant-commander or under is known as "doctor." In the other branches only rank is used.

Regrets for those in the services read the same as for civilians, though the correct rank designations should be used.

INNER ENVELOPES

Q: *I am sending invitations to everyone in the family including my grandparents and my aunts and uncles. It seems so cold to refer to them as Mr. and Mrs. on the inner envelopes.*

Go warm and affectionate all the way, so grandmother, grandfather, and aunt and uncle it is.

TIMING FOR MAILING INVITATIONS
AND RETURN RESPONSES

Q: *When are wedding invitations sent out and how much time does one give guests to respond?*

Three to four weeks for wedding invitations, though I prefer four to five. However, some books say up to six weeks ahead for large formal weddings whose guests include people coming from foreign countries.

Replies should be returned the week invitations are received, if possible. Ten days is the average time for responding.

RETURN ADDRESS

Q: *After ordering an engraved return address on the wedding envelopes, I read in my book on etiquette that you can handwrite the return address or even have address tags affixed but never engraved. Should I have them redone? Surely the woman in the store would not have suggested it if it wasn't correct.*

The engravers did not mislead you. An engraved address on the front top-left-hand corner of the envelope is lovely and meets post-office requirements, though most people have the address printed on the back flap of the envelope. Your book on etiquette is outdated. At one time it was not considered correct to put a return address on the envelope, making it impossible for the post-office to return undeliverable pieces of mail.

POSTPONED OR CANCELED WEDDINGS

There are many reasons why a wedding is postponed. Sickness or the death of a close family member is the most common reason, or it might be that the bride or bridegroom is in the military and cannot participate in the proceedings.

Postponing a wedding before the invitations have been sent is comparatively easy, though it may be terribly hard to handle the turn of events. Inform those you have verbally invited; however, should a lot of people be involved it is best to notify them in writing.

If the invitations are already engraved and a new date has been set, I prefer changing the date on the invitation by hand as neatly as you can. Or insert a handwritten note saying that the date has been changed. It would read: "Please note: the wedding date has been changed from ____ to ____." However, there is always a chance that the note may be overlooked.

If a formal wedding has been postponed but another date has not been set and there is enough time, formally worded printed cards should be sent:

Due to the death [or sickness] of _____
[or no reason need be offered]
Mr. and Mrs. James Person Ode
announce that the marriage of their daughter
Jill Candace
to
Mr. Frederick Eldon Hampenstance
has been postponed

This may mean that there will be a private ceremony and a small reception or that the wedding will take place when the family feels more festive. It might be that the reason for the postponement is private but not because of a sadness.

However, if the invitations have been mailed you must act as quickly as possible and gather as much help as you can. The postponement should be made in the name of the host and hostess. Obviously there will be no time to lose. A month will give you time to mail a letter to everyone who was sent an invitation but a week will mean telephone calls or telegrams, notifying first those who have to travel a distance. If time is on your side then have a card printed in the third person:

Mr. and Mrs. James Person Ode
announce the marriage of their daughter
Jill Candace
to
Mr. Frederick Eldon Hampenstance
will not take place

or

The marriage of
Jill Candace Ode
to Frederick Eldon Hampenstance
will not take place
[has been canceled]
[has been postponed]
[has been indefinitely postponed]

I prefer the second version because it is shorter and looks less like an invitation.

INVITATION TO THE BRIDEGROOM'S FAMILY

Q: *I am told to send the bridegroom's family an invitation. That's ridiculous . . . we shall insult them sending an invitation to their own son's wedding as if they needed one to attend. Is my daughter right in insisting I do so?*

I understand how you have interpreted the action but the invitation is not sent because the bridegroom's family need one to know they are invited to their son's wedding. It is sent accompanied by a note saying you thought they would like to receive one through the mail as a keepsake.

HE WHO RECEIVES

Everyone in the bridal party receives invitations, as does the clergyman or woman, if invited to the reception. Invitations should go to fiancé(e)s of the bridal party and to those who are dating someone on a steady basis, though not to their casual friends.

... AND GUEST

LADIES AND GENTLEMEN, take care to evaluate the relationships of attendants and their sweethearts and use the phrase "and guest" with discretion.

A young lady's steady date was asked to be his friend's best man. The couple had been seeing each other for some time and expected to become engaged. The future bride and bridegroom and the soon-to-be betrothed had double-dated often. However, the latter did not receive a separate invitation to the wedding but found that the best man's invitation listed his name on the inner envelope with the words "and guest" underneath. Naturally she was hurt. Why, she asked her sweetheart, wasn't she sent a separate invitation and, barring that, why was she referred to as "and guest" when they knew her name?

The first flush of anger had her thinking she would not attend the wedding. Her second, calmer, reaction was that she would attend but not go to the prewedding showers.

Note the repercussions over the thoughtlessness of changing a close relationship to an "and guest."

GROUP INVITATION

Q: *I am inviting the entire office to the church only. Do I have to send separate invitations?*

The most efficient way is to put the invitation on the bulletin board noting the department in which you work.

ACCEPTANCES AND REGRETS

Formal wedding invitations are answered in one's own handwriting using black or blue ink on good-looking paper and following the way the invitation is worded:

Mr. and Mrs. Invited Guests
accept with pleasure
Mr. and Mrs. James Person Ode's

kind invitation for
Saturday, the sixth of June
[time optional]

It is unnecessary to repeat the entire invitation line for line, as was once demanded, because it is tedious both to the sender and to the recipient. Address the envelope to your host and hostess, a custom that differs from other social occasions when only the name of the hostess appears.

If one member on the invitation is able to attend but not the other, write the name of the person who accepts on the first line:

Mrs. Invited Guest
accepts with pleasure
Mr. and Mrs. James Person Ode's
kind invitation for
[etc.]
Mr. Invited Guest
will be unable to attend

Q: *How do I respond to a formal engraved wedding invitation from the bridal couple themselves? Also, whose name appears on the return envelope?*

Whether accepting or declining, the formal wording is:

Mr. and Mrs. Invited Guests
accept with pleasure
[or regret that they are unable to accept]
Jill Candace Ode's
and
Frederick Eldon Hampenstance's
kind invitation to
their wedding ceremony and reception

If you are not sure whether the couple is living together, address the envelope only to "Ms. Jill Candace Ode."

WRITER'S CRAMP SUFFERERS

Q: *I feel uncomfortable answering a formal wedding invitation the traditional way. It seems so pretentious and so I am always late in responding. Why can't I write that I will attend?*

Many people feel self-conscious about writing in the third person and following the invitation line for line. I think it a great way to accept or regret without having to give an excuse. You should think of this short note not as a formal statement but as a convenient reply:

Miss Sally Shy
accepts with pleasure
Mr. and Mrs. Host's
kind invitation for
Saturday, the sixth of June

This is easier for some people who dislike composing letters. Your hosts, after waiting for responses to come in, will not care whether you respond in the formal way or not if you respond in time. So feel free to handwrite the type of note that reflects your style.

REGRETS

Q: *How do I decline a formal invitation?*

Mr. and Mrs. Sanford Shy
regret they are unable to accept
Mr. and Mrs. James Person Ode's
kind invitation for
Saturday, the sixth of June

Again, writing in the third person removes the burden of making any excuse, especially if declining is to retaliate for the bride's not attending your sixth birthday party. If you are close to your hosts then a warm note telling them why you are unable to attend would be gracious.

GUESTS' RESPONSES

LADIES AND GENTLEMEN, since your hosts are gracious enough to send an invitation four weeks ahead of the wedding day so that you can reserve the date, try to send replies promptly. Acceptances or regrets should be mailed at the time invitations are received. Most families have a limited guest list, and though they will be disappointed should you have to refuse, your prompt regret will enable them to invite someone else. Delaying your response means that not only will your hosts be unable to ask an alternative in your place but, as the wedding draws nearer and they have to notify caterers how many guests to expect, they will be charged whether you show up or not.

RESPONSE CARDS VS.
HANDWRITTEN ACCEPTANCES

For years I have been asked whether it is correct to enclose response cards with wedding invitations instead of expecting the traditional handwritten reply. For the first time, recently, someone telephoned to ask if it still is considered in *good taste* to put "please respond" on the invitations. That is how much attitudes have changed toward response cards.

The questioner's friend told her that the handwritten reply was outdated and response cards were considered correct. The bride did not like nor did she want to *have* to send them and, of course, her friend was wrong.

Most books on etiquette positively shudder in one's hands when the words "response cards" leap from the page. These impersonal cards are for business affairs, not for social occasions, the experts say. The correct way to answer a social invitation is to write an acceptance or a regret by hand in black or blue ink on fine letterpaper following the style and formality of the invitation itself.

Because people are both tardy and forgetful about answering invitations, answer or response cards are a practical solution—though not foolproof—for large social functions such as weddings. Those invited are requested to send the cards back in the stamped, self-addressed envelopes by a specific time so that the hostess can notify the caterer how many guests to expect.

Easy? There are those who find even that hard to do, but most are relieved from the burden of replying the formal way.

Though I prefer the more gracious handwritten reply for social functions, the answer card is also acceptable. It offers a compromise for those who dislike any type of response inserts because they think people should be able to write an acceptance or regret by hand and respond immediately. But practicality makes it necessary to "urge" people to answer by making it easier to do so.

To have some control in this area, you write the names of the invited guests on the top of the answer card:

Mr. and Mrs. Barnetta
[remember, surname only]

accept

regret

Saturday, June sixth
[Place of reception]

This style repeats the surnames on the inner envelope of only those being invited and is less confusing than the response card that asks how many people will attend. To me, "Mr. and Mrs. Barnetta" adds up to two people.

The other style, which I look upon as the "response card," gives guests a time span, also designed to elicit a prompt reply:

Please respond by May 22nd.

M _____

will ____

will not ____

Number of Guests ____[optional]

Asking for the number of guests accepting is confusing and might give the impression that others not listed on the inner envelope could come to the wedding, which is not so.

Include a stamped, self-addressed, printed envelope with the answer and response cards.

Some people who plan to mail invitations early have a few response cards printed without the response date so that they can be used for the alternative guest list should they have a refusal or two.

STAMPED ANSWER-CARD ENVELOPES?

Q: *To cut expenses, I want to send answer cards with matching envelopes but would omit the stamp. My fiancé is surprised by my decision. Is it a must?*

It is not a must but appropriate and gracious. If you send out 100 invitations the cost, currently, is twenty-two cents per card. Your total expenditure for the stamping of the response card envelopes would be $22.00.

RÉPONDEZ S'IL VOUS PLAÎT

Q: *Because I am such a busy bride, I would like to use response cards indicating a time within which people should answer. If I just have an R.S.V.P. on the invitation, I will end up having to wonder how many will show up at the wedding, since people are tardy about answering. However, I am marrying into a socially correct family, especially my fiancé's grandmother. She knows all about the dos and donts and is terribly particular about every aspect of the niceties of life. I know she won't approve. Are response cards still unacceptable?*

Grandmother will not like the idea of response cards. She will probably say, "People should know how to respond to a social invitation. Response cards are rude since they assume that the recipient of the invitation does not know how to write an acceptance."

First, I will let you in on a well-known secret: some people never answer, whether what is expected from them is a hand-written note or merely writing their names on a card and checking off the "will attend" or "will not attend" box. They either don't show up or they come without warning, leaving the hostess to wonder if there is enough food to go around. But the return envelope does help. People tell me that when they receive a business bill, the last to be paid are firms that do not include self-addressed return envelopes.

My father used to say that the answer was in the question, and he was right. Even though you might view the matter as not too important, you still ask it because it is meaningful to your fiancé's family and you want to show yourself in a good light.

You have to choose either courtesy to your fiancé's grandmother or convenience to yourself. I would use the R.S.V.P. for the sake of his family. About seven days before the wedding contact those on your side who haven't answered. Ask his mother to take care of the tardies in her family.

LADIES AND GENTLEMEN, you see what trouble you cause when you do not answer an invitation on time?

Q: *I've always disapproved of response cards but they are beginning to seem less distasteful, especially when I receive wedding invitations with more than one set of sponsors. They may ask for an R.S.V.P., but to whom does one respond? This last invitation has me completely frustrated, since the bride and groom, her parents, and his parents are co-hosts. Also, the return address embossed on the back flap of the envelope is so faint I can't make it out.*

It is unfortunate there isn't an address underneath the R.S.V.P. on the left of the invitation.

It reminds me of a funny cartoon in the *Washington Post* depicting the family posing for a photograph at a wedding. In a separate insert family members were outlined in silhouette and numbered. Corresponding numbers above listed their relationships to the bridal couple: the bride's mother and her new husband; her father and his live-in mate; her grandmother and step-grandfather; the bride's ex-husband, with his wife and adopted child who looks like . . . It made an intimate family grouping. I hope invitations don't become that complicated.

To restore the address on the envelope, try rubbing a pencil carefully over the embossing so that the impression will show clearly. Now you have the address, I hope. Should you not recognize the address, look in the telephone book or, if the address is not local, directory-assistance telephone operators should be able to find the address for you. If that doesn't work, telephone the people whose names on the invitation are known to you to ask who is handling the replies. Another suggestion that I have offered is to write your response, enclosing it in a stamped blank envelope, and put it into another envelope addressed to the people you know asking them to write in the correct name and address and forward it.

INFORMAL RESPONSE

Address the letter to your hostess:

Dear Jill,
    John and I will be delighted to attend your wedding. Seeing you as a bride standing next to Frederick on your special day will make us very happy.

Love,
Cynthia

TELEPHONE RESPONSES

Q: *We are sending informal wedding invitations with telephone regrets only. Some people say R.S.V.P.s with a phone number are a better idea.*

    The same problem exists in both cases. How do you get people to respond? With telephone R.S.V.P.s you at least have an idea of who is not able to attend. Then, as time draws near, you have a choice of checking with those from whom you have not heard, enabling you to know how many to expect.

Q: *How do I address an envelope to a couple who are living together but are not married? I don't think separate wedding*

*invitations would be appropriate. Also, I have three girlfriends
who share an apartment. Is it proper to send one invitation to
the group?*

A joint invitation is suitable for a couple living together:

Ms. Sylvia Anders
Mr. George Gordon

The inner envelope should also have both names on separate
lines, but do not use first names.

According to strict etiquette, adults in the same household
receive separate invitations. A group invitation would be appropriate only for an office or an organization so large that it would
be an otherwise impossible task.

CORRECTION DILEMMA

Q: *Invitations to my daughter's wedding will go out Monday,
June 22. At the time I ordered the response cards I thought that
July 10 would be a reasonable time for people to reply to our
invitation for August 8. Besides, the caterer wanted a firm guest
count three weeks before the wedding. Now I have been told I
should have given guests more time. Do you think it would be
all right to hand-change the date to the 20th? The gold lettering
could be altered with gold ink.*

A three-week guarantee date to the caterer is unrealistic. Call
and say the responses will not be coming in promptly enough to
enable you to give them a firm count.

If you were going to change something on the invitation itself,
I would say that you should not touch it unless the correction
was an absolute necessity and there was no time to have them
reprinted. The response card is not as important, so if you feel
strongly about it go ahead and change the date. People will think
it was a printer's error. But think about it. The invitations will
arrive no sooner than the twenty-seventh. That will give guests
thirteen days to reply. But many people are late in responding
anyway, so it really doesn't matter. However, it would matter if

it were the other way around and you had only allowed a week's time to hear from everyone.

CASH BAR

Q: *Where do I put "cash bar" on the wedding invitations? I want people to know that they can have hard liquor but at their own expense.*

As is my policy, I must tell you frankly that including the words "cash bar" on the invitation, much less the idea of having people pay for their own drinks at the wedding reception, is not considered in good taste. As host and hostess, you decide what to serve at the wedding as you would if guests were being entertained in your home.

Arrange your wedding and reception within the framework of what you can afford. Those who can't afford or do not wish to serve hard liquor substitute for it another drink such as wine, champagne punch, or fruit punch. Your guests will be able to withstand the trial of not having spirits for a period of less than four hours.

Someone I know received a "cash bar" invitation, and if you saw her "can-you-believe-this" expression when she pointed to the lower-right-hand corner where the words were printed you might think twice about including it on yours. "His folks must be mortified," she chuckled. That, of course, didn't prevent her or others, who had also expressed surprise at the invitation, from attending the wedding. She said it was a fun wedding and many people bought their own drinks . . . but it still is not considered proper . . .

NO SMOKING, PLEASE

Q: *Where on the invitation can the words "no smoking" be printed? I want people to know that I find it offensive.*

It is not appropriate to have "no smoking" or any other comment on the wedding invitations. I am not sure how you should make your wishes known. Guests certainly would not smoke during the ceremony, so your concern is at the reception. You could have small place cards on each table requesting that guests do not smoke, which might result in more people on the veranda than at the reception.

YOUR PRESENCE BUT NO PRESENTS, PLEASE

Q: *Where do I put "no gifts, please" on the wedding invitation? We have been married before and would prefer no gifts.*

It is considered inappropriate to refer to the possibility of receiving or not receiving presents on the invitations. Such offerings are supposed to be voluntary. Aren't there a few people who could pass the word to friends and relatives?

The only other way I have seen this request handled is by inserting a handwritten slip of paper with "No presents, please," or, if you prefer, "No gifts, please."

ARE WE OR AREN'T WE?

Q: *I've received an engraved, formally worded invitation to a house of worship. It's from out-of-town friends to their daughter's wedding. An R.S.V.P. is listed at the bottom-left-hand corner but there is no mention of the reception. Does that mean we are invited to the ceremony only, or that there is not going to be a reception?*

When there is an R.S.V.P. on the invitation it means there will be a reception after the ceremony and that you are invited to both. Apparently the reception will follow on the church premises.

Your hosts could have avoided confusion if they had included a last line:

Reception following in
The Fellowship Hall

R.S.V.P.

A house of worship holds many more people than a reception place, so declining the invitation to the ceremony is not required. A reply is requested only when a reception is to follow, because your hosts have to notify the caterer of the number of guests to expect.

Q: *What does it mean when an invitation to an out-of-town wedding is received and there is no "please respond"? I have sent a wedding present, since I am the bride's great-aunt, though I am trying to interpret to what I have been invited.*

I am mystified also. You are a close relative and live out of town, so it seems unlikely that you would be invited to the ceremony only, though that is what the invitation indicates. My first inclination is to tell you to check the envelope for the reception card, but the reception card would be hard to overlook. There is no other solution than to telephone your niece and ask her. A few days later the caller said she had spoken to her niece who stated that she had not bothered to enclose the reception card because she was not expecting her aunt to make the trip.

I made no comment and thanked her for the feedback. But really, ladies and gentlemen, that was not nice, was it? Even if her family's intentions were good they should not have made up their aunt's mind for her, but allowed her to accept or decline as she wished. On the other hand, even if they were keener on her present than on her presence (they certainly conveyed that message) they should have waited to send a marriage announcement after the wedding—the result would not have had the same unfortunate appearance.

I think our gentle aunt's niece had a twinge of conscience. She has been making solicitous telephone calls to her relative ever since.

INVITATION TO CHURCH ONLY

Below is a question that I included in the introduction to this book because it is an example of a misleading query.

Q: *When invited to the church ceremony and not to the reception, is it obligatory to attend?*

An invitation to the church ceremony carries no obligation on your part; not even a reply is expected.

LADIES AND GENTLEMEN, after a few minutes of discussion I found I was speaking to an employer's wife who had received a ceremony-only wedding invitation from an employee, a young man who had worked for the firm a number of years. Apparently Mr. and Mrs. Employer had entertained the young couple in their home and expected to be included in the reception list. Yet when the invitation arrived they were surprised and confused to find they were only invited to the ceremony. They were in a quandary and really did not want to attend, although they had decided to send a present.

I did not voice my opinion because it is not my place to cause any more resentment than is already apparent; however, I wondered to myself why the bridegroom or his bride would chance antagonizing his employer and wife like that. It did not seem sensible to me. Aside from questionable good taste, how could it promote goodwill? There may have been a good reason for the engaged couple's action, though I became tired of speculating what that could be.

As I said in the introduction, the young man shrugged away his involvement in the decision by saying that the bride's side were responsible for the arrangements. I am uneasy about his unwillingness to look after his own interests by allowing himself to be placed in an awkward position. Being in love is no excuse for allowing a slight to one's employer. The young couple must realize the worth of the other's business and personal relations, from which both benefit.

It bears repeating that relationships can be established and reinforced by recognizing subtle nuances, or destroyed by thoughtless actions. I have uncomfortable feelings about church-only invitations, though they do allow people to come to church to see an acquaintance marry.

LOVE ME, LOVE MY . . .

This question brings to mind the embarrassing situation in which a family found themselves when they sent a wedding invitation to a couple. On the inner envelope they wrote "Mr. and Mrs. Barnetta." The response card was returned indicating that four people were coming—Mr. and Mrs. Barnetta and their two children. The bride had not invited any youngsters, due to guest list restrictions, and if the Barnettas had been allowed to bring theirs, others' feelings would have been hurt.

One way of avoiding the "no children" problem is to have a third party pass the word to family and friends when the decision is made. It should not be printed on the invitation; it is a tasteless phrase.

Like the Pied Piper, some parents think their children should follow them everywhere. They should never assume that their youngsters are automatically invited. As with all who receive invitations, only those names on the inner envelope are invited to the wedding.

The bride has the option of writing or phoning the Barnettas. She should try to say something about treasuring their friendship and how happy she is they will be able to come to the wedding, but there seems to be a misunderstanding about the children. As much as they want all the children to come, the guest list had to be limited.

Now, as I have written elsewhere, advice is only as good as the receiver's ability to take it. When you are in a fix ask yourself whether it is a sensible decision or will it cause more problems. It may be a better solution, and the results less painful, to allow Mr. and Mrs. Employer, for instance, to bring their children and afterward, should anyone express surprise, explain that it could not be helped.

NOT SURE CHILDREN ARE INVITED?

If children are invited to the wedding, their names would be listed on the inner envelope, so my first instinct is to leave them home without investigating further. But if you have reason to believe they are invited, and I would suggest that it be a strong reason, why not try an ancient remedy—ask.

How do you ask? If not directly to the principals, speak to a member of the family. Start the conversation with: it is fine either way, and I know this is a delicate question, but are our children invited? You will have avoided the possibility of embarrassing your hosts or yourselves by taking the uninvited.

Q: *I am the mother of the groom and I'm afraid I have made a mistake. My brother phoned to say a friend of mine called him to ask if her children were invited to the wedding since the invitation read "and family." I am mortified because I gave the list that way to the bride and it was decided early not to invite young children, only teenagers and up. I don't want to hurt my future daughter-in-law, who is such a sweet girl, and neither do I want to hurt my friends. How shall I handle it?*

Your friend is a sensitive person. She must have been surprised to find her children were invited, and, knowing mistakes can be made, she asked your brother to straighten out the matter. You can let your brother handle it or call yourself.

MARRIAGE ANNOUNCEMENTS

Announcements follow the same form as the invitations. When issued by the bride's parents:

Mr. and Mrs. James Person Ode
have the honour of
announcing the marriage of their daughter
Jill Candace
to
Mr. Frederick Eldon Hampenstance
Saturday, the sixth of June
One thousand nine hundred and eighty-seven
New York City

or

Mr. and Mrs. James Person Ode
and
Mr. and Mrs. Harold Dean Hampenstance
have the honour of announcing
the marriage of their children
or
announce the marriage of
Jill Candace Ode
to
Frederick Eldon Hampenstance
Saturday, the sixth of June
One thousand nine hundred and eighty-seven
[Place of worship optional]
New York City

Because the bridegroom did not fall out of the sky and land ready-made on the bride's doorstep, I prefer the second version, since it is a more complete announcement.

COUPLE ANNOUNCING

Jill Candace Ode
and
Frederick Eldon Hampenstance
announce their marriage
on Saturday, the sixth of June
One thousand nine hundred and eighty-seven
in New York City

BRIDEGROOM'S PARENTS ANNOUNCING

Q: *The bride's parents are not going to send wedding announcements. Are we, as the groom's parents, forbidden to do so? It is extremely important to us to send them to the many people who were not invited to the wedding but need to know the news.*

At one time all announcements to do with the engagement and marriage were issued by the bride's parents. The needs of the bridegroom's parents were limited by that custom but now his parents are recognized as parents. Though the engagement announcement reads as if sent by the future bride's parents, after the wedding the parents of the bridegroom are free to send announcements of their son's marriage, even if the bride's parents think it unnecessary. You do not need their permission, for you are making a true statement that is considered in good taste.

Mr. and Mrs. Harold Dean Hampenstance
announce the marriage of their son
Frederick Eldon Hampenstance
and
Jill Candace Ode
daughter of
Mr. and Mrs. James Person Ode
Saturday, the sixth of June
One thousand nine hundred and eighty-seven

or

Mr. and Mrs. Harold Dean Hampenstance
have the honour to announce
the marriage of
Miss Jill Candace Ode
daughter of
Mr. and Mrs. James Person Ode
to their son
Mr. Frederick Eldon Hampenstance, [etc.]

ANNOUNCEMENT BLUES

Q: *I have conflicting feelings about wedding announcements. It would be practical to send them but doesn't it seem as if we are asking for wedding presents?*

Printed marriage announcements should be looked upon in the same way as a newspaper piece. It informs the recipients of the change in status of these two people. It is true, however, from inquiries I receive at the desk that some people do not know whether a present is expected of them.

As with church-only invitations that exclude the recipients

from the reception, some people are troubled about marriage announcements that are mailed soon after the wedding has taken place to those not invited to the event. To them it appears to say that a marriage has taken place to which recipients were not invited and that presents are expected.

Neither is true. Most people understand that it is impossible for everyone to be invited to the wedding. A *present is neither obligatory nor expected,* and is voluntarily sent based on the recipient's feelings toward the bridal couple or their parents.

LADIES AND GENTLEMEN, as with so many of the questions throughout this book, most cannot be answered by saying "yes" or "no," and "maybe" is evading the issue.

DO SOS AND NO NOS

- Abbreviations are not used on the invitations. Every word and numeral are spelled out except Mr., Mrs., Dr., Jr., Sr., and R.S.V.P. (though some prefer "junior" and "senior" spelled in lowercase letters, for the most formal invitations).
- The exact time the wedding is expected to begin is the time listed on the invitation.
- Nicknames are not apropriate, even if you think no one will recognize your name. Most people realize that Bill is an abbreviation of William and Meg is a shortened version of Margaret. Besides, marrying is an adult thing to do and everything attached to the arrangements should be also.
- There is a difference between the meaning of "junior" and "2nd." "Junior" means the son has his father's name: "Mr. James Person Ode, Jr." When "junior" has a son who is named after him, then his son would be "James Person Ode III (3rd)." Grandfather becomes a "senior," father is a "junior," and grandson is "the third." Now, here is the tricky part: being named "the 2nd" or "3rd" indicates that the gentleman has a relative's name, but not necessarily his father's; he might be named for his grandfather or an uncle. Note that the "III" can mean that he is named after his father or another relative.

- Your guest list should be checked for the correct spelling of personal names as well as names of places and street numbers. Such mistakes are embarrassing.
- The rank of those in the armed forces, as well as the titles of clergy and other titled people in America and foreign countries, should be correctly addressed on your invitations.
- Buy enough stamps for every envelope and for answer cards, should you decide to include them. Buy a block of festive-looking stamps at the post office so that the outer envelope and the enclosure envelope will match. This little effort makes a nice touch.
- Personal notes are never written on the invitation itself.
- Ask engravers for the envelopes early so they can be addressed ahead of time.
- Check all addresses to be sure that invitations, once mailed, will not go astray.

    The ZIP code should be correct. Don't be under the impression that the post office will automatically know the correct one. I am told that when a letter has an incorrect ZIP code the letter is separated from the daily mail and has to go to another area to be sorted, causing a delay. I have had mismailed letters returned but too late to rectify the situation. Incidentally, the post office sells a ZIP code book that covers every city and town in the entire United States. Every post office in the country has a ZIP code book displayed for your use.

- The return address should be legibly listed on the outer envelope. The post office prefers that it be placed on the front top-left-hand corner of the envelope. Most people, when they have formal invitations, like the return address embossed on the back flap. For practicality's sake, think about engraved or raised lettering or even stickers. I know stickers don't compare in elegance, but they can be seen clearly.
- Order twenty-five more invitations than the actual guest count to allow for errors, or to send to alternatives on your guest list should you receive some early refusals.
- Matching ink is used on the outer envelope, but should this

be hard to obtain, it is never incorrect to use black ink—
in fact, it is traditional and still the most used.
- Proofread the invitation—*every* character on *every* line of
the entire invitation and also on the inserts such as the
reception and response card. Proofreading is difficult because the eye expects to see the word spelled correctly, so
a misspelling can be easily overlooked. Can you tell me
what is wrong in the following?

Mr. and Mrs. James Person Ode
request the honour of your presence
at marriage of their daugther
Jill Candace
to
Frederick Eldon Hampenstance

Did you catch the mistakes? "The" was omitted from the
third line—"at *the* marriage"—and "daughter" is mis-
spelled.
- The inner envelope is addressed only to the actual people
you wish to come to the wedding. Note that first and middle
names are omitted:

Mr. and Mrs. Jones

If you are asking their very small children, list them on
the inner envelope under their parents' name according to
age:

Jonathan, Jennifer, and Sarah

"And Family" on the outer envelope is not considered appropriate.

Young people in their teens can be listed on the outer
envelope under their parents' names:

Mr. and Mrs. Invited Guest
The Misses Guest
Master Guest

Those sixteen and over should receive separate invitations, or a joint invitation can be sent:

Mr. Jonathan Ode
The Misses Ode

More than one young gentleman would be addressed:

The Messrs. Guest

- The easiest way to stuff the wedding invitation envelopes is to pretend you are the recipient. When the envelope is opened you should first see the handwritten name(s) on the unsealed inner envelope showing who is invited to the event. As you turn the envelope over to withdraw the contents, the engraved wording should face you. The enclosures are in front of or within the fold of the invitation so they will not be overlooked.
- Tissue sheets are used for engraved invitations to prevent smudging but are unnecessary for printed ones.
- All invitations are mailed on the same day.
- Invitations should be sent from three to six weeks before the wedding. I recommend four to five weeks.
- Invitations are sent to everyone—including parents of the bridegroom, members of the wedding party, and the officiant and spouse (if friends)—as well as friends and relatives in mourning.
- Guests who are engaged should ask the bride if it is possible for their fiancé(e)s to be invited. A separate invitation should be sent unless there is a shortage; in that case, on the inner envelope write the new guest's name under that of the person originally invited:

Miss Betrothed
Mr. Troth

- LADIES AND GENTLEMEN, do not bring an uninvited guest because it is lonesome to go without a companion. A wedding is not that sort of social occasion.
- Maps and enclosures helpful to invited guests, especially those who live out of town, can be included with invitations or sent separately after acceptances have been received. (Don't groan at the possibility of addressing more envelopes, just choose the first option.)
- Guests reply immediately whether they can or cannot attend. If there is no answer card, write your response by

hand. The formal way is to follow the invitation line for line:

Mr. and Mrs. Invited Guest
accept with pleasure
[or regret they are unable to accept]
Mr. and Mrs. James Person Ode's
kind invitation for
Saturday, the sixth of June

Or, write a letter of acceptance or regret in the first person.

OFFICER RANKS FOR MILITARY AND NAVAL SERVICES—SOCIAL OCCASIONS ONLY

NAVY

Admiral and Mrs. Thomas Thomason
Vice Admiral
Rear Admiral
Commodore
Captain
Commander
Lieutenant Commander
Lieutenant
Lieutenant, junior grade
Chief Warrant Officer
Warrant Officer
Ensign

ALL OTHER BRANCHES

General and Mrs. Thomas Thomason
Lieutenant General
Major General
Brigadier General
Colonel
Lieutenant Colonel
Major
Captain
First Lieutenant
Second Lieutenant

CIVILIAN TITLES

If you are not sure of a dignitary's title or how to address him or her, telephone the person's office or speak to the Protocol Office.

When the position is the only one, then it is not necessary to write the person's name.

Planning
the Wedding

Where, When, and Who

$\backsim\!\!\mathcal{W}$edding planning—a time for imagination stretching; a time to draw on one's talent for tact and diplomacy; a time for problem solving.

A wedding doesn't just happen, it is organized. That is why books like this one are invaluable. Talking to friends who have gone through the experience and trying to envision the event from beginning to end are helpful too. The mind's eye should walk through the proceedings step by step.

Once the dazzling array of wedding plans has been carried out, one can appreciate what it takes to arrange a diplomatic or political dinner, a business function or a church affair honoring the bishop. But while there are similarities, such occasions cannot present the emotional aspect of getting married.

The initial excitement of the engagement is now fused with thoughts of upcoming nuptials. Decisions must be made on the style of the event and where the ceremony is to be held—in a house of worship, one's own home, a rented historic mansion, a hotel, or a park setting. Also, what type of reception will fit into the budget—is it unlimited, or will every dollar count each step of the way? What about the guest list?

Find the most professional services that can be afforded. Word-of-mouth recommendations are often the best. The least experienced firm may charge only a little less or about the same as the most competent.

It may be true that the wedding is for the bridal couple; after all, it is their statement and no other step they take in life will be as important as this one. Often, at the point of marrying, the espoused are broadening their world and are becoming independent of their parents. Isn't that what is hoped? But though their ideas about the best kind of wedding may not encompass the needs of their parents, sons and daughters should realize that they have not grown up in a vacuum. Neither should they dismiss the people who have been part of the family's extended structure—their parents' lifelong friends and associates, as well as other family members. Whether young people recognize it or not, they have benefited in intangible ways from their parents' relationships. All have been enriched by sharing the joys and hardships of parenting.

On the other side of the coin, parents shouldn't negate the importance of friendships and ties the young couple have made. It may be true that some of these bonds have not had the test of time but they are as necessary to the young couple as their parents' are to them.

A "mommy-and-daddy wedding" (I am not using this term in a derogatory way but with affection) describes the occasion for young people who are barely finished with their studies or who have just started working. They live on campus or share an apartment with roommates but come home for Thanksgiving, Christmas, and summer vacations, and are still very much part of family life. Whether they live at home or away from it, their lives are still centered in their parents' home. Friends do not make up the entire wedding list. The wedding, then, is shared by both families and by the friends of their parents. This is a wonderful event, a symbol of parental caring and of glowing youth.

An independent couple's wedding might have a different emphasis. Generally, this pair are in their late twenties or older with established careers, and have lived independently of their parents for years. Their friendships and life styles are set. Whether parents are planning the wedding or not, the people invited are usually friends of the couple, along with business associates and close family relations on both sides. Together they make wedding arrangements and parents generally take the position that it is completely up to the lovers' taste.

There are both younger and more mature adults whose parents sponsor them but who have chosen a small intimate wedding not involving business or social acquaintances, keeping the guest list to relatives and intimate friends.

There are so many points of view to consider. What do the bride and bridegroom wish, and how pliable and accepting are the principals? One couple said of their daughter that she had such way-out ideas that they wouldn't have been surprised if the girl had worn a burlap wedding dress and a wreath of eucalyptus in her hair. But if that is what she wants on her wedding day, that is the way it should be. They might be surprised one day to find their free-spirited daughter saving magazine clippings of white bridal slippers and nymphlike wedding frocks.

And has anyone ever listened to an excited mother planning her daughter's big day as if she herself were the bride? Meanwhile, her daughter, a self-supporting young lady who has an executive position, confides that all she really wants is a small wedding, a simple outfit, some champagne, and a string quartet. Instead, she finds herself in a frothy wedding gown and a cathedral-length train at an ultra-formal wedding. Walking in her mother's path, her mother's words, "Our wedding, our wedding," echoed in her ears.

Then there is the danger of distancing one's self too much from the proceedings. One young lady said that her mother's experience with her own mother over wedding arrangements twenty years before had made her so conscious that it was not her wedding day that it was hard to get her input, which the bride would have welcomed.

There is a middle-of-the-road approach—a meeting of minds. Communicate, talk about it openly. It may lead to the start of a lovely mother-and-daughter (or parent-and-daughter) relationship. After striking out for independence and achieving it, the act of getting married can bring to both the bride and the bridegroom a new realization of the importance of the family circle.

FORMAL, SEMI, INFORMAL?

Q: *What is the difference between semiformal and informal weddings? I thought the terms were similar in meaning.*

There are varying degrees of formality: *informal, semiformal, formal,* and *very formal.* Remember, they are all "formal" to one degree or another, which means they follow certain guidelines— in this instance, guidelines encompassing weddings.

Very formal or *most formal* means that the bride wears an elegant style of wedding gown with a cathedral train, a long flowing veil, and a full bouquet; her bridegroom is dressed in formal wear suited to the time of day when the event takes place. She can be surrounded by an entourage of up to twelve: maids, flower girls, and ring bearers—all appropriately attired. The number of ushers is set at one per fifty guests. It is up to the bride whether to balance maids and men for a uniform wedding party. The ceremony is held in a house of worship, a hotel, or a place large enough to hold two hundred or more guests. The reception includes all the elements of a grand ball. This sort of wedding takes the most detailed planning.

A *formal* wedding, with the reception afterward, is neither as elaborate nor as large an event as the *very formal,* and there is generally a guest list of up to a hundred and fifty people. Though the arrangements are not as lavish, the place for the ceremony may be the same and there may be little difference in the elegance of the bridal ensemble or in the number of attendants.

A *semiformal* wedding indicates a more moderate degree of formality for the ceremony, dress, and reception. The bride still has a choice of a long wedding dress with a short train and an elbow-length veil or, if she wishes, ankle, tea, or street length. The bridal party is smaller in number. A buffet reception is served.

Informal implies a more casual approach. However, the couple still exchange marriage vows whether they are married in a park by a justice of the peace or in a chapel, the rectory, at home, or any suitable place befitting the dignity of the occasion. Though the guest list is generally limited to people close to them, there is some sort of gathering afterward at home or in a restaurant. In no way does an informal wedding mean holding hands alone under the stars and declaring eternal love. Nor does it mean casual manners, a bathing suit for the lady, and a torn jacket, tieless shirt, and gardening slacks for her swain.

Past informal is the only fitting category for the young lady who called one Friday afternoon to invite me to come that evening to a telephone booth on a street corner to witness her solemn exchange of marriage vows. I declined, since I couldn't envision myself packed like a sardine, crushing the bridal illusion during this ethereal event with, I imagined, AT&T officiating. I have only one regret. I did not ask if her bridegroom was going to be crowded into the booth with her or if he was waiting in a phone booth in Alaska. If it was Alaska, I hope she knew that in some areas in the United States you cannot be married by telephone.

Q: *How does one determine the formality of a wedding?*

One misconception is that the time of day is the deciding factor. It is not. Unlike other occasions, when the dress code suits the time of day, it is the formality of the bride's outfit that counts. If she wears all the features that go into an extremely elegant wedding dress with cathedral train, then everything to do with the wedding is formal.

WHO CHOOSES CHURCH AND CLERGYMAN?

Q: *Who chooses the church for the wedding ceremony, me or my girlfriend?*

The bride and her family.

Q: *Oh. [Silence.] Er, who chooses the minister?*

The bride and her family. But you could ask to have your minister co-officiate if you like.

[Click. Dial tone.]

LADIES AND GENTLEMEN, trouble in paradise?

CLERGY

Choosing a clergyman is generally the prerogative of the bride and her family since traditionally the bride is married from her parents' home and in the house of worship in which she was brought up. If the bridegroom's family has someone they wish to co-officiate then it should be discussed with the bride's family and the officiating clergyman.

CLERGY'S FEE

Q: *As the bridegroom I understand I pay for the minister. How do I determine the fee? I feel self-conscious about asking directly.*

You do not have to ask the officiant directly. Try calling his or her secretary, who will give you some indication of the fee involved. Sometimes, however, they are reluctant to quote an exact amount because the figure represents a donation to the clergy or the church and it is therefore left up to the donor to decide what would be appropriate.

A church secretary told me that when pressed she suggests a figure of no less than fifty dollars. Some ministers view their role as officiants at weddings as part of their ministering to the congregation.

An important part of today's approach to marriage is the marriage-counseling sessions the clergyman has with the young couple. I am told at least one is customary and some clergy hold one with the bride alone, another with the bridegroom, and a third with both. Then there is the rehearsal a day or two before the wedding day. All this takes time.

I have read that the honorarium should also be based on the size and formality of the wedding as well as the above-mentioned information. But I think that presupposes that the more formal the wedding the more generous the donation.

In Jewish weddings, when the rabbi conducts the ceremony and the cantor sings, both are paid. Those rabbis who do interfaith ceremonies are sometimes more expensive.

The clergy often share as co-officiants in a wedding ceremony with the visiting clergyman (such as the bridegroom's religious adviser) as the assistant—unless the visitor is a high-ranking personage such as a bishop. The donation would still go to the home minister, though a further contribution might be sent to the actual officiant. A present, rather than a fee, would be given to a friend who officiates.

When the clergy is asked to conduct a ceremony to take place in another area, travel and lodging expenses are paid for by the family. If a male officiant is asked to wear formal attire that he does not own for the occasion, the cost of renting the outfit again falls to the family.

ROLE OF THE OFFICIANT

The marrying couple should know that an officiant is *not required* to perform a wedding ceremony if he or she has doubts about the suitability of the circumstances. Officiants judge legality and propriety according to their conscience.

Propriety? Suppose either of the two young people is underage. They want to marry and are equipped with the necessary license, but a sixth sense tells the officiant that though they seem to have a parent's consent, this should be checked.

An important prerequisite is that both parties must be of sound mind and marrying of their own free will. This is found in most religions.

Legality? The license has expired.

WHO MAY MARRY?

Although the law of the land might not coincide exactly with that of the various religions, there are areas that are closely linked.

Every state in America has its own marriage laws, some more stringent than others. But all follow to one degree or another the prohibitions on who may marry.

Below is the list from the state of Maryland: it starts with the statement that a marriage must be between man and woman.

A man shall not marry:
> His grandmother,
> His grandfather's wife,
> His wife's grandmother,
> His father's sister,
> His mother's sister,
> His mother,
> His stepmother,
> His wife's mother,
> His daughter,
> His wife's daughter,
> His son's wife,
> His sister,
> His son's daughter,

His daughter's daughter,
His son's son's wife,
His daughter's son's wife,
His wife's son's daughter,
His wife's daughter's daughter,
His brother's daughter,
His sister's daughter.

A woman shall not marry:
Her grandfather,
Her grandmother's husband,
Her husband's grandfather,
Her father's brother,
Her mother's brother,
Her father,
Her stepfather,
Her husband's father,
Her son,
Her daughter's son,
Her husband's son,
Her daughter's husband,
Her brother,
Her son's son,
Her son's daughter's husband,
Her daughter's daughter's husband,
Her husband's son's son,
Her husband's daughter's son,
Her brother's son,
Her sister's son.

The list of prohibitions is specific within each religion as in civil law, though, I repeat, with differences. Such marriages, to say the least, are void. You will notice that not only blood ties (consanguinity or kindred) but those related by marriage (affinity) are forbidden. If you are thinking of marrying a relative, it is wise to check with your religious adviser and with the marriage laws of the state and country in which you live. In Greece, for instance, because marriage is forbidden between children who have the same godparent, an adult can only assume the role of godparent to children of the same sex.

The union of close blood relatives is harmful to offspring when carried from one generation to another, because negative traits or genes are reinforced. It happened in the Russian royal family. Queen Alexandra married her cousin, Czar Nicholas; the only male heir she produced was born with hemophilia, a disease dreaded even more a century ago than it is now. The ancient Egyptians did not know of the danger of constant intermarriage. Pharaohs were allowed to marry only their sisters, to ensure the line of succession within the family, but over the years the dynasties died out, for their children could not survive such severe inbreeding.

MARRIAGE LICENSE

A marriage license is in actual fact a permit to marry. It authorizes that:

The couple are free to marry each other.
Papers proving a divorce or widowhood have been produced.
Both are of legal age according to that county's laws. If not, parental consent must have been obtained.
The necessary requirements, such as blood tests—where stipulated—have been complied with.

The age below which applicants are not allowed to marry without permission of both the state and parents or guardians varies from state to state. There is such a wide range of ages, from twelve to eighteen—usually younger for women than for men—that knowledge of current laws in your particular state for both male and female is required.

In England and Wales, the law states that those under sixteen are not permitted to marry and those under eighteen have to have parental consent. There is another regulation that says "both parties must be respectively male and female by birth."

The United States government prints information booklets on practically every subject you can think of. Should you want those on "Where to Write for Marriage Records" and "Where to Write for Divorce Records," write to:

Superintendent of Documents
Government Printing Office
Washington, D.C. 20402

As of this writing, only a handful of states do not require a blood test. Some of those insist on medical certificates, though.

Having obtained the permit to marry (the marriage license), the engaged couple may exchange nuptial vows *within the life of the license* and *within the area* (i.e., the same county) where they received the license.

An expired license is invalid. An officiant cannot perform the ceremony before the marriage license is valid or after it has expired. It is interesting to note that, according to the law of Maryland, the marriage would be recognized but the officiant and the couple could be subject to the penalties of the law.

One of the differences in law between states is in their recognition of common-law marriage, when the couple are not legally married but are living together. Maryland does not recognize common-law marriages. Yet if a couple have lived together in another state that recognizes this type of union, Maryland will accept that the couple are married when they take up residency in the state.

A marriage license is similar to the issuing of a driver's learner's permit. After establishing that the person is of age, can read, understands the driver's manual, and that his or her vision is not impaired, a temporary license gives permission to learn how to drive a vehicle. Once the test is taken and passed, a permanent driver's license is issued. That is the one that counts, and so it is with the marriage certificate.

MARRIAGE CERTIFICATE

The marriage license is a permit that allows an officiant to perform a marriage ceremony. The marriage certificate is the official document stating that the marriage has taken place. After nuptial exchanges, the officiant, the bridal couple, and two witnesses sign the marriage certificate in triplicate: one is mailed to the bride and bridegroom, the other is for the officiant to send to the state, and the third for the officiant's file.

CIVIL CEREMONY

Q: *My fiancée and I are being married at the courthouse in a civil ceremony. My mother says it is a cold and impersonal way to get married so we would like to compose our own vows; do you know if the officiant will allow it?*

I cannot give a direct answer because the law varies from county to county and state to state. But no matter where or how you marry, either you or your fiancée must appear in person to obtain a marriage license. Ask the ground rules at that time, or I am sure they accept telephone information calls. If they don't permit changes in their standard service, maybe one of their officiants will make "house calls." If so, ask whether he or she would incorporate the vows you wrote into the ceremony.

In Maryland's Montgomery County there is a standard civil marriage ceremony with no deviations from its nonreligious wording. The ceremony takes place in the Marriage Room, which has about five rows of benches for guests. The Clerk of the Court asks the bride and bridegroom to sign the register: the bride on the pink line, the bridegroom on the blue; one or two witnesses sign on the red line. With backs to the company, a female witness on the bride's left and a male witness on the bridegroom's right, the bridal couple face the Clerk, who conducts the exchange of vows in a ceremony that lasts no more than several minutes. It can be a double, single, or no-ring ceremony. Some couples do not want a ring ceremony because they will be repeating the process in a house of worship at another time.

Cold and impersonal? Well, it can neither compare with the excitement that builds up with planning a wedding nor with the traditional and emotional response of a ceremony that combines the beauty of pageantry and the intimate feeling of being surrounded by relatives and friends. But it does suit the needs of people who do not want a fuss. It is short and simple.

I understand that most couples wear smart daytime clothes and have at least two people accompanying them. The day I visited I was asked to be the sole witness for one couple who came alone. For their no-ring ceremony the bride wore an extremely casual pair of pants and an Eisenhower jacket; they looked as if this was one of the errands they had to run that day and had barely time to accept my good wishes and those of the Clerk's. It was true! Time was of the essence, since both were in the military; one was being transferred and to be together they had to be married as soon as possible so that their branch of service could process their papers. Later they would have a religious ceremony with their families present.

Q: *I'm in my early thirties and would like to wear a traditional wedding dress. Do you think it foolish?*

You are talking to a mother of two grown sons, and from my point of view you are what I call a young woman. If you have not been married before you can choose to dress as a traditional bride, as long as it is in a style and tone that suits your personality—a good suggestion for everyone whatever one's age.

Q: *My daughter has been living with a young man. Now they are getting married and she wants a wedding. How do you go about arranging a formal wedding under those circumstances? I am also receiving hints from my mother about the propriety of it all.*

Your daughter is marrying out of your home, under the umbrella of her parents, and that is how you should look at it. How do you feel about having the wedding?

Q: *I would like her to have a wedding. Not that I don't have conflicting feelings about their living together; I am quite conventional and also wonder about the reaction of my family and friends.*

Assume the attitude that you are glad they are taking the step and go on to plan the wedding without thought to the young couple's life style. Your daughter and her fiancé have decided they want to spend the rest of their lives together and the wedding is the symbol of the decision. As for the reaction of friends and relatives, they will come and dance at the wedding.

Maybe young people will conduct themselves differently in the future, but right now their approach is so open that they do not bother to hide even the most intimate of relationships. So many think nothing of it. I have heard young adults who are living together or have a liaison make remarks about promiscuous people. Apparently that is where the line is drawn.

Q: *This wedding is driving me wild. First my daughter didn't want a wedding, though she hasn't been married before. Then she said okay to a simple one—no show because she was a bridesmaid at two separate weddings and thinks them "stagey." But what does a "simple wedding" mean? She wants to walk to the altar unescorted. That's not simple—that's awkward. She has a loving and handsome father to escort her. We are a modern Jewish-American family but my secret desire is for both me and my husband to escort her. However, at this point, I would not dream of suggesting it. Her bridegroom is going to slip into the room somehow, and, like a theater in the round, guests will be seated in a circle with the wedding canopy centered. What can I say to her?*

Some young people have conflicting feelings. They want to be part of the whole and yet somehow be different, not always realizing that the wedding ceremony carries on a tradition that couples have taken part in since time immemorial—with variations according to cultural backgrounds.

In today's society, the bride wears a dress that is generally different from any other she will wear during her lifetime but whose character is the same as most bride's dresses. Whether the bride walks alone or is escorted by her father, both parents, or by her honor attendant, those steps that lead her to her waiting bridegroom are separate from any she has taken before. No matter that the bridal couple have written their own vows—those utterances are still promises they make to each other. There is no other day in one's life such as this one. Though it is repeated with minor changes for all marrying people, it is a special day for the individual couple and for their families.

I believe your daughter will rethink walking to the altar alone, especially if you talk to her in a quiet, reasonable manner and explain that it is an honor she would not want to deny her father. If things calm down a little, you might even be able to sneak in the idea that you would like to walk by her side as well. Use your intuition; don't suggest it unless you feel it will be accepted as a possibility, and don't be disappointed if it is turned down.

The ceremony-in-the-round idea would not work in most houses of worship where the benches are stationary. But it's an appealing idea. Arranged properly, it would create the "difference" your daughter seems to want. The result is almost the same, though, since some guests will be facing the couple while others will not. Be sure that there is ample aisle space for the processional and that there are aisles for guests to maneuver to their seats.

Point out to her that there is a feeling of privacy she may want to retain as she and her bridegroom face the rabbi to make their vows. As public a wedding as Prince Charles and Princess Diana had, the cameras were not allowed to take a front view of their faces during the ceremony. Queen Elizabeth felt they should have those moments without the world looking on.

Q: *My son has decided to marry a girl he met at college whose background is different from ours. Up to the time we visited her parents I didn't realize how different suburban and rural people can be. Since then I am actually sick with worry about this wedding and have told my son I can't invite my family or my friends to the wedding.*

The ceremony, an interfaith one, will be held in a motel reception room where guests will be seated at round dinner tables already set for dinner. There will be a center aisle for the procession and programs, like those used in church, will be distributed.

These arrangements are completely alien to any wedding that I've attended but, to top it all, at the reception after the ceremony there will be limited champagne, enough to toast the bridal couple; plenty of beer and wine; and if guests wish hard liquor, there will be a cash bar!

At this point I couldn't contain myself. When I objected to having guests pay for anything at a wedding, they said that the bar will be in another room so no one will see money change hands.

Have you heard of such arrangements?

Even though a wedding is held elsewhere, guests should be treated as if they were coming to your home. As hosts you could choose not to serve hard liquor but punch and wine only. However, you do not expect guests to run to the local pub for a shot of whiskey. Most people will agree that a cash bar at a wedding is in poor taste. Having said that, it should be added that it might not be so unusual in rural areas to have a cash bar. That fact does not make it any more acceptable but it may be an explanation.

Programs, however, are not unusual in some parts of the country, though they are mostly used for church wedding ceremonies.

For the ceremony, you might suggest to your son that chairs be placed in rows right and left of the aisle. While people are standing in the receiving line, which could be held in another room, have the staff briskly rearrange tables and chairs for the reception. But this might not be to her family's liking, just as you find their customs not to your taste.

The bridegroom's family has a limited say in the wedding proceedings if the bride's family is doing all the arranging. But think clearly a moment: your son will be hurt if his family is not invited to the wedding—it is his family, not just yours. You could tell your people that they are coming to a country wedding that is a bit different from what they are used to attending—it might be fun for everyone.

LADIES AND GENTLEMEN, during a subsequent phone call with the young man's mother I had a sudden feeling that the bride's family had put on the "we're hicks from the hills" act for his parents. If the young man's mother was worried and clearly thought the match unsuitable, it is possible the other side felt the same way. Her son seemed to be wavering. I wonder how that situation turned out.

WEDDING DAY—HIS DREAMS AND HERS

LADIES AND GENTLEMEN, I find it fascinating to discover how people come to certain conclusions. Sweethearts decide to marry but each envisions the events of the wedding day in the opposite manner. Both have been married before, she in a single-ring civil ceremony with a small reception at a restaurant. He was the resplendent bridegroom exchanging wedding rings with yards and yards of bridal illusion and calla lilies. Now she wants to look "bridey." Not, she promises everyone, that she will wear a veil and look like a floating virgin. And at the reception, she says enthusiastically, they will invite everyone. He, on the other hand, has gone through the whole bit and now would like to be married quietly in a single-ring ceremony in a judge's office and later have a few select people to wish them well.

Can't you just see where both are coming from? Having had broken marriages, apparently not without scars, they do not want to have a wedding resembling what each had the first time they were married.

They will probably find a happy medium. It is hoped he will be reassured that he will not have to grope for the garter and that she is going to look splendid in an off-white tea-length dress with maybe a picture hat and a delicate bouquet. The ceremony will suit a mature couple's taste and the reception will be attended by those they really want to invite.

One recurring theme that keeps drifting my way, and is a concern mainly expressed by young professional men and women, is: what if he suffers from male ringophobic *malade imaginaire* (or, in Latin, *sexus masculina*) disorder? While most men are comfortable wearing a wedding band, some men just do not like to wear jewelry and some women just do not like the idea that some do not like to wear wedding bands.

Why, she asks, should I wear one if he does not?

He says that the wearing of a ring by either sex does not promote constancy and that those who want to be unfaithful will not be deterred by a ring, unless, when fancy is tempted, it has some magical power to prod the conscience.

There is a difference between a man who will not wear any jewelry and one who rejects a wedding band per se. My husband has an aversion to jewelry that he cannot explain. At this writing, the only adornments he has ever worn are cuff links when he has absolutely no choice and a watch when he travels. Even if he did not have this dislike, his work with high-voltage technology would prohibit the wearing of metal of any kind. Surgeons have to divest themselves of ornaments when operating, as does everyone connected with the scrub room of a hospital.

Ms. Ring might choose to wear a wedding band or not. However, women have a certain amount of protection from unwanted attention when they wear one—though only from those who seek a carefree relationship. Even a divorcée will suddenly sport one when it suits her purpose, and, just as she can produce a ring, he can secrete his away.

Unlike a tetanus shot, wearing a ring does not give anyone immunity from the "wandering desire virus," which can attack either sex. Marriage is built on mutual trust. The confidence men and women instill in one another is not derived from wearing a wedding ring.

Though the exchange of wedding rings is an integral part of Eastern Orthodox rites, double-ring ceremonies in Protestant and in Jewish Conservative and Reform wedding ceremonies are a fairly recent introduction. This is based solely on choice and is not a religious belief or rite. The single-ring ceremony is still observed in most Orthodox Jewish weddings since the ring is traditionally the symbol of something of value presented to the bride by the bridegroom. The giving of the ring was depicted by Egyptians over 4,500 years ago, and was considered "earnest money," a sign of good intentions.

SINGLE RING

When I asked a young bride why she and her husband had had a single-ring ceremony, her answer surprised me. Though the bridegroom would have acquiesced in a double-ring ceremony, he was not keen on wearing a wedding band. She felt that there was no point—perhaps even a hint of insincerity—in having a double-ring ceremony if he was hesitant about wearing one. To her, the vows were the most meaningful part. Besides, when she analyzed it, the single-ring ceremony was traditional and everything about their wedding was old-fashioned.

Though I did not say so, I see no contradiction in having a double-ring ceremony and not wearing the wedding band afterward, even if the wearing is important to the bride. It is the beginning of the gentle art of successfully living together. No longer do we expect to think and feel as one—an impossible expectation. Each is recognized as an individual; marriage makes us separate and yet together in a special way.

SICKNESS OR DEATH IN THE FAMILY

Q: *Although my father is ill he insists we go ahead with the wedding as planned. Aside from the heartbreak, I am terrified lest he pass away at the time of the wedding. Do you know of others' experiences and how they handled it?*

There are gigantic feats of strength that are exhibited at special times. Some people go along with the stricken person's wishes, feeling that it gives them solace and something else to concentrate on during a difficult time.

It happened at my brother's wedding; a seriously ill loved one left the hospital in a wheelchair to witness the ceremony.

My son was at a wedding where the father of the bride was terminally ill. The morning of the wedding he was too weak to move. When he insisted on attending his daughter's wedding, two of his cousins took him into the shower until the warm water had loosened his painracked body enough to enable him to dress. At the reception he danced with his wife and his daughter and refused to listen to anybody's suggestion that he slow down. After all, he hadn't been expected to live long enough to see the wedding at all. It was the best gift he could have given his family and so moving that everyone at the wedding was deeply affected.

Another good example is of an engagement announcement in the newspaper. It was almost the deadline for the Announcement Desk. I received a call from the mother of the engaged girl saying that it was important to have her daughter's engagement announcement in the next insertion date. She went on to explain that her husband, though alert, was at death's door and knew it. He wanted to be able to read of his daughter's betrothal in the newspaper. Naturally the announcement appeared.

After the gentleman had died, his wife telephoned. She told me that the preparation of the wording, the expectation of reading it in the newspaper, and finally its appearance with a photograph of his child worked not only as a distraction but as a sense of completion. I admired that family's strength, caring, and control.

An acute sickness or the passing away of an immediate family member at a time like this brings immediate meaning to the saying "Life is bittersweet." Whether to go ahead with the proceedings is a decision you must make with your fiancé, your side of the family, and with a religious adviser, if you have one. Some religions have specific guidelines and not all necessarily recommend postponing the wedding, so check those areas. You might want to tone down the festivities but be subtle about it.

THREE-HOUR LIMIT FOR WEDDING

Q: *Is three hours enough time in which to have a wedding ceremony and reception? My son is being married in Los Angeles, California. He and his fiancée are planning a wedding with a tight budget. There is a lovely outdoor site overlooking the Pacific that they can rent which is not exorbitantly expensive. The place is booked solid but they have a three-hour span available. There will be about 150 guests, mainly their friends, since both families live great distances away.*

Will both the ceremony and reception be held in the same place?

Q: *Yes.*

You would have to ask how long the caterer needs to set up and clear up after the event. Then the officiant and guests must be on time, which is not always possible if you live in a congested area. Everything would have to be timed precisely, and you wouldn't want the appearance of rushing through the wedding. It can be done, but the chances of something going awry are greatly increased.

The ceremony should take less than half an hour. Dispense with the receiving line or shorten it to only the mothers and bridal couple. Since you mentioned that the site might be available a little earlier though the ceremony could not take place then, maybe the couple could receive beforehand. A cocktail reception with hors d'oeuvres and a wedding cake or a champagne buffet might be perfect following an afternoon ceremony.

CONFLICTING DECISIONS

Q: *We are planning a small but elegant wedding. Her parents are paying for the food, mine for the liquor and flowers, and my fiancée and I for the rest of the expenses. But suddenly there are little annoyances that are cropping up; the photographer, for instance, is much more expensive than we realized. Also there are differences in opinion about what constitutes an elegant wedding. I don't know what I expect you to say but have you had any experience in this area?*

Decision-making is difficult when three couples—six minds—are involved in the planning. There would be less controversy if only one side of the family made the decisions, even while encouraging input from the other side.

Trouble begins when expenses exceed the budget and everyone must agree on the cuts that could or should be made. One wants continuous music, the other large floral centerpieces for the tables. Some families can avoid the tug of war, others cannot seem to let go of an idea. The key, I suppose, is compromise.

Now you have to take a stand. One couple must have veto power, and since it is your wedding it will have to be you and your fiancée. The way to accomplish this is to forget who is paying for what. Add up your resources. Decide what are the most important aspects of the wedding. Make the decision on what constitutes an elegant wedding in your eyes.

MY TOWN OR MY FAMILY'S

Q: *I am a twenty-nine-year-old single lady who is planning to be married in December. I have lived away from my home state for eleven years. My future husband is a native of the state in which I now live.*

My family, relatives, and friends back home want me to come there to be married; my friends and acquaintances where I live now want me to have the wedding here. My fiancé says it is up to me but I am really torn. The decision is a tough one, because I promised my mother back in 1975 that I would come home to be married. I don't want to disappoint her. Although I visit my

*family and home church an average of seven times a year, I feel
that the church I now attend is my church. Do you have any
advice on the subject?*

"My town or my family's?" is a not uncommon question
now. On a large piece of paper head one side GO HOME and the
other side STAY HERE. Divide the two columns into four. Under
GO HOME list PROS and CONS; do the same under STAY HERE.

The first pro under GO HOME should be the promise you made
to your mother. Even though you made it years ago, it is still a
vow that should be kept, unless you can ask her to release you
from it. She may realize the oath is difficult to keep and that it
would be unfair to hold you to it. On the other hand, when you
left that is exactly what she may have anticipated, being willing
to part with you if you would not grow away from your family.
Apparently you have not, since you go home several times a year.

Decide whether the wedding you would have in your adopted
town would match the warmth and love that would envelop you
when encircled by your family and friends as you stand before
the clergyman performing the ceremony in the church in which
you grew up.

You probably would not feel the conflict if you had lived
away but did not go home much, or had severed your relations
with the home church.

There is also a key in your choice of words when, in your
letter, you say "My *parents, relatives, and friends* want me to
marry there" which indicates a closeness; referring to those in
the town where you live your wording is different, "My *friends
and acquaintances*"—not as warm a phrase.

If you are thinking of the bridegroom's side of the family, it
is generally expected that they would travel to the bride's home
for the wedding—it is traditional for the bride to be married from
her parents' home. Your good friends will make every effort to
dance at your wedding.

No matter where nuptial vows take place, you could, if you
wish, have a reception in the other town for those who will be
unable to go to the wedding. Everyone loves a party.

Q: *My daughter is being married; we are Jewish but her fiancé
is not. That, at the moment, is not a problem.*

Our family situation is complicated. My husband died and ten years ago I remarried. However, my daughter doesn't get along with her stepfather.

I thought she would ask her older brother to escort her to the altar but she wants her grandfather to do so instead. Also, although I have not suggested it yet, can I walk with them as is the custom of Jewish parents? Or, if that is not appropriate, could I stand under the canopy with her?

You seem puzzled about her wish to have her grandfather walk with her to the altar. Maybe he has been her confidant.

Q: *Not really. I just mentioned it in passing; it seemed to me that she would want her brother to do it.*

Is the grandfather on the bride's paternal or maternal side?

Q: *Maternal.*

Though it has nothing to do with age, it may be that her grandfather seems more suitable as a mentor and her brother too young. By the way, have you mentioned that you would like to walk with her?

Q: *No, not yet. I have too many cobwebs to clear first and we have only just begun to plan the wedding.*

Before you speak to your daughter regarding her choice of escort, how does your husband feel about not being asked?

Q: *He understands the situation and did not expect to do the honors.*

There are several things to begin thinking about, though you do not have to answer now, such as: will the couple have an interfaith ceremony?

If you have a traditional Jewish ceremony, not an interfaith one, and your daughter walks between you and your father, will the bridegroom's parents want to participate and stand under the canopy with their son? Some people find it touching, others are not used to the idea.

Some decisions will fall into place about the ceremony after your daughter and her fiancé have the advice of the clergy involved in the marriage rites. But whether to suggest walking down the aisle with your daughter is another question.

A wedding is a unique event in many subtle ways. The differences between your daughter and her stepfather have been, until now, strictly a private affair and only a few have been privy to the dissension.

However, a wedding brings together two families and a company of people on both sides. Now it is a public matter.

If you alone walk with your daughter or accompany her with her grandfather, wouldn't this point up the problem between your daughter and her stepfather—your husband of ten years? Though your husband understands and accepts the fact that he will have no part in the proceedings, he might not really comprehend the story it tells until the wedding day. I feel there would be less speculation if her grandfather did the honors alone.

LODGINGS FOR OUT-OF-TOWN GUESTS

Q: *We have reserved a block of rooms at a motel for out-of-town guests who will be attending our wedding. How do we let them know that they are responsible for the bill?*

When you reserve a block of rooms, most hotels and motels offer reduced rates and ask for your guest list. They send the information. If they do not have that arrangement, you mail the material with the rates clearly marked.

Q: *Does the bride take her father's left or right arm when he escorts her to the altar?*

Ask the officiant for advice. Generally, the bride walks on her father's right, which makes it easier to maneuver as they arrive a few paces from the bridegroom. She switches her bouquet to her left hand and the bridegroom stands on her right. Father stands on the left facing the minister to give the bride away (if that is part of the marriage rites) and then joins his wife, who is sitting in the first pew, left side of the aisle.

For the recessional the bride and her husband face the congregation, after which she takes his right arm for their first walk together as a married couple.

This procedure is reversed for a Jewish wedding if the father escorts his daughter alone, because the bride's family customarily sits to the right of the aisle and the bridegroom's side on the left.

LADIES AND GENTLEMEN, in medieval times a lady walked on her champion's left because his right arm had to be free to draw his sword in case of trouble. Later, a gentleman escorted his damsel on the curb side of the street so that it would be he who would be splashed with mud by galloping horses and carriages.

Q: *At our wedding ceremony, we, the bride and bridegroom, are going to walk to the altar together. Do we hold hands or walk arm in arm, and am I on his left or right?*

Since your bridegroom is escorting you, entwine your arm in his as you walk on the side suggested by the officiant.

Q: *Have you heard of attendants alone or with guests giving the bride away? Right now it is being debated whether just attendants or the whole company stands and says, "We do."*

I do not know of anyone who has done that. However, what the bride and bridegroom have to do is discuss it with the officiating minister, who may or may not give permission. Generally, only a parent, a relative, or a friend who escorts the bride to the altar gives the bride away—it is a solemn service.

SHIVAREE

Q: *My future husband has just told me that he belongs to a club which follows the practice of serenading newlyweds on their wedding night. I think it is tacky and will feel terribly embarrassed by this show of attention at our hotel. What do I do?*

Either you are funning me or he is teasing you. But if what he says is true, *firmly* convince him to keep the name of the hotel a secret from everyone—as newlyweds have done, until recently.

LADIES AND GENTLEMEN, I treated the question seriously but I think it was a put-on. Actually, it started me thinking. The practice the young lady was talking about is a genteel equivalent of the old-fashioned "shivaree," a sort of cat-and-mouse game.

In some rural areas it was the custom of townspeople to try to guess where the bridal couple were spending their first night together (a quaint custom in itself by today's standards). They would surround the house while banging on pots and pans, creating a frightfully discordant row. The newlyweds would try to avoid the shivaree by keeping their hiding place secret, a practically impossible task in those days. Some couples were painfully sensitive about the hazing; thicker skins knew full well that they had done it to others and now it was their turn.

EVERYTHING THE COUPLE SHOULD KNOW

Whether yours is a formal or an informal wedding, the first order of business is to satisfy the old bridal rhyme, to which, with apologies to Mr. Anonymous, I have added something new of my own in italics.

Something OLD—*a link with the past*
Something NEW—*a marriage to last*
Something BORROWED—*a friendship of giving*
Something BLUE—*a sky full of living*
And a SIXPENCE in your SHOE—*for good fortune*

So "old" can be an heirloom cameo; "new" might be your wedding gown or your stockings; borrow your aunt's lace handkerchief, and accent your lingerie with a blue ribbon . . . and a shiny dime can be your sixpence.

Now let us talk about the schedule before the actual wedding day. There are three questions to be answered before deciding on the type of wedding to be planned. What degree of formality will it have? How much money can be spent? How big is the guest list?

It is unrealistic to plan a *very formal* wedding with a meager pocketbook. The key word is "very," and it is synonymous with "more"—a *more* expensive wedding dress and accessories, *more* invitations, a *more* elaborate reception, *more* attendants, which means *more* flowers and *more* money to be spent for presents. And it would be a big mistake to suppose, as someone once said to me, "budgets are made to be broken." That philosophy will cause headaches, not happiness.

- If the bridegroom's family intends to contribute toward some of the expenses, they should make the offer early.
- His family should give the guest list, along with correct names, addresses, and ZIP codes, to her family as soon as possible.
- Although a wedding date has been agreed upon by both the bridal couple and their families, it is best to have some alternative time of day and dates from which to choose. The officiant, the house of worship, and the reception place have to be coordinated—especially if the wedding has been planned for a busy time of year.
- The betrothed should make an appointment with the officiating clergy for marital counseling and wedding planning. Since each institution has guidelines for music and the proceedings of the wedding, discuss any major preferences in the ceremony or in the music.
- Keep records by using file cards. As the invitation list is gathered, on individual index cards and in alphabetical order, write the names of potential guests with their addresses and telephone numbers. Note the relationship of the guests to the bride and bridegroom; both will find it useful information. Names on the "absolutely sure" list should be kept in one file, the "maybes" in another. After the invitations have been mailed and replies start coming in they are meticulously entered on the index card; "yesses" in one file, "nos" in another. As presents are received record the type of gift, the arrival date, and also the day the thank-you note was sent. I understand that the file boxes serve as silent

reminders to keep up with notes of thanks, especially if they are painted a bright red.

- When choosing where to hold the reception, remember that too large a place creates a cold atmosphere. Too many people crowded into a small hall is uncomfortable.
- When the type of wedding is being decided on, thoughts should center around the bridal gown, veil, and accessories as well as the bridegroom's attire and accessories. Once the bride's ensemble is planned, the decisions about the color scheme for members of the bridal party, flowers, table coverings, etc., can be coordinated.
- Choose honor attendants as carefully as you would their clothing and don't be shy about asking for their help—that is their function.
- Choose bridesmaids and ushers. The number should be determined by the size of the wedding. One usher for fifty guests. Think about including your fiancé(e)'s brothers and sisters.
- Ask relatives and friends to put up out-of-town bridesmaids and groomsmen. If not, hotel expenses will be your responsibility.
- Arrange with a motel to reserve a batch of rooms for out-of-town guests—their expense, but they benefit by the group rates you can get.
- Mothers coordinate color, length, and style of dresses. It is customary for the bride's mother to make the decision first so the bridegroom's mother knows just what to pick.
- Photographer: hire a person with experience shooting weddings and ask to view wedding portfolios. If you wish to announce in the newspapers, discuss having a black-and-white glossy print taken.
- Music: discuss what type of music is preferred for the ceremony and reception. Make an appointment with the musicians to hear them play at a wedding.
- Engravers: order invitations (add twenty-five more than guest count); wedding announcements; informal and formal cards. Proofread carefully to see that the wording is correct.
- Caterer: when going over the menu, keep in mind that the

choice of food for a buffet reception should be easier to manage than that for a seated dinner.

- Order the wedding cake and, if you will be having one, the bridegroom's cake.
- Florist: since you now know your color scheme you can select the necessary floral arrangements.
- Limousine: this service might be useful if many out-of-town guests fly in and transportation is needed; also useful to transport bride and bridegroom from the ceremony to the reception.
- Discuss wedding-trip plans and wardrobe needed for the climate. Make transportation and hotel reservations as early as possible.

    Traveling overseas? Check that passports are up to date. Should you need new ones, have passport photographs taken. Have necessary inoculations. It is best to call the Passport Office for special information about your honeymoon destination. Plan the trip from the reception to your honeymoon destination.

- List papers that have to be changed to Mr. and Mrs., such as insurance policies, bank accounts, wills, and all legal papers. If the bride is changing her name on documents and licenses, add those to the list.
- Make an appointment for fitting of wedding dress; take wedding shoes to ensure dress will be the correct length. Have you worn the shoes in the house so they will be comfortable on the wedding day? Also check with maids about their fittings.
- The bridegroom, his ushers, and the best man should go for their fittings; while there he orders accessories for his groomsmen.
- The bridegroom blackens the soles of his shoes if he and his bride have to kneel during the ceremony.
- For ease of mind, any shopping should be accomplished as early as possible, especially for the bride and bridegroom's wedding bands, if they are to be engraved.
- Visit bridal registry together to select china, crystal, and silver patterns, and other sundry household items.
- Before going for marriage license, telephone the Marriage

License Bureau for its policy on obtaining the license and
to find out whether blood tests are necessary.

- It is a good idea for both bride and bridegroom to have
complete medical checkups.
- Plan bridesmaids' party, if you are giving one.
- Plan bachelor party (optional).
- Discuss guest list for rehearsal dinner.
- To the bride: consider having a hairdresser arrange your
hair to suit your face and veil. Have your nails manicured
and, if you need help with your makeup, consult a cos-
metician; have her make you up once before your wedding
day to see if you like the results. Try for a natural and not
too dramatic look.
- To the bridegroom: judge the proper time to have a haircut
so that your hair will look just right on your wedding day.
- Arrange rehearsal time for the wedding ceremony. Notify
the bridal party and be sure to stress promptness. The rehearsal takes place a day or two before the actual wedding day and depends on how easily everyone can be
gathered together. During the rehearsal the bridal party
are walked through the procedure but actual words are not
exchanged.
    Everybody should concentrate on their roles in an effort
to achieve a smooth processional. The fun takes place later
at the rehearsal dinner.
- Time the trip to the house of worship and add a few minutes
in case of traffic so that you and the wedding party will be
able to judge prompt arrival time on the wedding day.
- Lists of names should be given ushers if there is going to
be special seating in the house of worship.
- Attendants should be enthusiastic about their friends' wedding plans; blasé just won't do.
- Best man: remind the bridegroom to prepare beforehand
the check to be given the officiant on the wedding day. A
note of thanks accompanying it would be appropriate.
- Choose going-away attire and honeymoon wardrobe.
- Pack for your honeymoon.
- A travel tip: expensive jewelry should be given to the care
of the hotel or ship steward during the day. You will be

invited into a private room and given a safe-deposit box
for your valuables. The key and box are assigned to you
for the trip. The jewelry can be retrieved at will.

• Don't forget to call the caterer with final guest count. Keep
in touch with the musicians, florist, and photographer.

• You and your sweetheart should not let anyone interfere
with your happiness. Because you are center stage, put on
happy faces, even when pressures mount.

• Keep up with thank-you notes.

WEDDING DAY

Take a cue from Shakespeare:

All the world's a stage,
And all the men and women merely players . . .

Calm is the secret to a lovely bride and a relaxed bridegroom.
What bride doesn't want to look serene when walking down the
aisle, and what bridegroom doesn't envision himself the confident
figure waiting for his bride at the altar?

Try to have all arrangements completed so that you have
some free time to rest on the day before the wedding. To do this
the rehearsal dinner should be planned two evenings before the
wedding if possible.

Even though there is a rehearsal dinner the evening before
the wedding and many guests are in from out of town, the dinner
should end at a reasonable hour. For some bridal couples the
wedding day starts early, because the photographer wants to take
formal shots when every one looks fresh.

• Try to rest at least an hour or two before dressing.

• *Check your lists:* do you have the license, wedding rings,
toiletries, extra hosiery for the bride, and a sewing kit for
an emergency? Passports, tickets, car keys, money, charge
cards?

• Before donning the wedding dress and shoes, apply all
makeup, perfume, and do all nail repair. Make sure that
polish and deodorant are dry. My friend told me of the

bride who walked down the aisle with tears streaming down her face because her wedding dress had a stark red splash of nail polish on the skirt.

Keep sharp instruments away from stockings as well as other clothing.

If not dressing at home, be sure all containers, such as lotions, nail polish and remover, makeup base, and face powder—everything that has a lid—are tightly closed. Pack these toiletries in a separate, securely closed case. Ziploc bags make excellent holders for items that are not self-contained since the opening closes as firmly as a zipper and they come in different sizes. I use them instead of makeup kits.

- Whether prone to allergies or not, don't try new products right before the wedding. All experimenting should be done at least a month before so that a reaction to a new perfume or mascara will have disappeared by the wedding day.
- The above advice is useful to the bridegroom. A new shaving lotion might be a nice change but be aware of the skin's reaction to it.
- If the bride is dressing at home, remember to place a sheet over the seat and floor of the car to prevent soiling the wedding dress. During her walk to the car, she should lift her dress over her arm and straighten it when seated so it will not crease.
- Both of you should mentally go through the main parts of the day:

The bride puts her engagement ring on her right hand.
The bridegroom remembers to bring the marriage license and wedding ring.
Remember to start left foot first when walking down the aisle.
Bride entwines her arm through the bend of her father's.
Bridegroom gives the ring to the best man.
Everyone walks at a slow pace but not a crawl.
Heads and backs should be straight, expressions pleasing.
Vows should not be loud, but neither should they be inaudible.
The bouquet should be held below the bride's waist and

below the level of her father's arm so it can be seen as well as look symmetrical and graceful.

The bridegroom should practice holding the ring so that he can slip it with ease and confidence on the bride's finger. If she is wearing long gloves, she should be able to slip her finger smoothly out of the slit of the glove. He should be aware that it is hard for the bride to move about in a wedding dress with a train, so he should pace himself without being obvious about it.

Remember, you are surrounded by an affectionate company, so there is no need to feel stiff and nervous.

• Have a nice life.

TOO LARGE OR TOO SMALL

Q: *We contracted for a reception hall and, due to a situation beyond our control, we find that the room is larger than we thought and it is too late to look for another. Besides, we will lose the deposit. Has anyone ever called with this problem and how was it solved?*

The manager of the reception site could make the room *look* smaller. It is done all the time by strategically placing screens surrounded by tall plants around the room—screens and plants can be rented. Even the way they set up the buffet tables, the wedding-cake table, and liquor bar can help matters. Your guests will never know the difference.

CHOOSING SITES FOR
CEREMONY AND RECEPTION

As you see with the problem above, careful selection of the house of worship and of the reception site is most important. You must be able to envision your company in those premises. Most places of worship can handle many more people than can reception places. Give or take a few guests, it is crucial to know how many people are going to be invited before choosing just where both events will be held. Many a dream of having the wedding at a preferred place has to be shelved because it is either too large or too small.

Should you select a house of worship for the ceremony and somewhere else for the reception, consider the distance between them. Out-of-town guests may be unfamiliar with the surrounding area and even with a map the reception site might be hard to find.

Because a sense of time and place and ambience is often appealing to bridal couples, it is popular now to be married and have a reception in a historic mansion or town home, especially in the city of Washington and the Virginia/Maryland area. Their handsome structures are imbued with the richness of this country's beginnings. The proceeds derived from such functions are used toward the houses' upkeep and restoration. Some examples are Woodlawn Plantation in Mount Vernon, Virginia, which is part of George Washington's original estate and filled with antiques and candlelight and sculptured gardens; the Decatur House, just a stroll from the White House and within the sounds of the bells of St. John's Episcopal Church on Lafayette Square; or the Oxon Hill Manor on the banks of the Potomac in Maryland, which rests on a site developed by the family of John Hanson, first President under the Articles of Confederation. In 1929, Cordell Hull, Secretary of State under President Roosevelt, built the magnificent Oxon Hill Manor, which has had as its guest President Roosevelt, among other notables. At one point it was burned almost to a shell and is now being restored by devotees of historic preservation.

Most manor houses have large rooms and some have original furnishings and paintings, as do town homes, though they are smaller in scale.

When contracting for a historic site you must expect to pay a fee by the hour for the use of the premises. Often you are obliged to engage a caterer from a list approved by the staff, since they know the layout and have worked there successfully. Commercial kitchens have been installed by some establishments but in others hot plates, serving pieces, place settings and cutlery, as well as tables and chairs, must be brought in by the caterer.

Other houses will allow you to bring your own food and supplies but it is important to check the kitchen facilities.

The contract might say whether or not you can have electronic music (stringed instruments are generally acceptable), dancing, and smoking. The premises must be left in good condition and generally there is a staff overseer.

Some rooms may be roped off, because during the day the mansion is a museum open to the general public and the furniture is old and fragile. This limits your access to the home. Another limiting factor is that certain sites allow receptions but not ceremonies.

In good weather, outdoor receptions can be held in the gardens of such houses, which are often extraordinarily lovely and spacious. The establishment might insist on the renting of a platform and a tent, which is a large added expense. Whether the wedding is held indoors or out, the guest list should be about the same since alternative plans must be arranged in case of rain. Rest-room facilities must be adequate for the number of people expected.

Like English gentry, some private owners of spacious houses rent in the same way that historic mansions and museums are rented. Aside from the above guidelines, it is advisable to check whether the owner has enough insurance coverage to handle an event such as a wedding. They must not only be insured against damage to *their* property and in case of a suit resulting from a business deal but also for the protection of persons renting the property.

An outdoor wedding and reception with the sky as a ceiling is considered by some a romantic setting in which to exchange marriage vows. National and state parks are available and the expense is negligible. Again, have alternative plans in case of rain, and please, near rest rooms, okay?

Business catering establishments such as hotels and restaurants can put everything at your fingertips. Luxury hotels offer varying package deals that sometimes include the bridal suite for use as a dressing place for the bridal party, if the ceremony is to take place on the premises, and for the wedding night. The catering department supplies a manager who can help guide you step by step through the proceedings during the ceremony and reception. They advise on the size of the banquet room for the amount of guests expected, plan menu and liquor needs, and suggest an adequate serving staff. Many people will use the facilities and catering of the hotel but hire other services, such as those of musicians, photographer, and florist, that are recommended to them by friends.

HOME WEDDINGS

Home weddings can always be successful if your house or apartment is large enough for the amount of guests expected. All guests are invited to both the ceremony and for the reception.

Some bridal couples choose to be married in a church or synagogue and then return to the house for the reception. Refreshments can be simple or more elaborate. A small group might be able to have a seated dinner but usually a buffet reception is best for a larger guest list.

If the ceremony is to be held elsewhere, the bridal party and intimates on both sides of the family sometimes have a photography session before returning to the house. Someone has to be at home to greet guests as they arrive because everyone comes at the same time—unlike an eight o'clock dinner party in your home when your company drifts in from eight until around eight-thirty.

The responsibility on the host family is, of course, greater than it would be if the entire wedding were held elsewhere. On this special day, much is demanded of them. When deciding on the budget for the wedding try to include the cost of a caterer and servers (bartender, etc.). Unless the hostess is an excellent organizer, managing alone will be a great strain and near impossible.

A friend of mine had a lovely home wedding for her daughter. She had the limited services of a caterer but mainly it was her own efforts and those of family and friends who helped cook and arrange the event.

The main pitfalls to avoid with a home wedding, she suggests, are overcrowding and not enough flatware and plates for food. In other words, have *more* than the guest count in case of an emergency. Also, she strongly recommends a bartender to serve drinks and a maid to clear the dishes.

A home ceremony and reception are a little harder to arrange and sometimes require removing or rearranging furniture. Choose an unobstructed area for the ceremony and decorate it with flowers and ribbons so that guests do not crowd around that spot but form a semicircle. Even if a garden ceremony is planned, the house may need the same rearranging in case of rain or an unexpectedly cold day, so it is best to be prepared. Touch base with the officiant for a list of items needed to perform the ceremony, though most do come prepared.

The mother of the bride should be at the door to greet guests as they arrive, and an usher or two assigned to take coats. Provide chairs for elderly people, who find it hard to stand for long intervals.

How the actual ceremony is arranged depends on the layout of the house. The family takes their place near the altar leaving an aisle for the small procession. The officiant stands facing the company, the bridegroom walks with his best man, the maid of honor follows, and then the bride is escorted by her father. Music can accompany the service but it should be suited to the size of the room.

After the ceremony has been concluded with the traditional nuptial kiss, but not before, the newlyweds then turn to both sets of parents for congratulatory hugs. Again, if the house lends itself, there can be a receiving line. However, if it is not convenient, the bride and bridegroom stand where they are to welcome all well-wishers.

At a home wedding, there is no moment that more suitably fits the mood everyone experiences after witnessing the exchange of vows than right after the ceremony. It is the perfect moment to toast the couple. Everyone is gathered near the bridal pair. The hostess has arranged beforehand that trays of glasses be filled with champagne, or whatever liquid has been decided for the purpose, and passed to guests. The best man offers the toast. Then refreshments are served.

If you prefer, you have the option of toasting the bride and bridegroom just before the cutting of the wedding cake.

Expenses

Inquiries made by the bridegroom's family generally concern the obligations of *his* family. The bride and her family, too, ask what are the responsibilities of *his* family.

Researching the particulars of the obligations isn't complicated. Most books on wedding etiquette suggest the same items, with minor differences. However, there has been a gradual change in attitude and expectation about who should undertake what, based not only on practicality but on a sense of fairness.

Traditionally, it is expected that the bride's family will pay for the complete event with some expenses being assumed by the bridegroom's family—if they offer. After all, the bridegroom of yesteryear, no matter what his education or prospects, undertook a lifetime of responsibilities—the support and care of a wife, children, and a household. Today's woman often comes to the marriage bed with a fine education and a career equal to her husband's. In most cases she can and does support herself—she is truly an equal partner in life. If a man expects that he should not have to pay alimony to a woman who is perfectly capable of earning her own living, he should not be surprised that some help is expected with the cost of the wedding.

But what would he say if the bride and her family wanted a large formal wedding and he could not see the sense in going to such an expense? As one young man told me: "A small event with a few necessary guests and you're just as married. What is more," he continued, "I'm taking on a lifetime of responsibilities and I don't feel like blowing my hard-earned savings in one day. My wife might work but I've seen enough of life to know that you never can tell what the future has in store. My parents are retired with an income greatly affected by inflation and I cannot deplete it further. Now tell me what my obligations are and I'll meet them."

So you see, rules are difficult to set. If the bride's family wants that type of wedding, they will have to do it with limited help from the prospective bridegroom. For the young couple, whether they have a small wedding or large, there is no other time when the outlay of money will be greater in comparison to their income. The grand event aside, from that point on they will not only have to clothe themselves but also furnish a household, pay medical bills, and keep a roof over their heads. No wonder that young man had such a sense of accountability.

Though I have listed the bridegroom's expenses separately from those of his parents, often the money comes out of one pocket. More than likely, if the bridegroom is young, his parents will be signing the checks. But should he be established they might share expenses, or he may assume all costs for his side. This also applies to the bride and her family.

The suggestions below are within the general guidelines but there are groups that follow their cultural customs and those customs should be respected.

BRIDEGROOM'S TRADITIONAL WEDDING EXPENSES
- Engagement (or other) gift to bride and the bride's engagement and wedding rings, which are no small expense.
- Marriage license
- Boutonnières for father and male attendants
- Bride's bouquet, if customary in your area
- Bride's going-away corsage
- Flowers for both mothers and grandmothers
- Gloves and ascots or ties for male attendants
- Wedding gift for the bride—optional
- Gifts for ushers and best man
- Lodgings for out-of-town attendants, unless the bridegroom's parents assume the cost
- Bachelor dinner—optional
- Clergyman's fee
- Transportation for himself and his bride from house of worship to reception—sometimes comes within the budget of the bride's parents
- Medical checkup
- Wardrobe
- Honeymoon

HIS FAMILY'S TRADITIONAL CONTRIBUTION
- Clothes for the wedding
- Traveling expenses and hotel bill for themselves and their children
- Wedding gift to the couple

- Rehearsal dinner—customary in some areas, optional in others
- Bridal album—her parents pay for the photographer but his parents pay for the selection of photographs they wish in the album

OPTIONAL OFFERINGS—the amount within his family's discretion
- Liquor
- Music
- Flowers
- Bridegroom's family may offer to pay for one or more of the above items.
- Guests whom the bridegroom's family wish to invite over the allotted amount, with her family's permission. That is not considered a contribution to the wedding expenses. Extra guests add to the number of flower centerpieces needed as well as the amount of liquor, throwing the budget out of line.
- Any extra items requested of her family for which the bridegroom's family promised to pay

BRIDE'S EXPENSES
- Bridegroom's wedding band. Some brides also give their future husbands a separate gift.
- Bridesmaids' gifts
- Bridesmaids' luncheon
- Medical checkup
- Engraved or printed stationery—informals, notepaper for handwritten thank-you notes and other correspondence
- Wedding gift book and wedding guest book

HER FAMILY'S TRADITIONAL EXPENSES
- Invitations—including all enclosures, as well as wedding announcements
- Costs of wedding ceremony—music, fees for house of worship, flowers, and other decorations
- Costs of wedding reception—music, food, wedding cake, gratuities
- Bride's wedding dress and accessories
- Personal and household trousseau

- Photographs, both formal and candid
- Flowers carried by bride's attendants (in some areas bride's parents buy all flowers except the bride's going-away corsage)
- Transportation for wedding party, the bridegroom's parents, and close relatives to and from house of worship and then to reception
- Accommodations for out-of-town members of wedding party
- Bridesmaids' luncheon
- Rehearsal dinner—if not hosted by his parents, a relative, or a friend
- Wedding gift to the couple

BRIDESMAIDS' EXPENSES
- Dress and accessories
- Travel expenses from her home to the bride's
- A present for the bridal couple
- A share in the "joint" gift to the bride and bridegroom
- Bridesmaids' party for the bride and bridegroom
- Shower gift—you don't have to give more than one or two shower gifts, no matter how many showers you attend.
- Your lodgings are provided by the bride and her family, as are the bouquets.

BEST MAN AND USHERS
- Wedding clothes—nice if you own suitable formal wear but rented otherwise
- Travel costs from your home to the bridegroom's
- A present to the couple
- A share in the "joint" present to the bridal couple

VARIATIONS ON A THEME

Q: *How do I invite his parents to contribute to the wedding expenses, which I hear is not uncommon today?*

It is not a usual practice for the bride's family to invite his parents to pay part of the wedding costs. I really do not know how you can do it without leaving yourself open to embarrassment. Generally it is up to his parents to offer.

A lot depends on how you have handled the relationship with his parents until now. It is so important that a meeting take place between parents right after their children decide to marry. For instance, did you discuss wedding plans with his family in the beginning? Did you give them an opening to express their opinion? If you had, that would have given them and you an opportunity for frank discussion. Or did you inform them that you are having a formal wedding, an open bar, a seated dinner and dancing, and that they will be permitted to invite a certain number with no leeway for extras—even though they might have expressed a willingness to pay for the overflow?

Q: *What can we expect the groom's family to contribute toward wedding expenses?*

Has there been an offer on their part?

Q: *No, but I think they ought to. I am the father of the bride; her mother and I are divorced now. When I was married my family undertook certain obligations even though the bride's side didn't approach us. We just said we would help.*

The general rule is that the bride and her family arrange the sort of wedding they can afford. If his family offers to help so that a more lavish affair can be given and the gesture is accepted— great. Should nothing be said on the part of the groom's family, it would be difficult to pry an offer from them.

Q: *My ex-wife called the bridegroom's family, who live out of town, and asked point-blank what they intended to contribute to the wedding. Their answer was that they will show up.*

I do not know how you can insist, especially if you and your ex-wife arranged the whole event and did not discuss the arrangements beforehand. The only option you have to keep expenses down is to limit the guest list. I've known people to drastically limit the bridegroom's guest list so that if his family needed extra invitations, it would be at their expense.

Q: *Naw. It's my daughter's wedding and I want her to be happy.*

PROMISE 'EM ANYTHING

Q: *My daughter's in-laws promised to contribute to certain extras for the wedding. Well, I paid for everything, thinking that when I sent them their share of the bill that a check would be forthcoming. So far we have not received a penny, though two months have passed. How do I handle such a touchy subject?*

Send your son-in-law's parents a reminder saying that the bill only includes those items for which they had assumed responsibility and which were not included in your budget for the wedding. Add that you would appreciate the money as soon as possible. Should this not work, talk to your daughter and her husband to see if they can help straighten out the situation.

If you had spoken to me before the wedding, when they originally suggested the extras, I would have advised that you arrange with the tradespeople to send his parents separate bills for those items for which they agreed to pay. It is more tactful and avoids embarrassment. If you had felt my suggestion crass, then I would have said that you would have a much better relationship with your daughter's in-laws in the future by being direct at the time. Now you are left with feelings of resentment and having been taken advantage of.

CHAMPAGNE PROMISES

A woman I know dealt with in-laws with champagne tastes. She and her husband paid for everything and arranged for an open bar and wine to be served at dinner. When her daughter came home from a visit to her future in-laws, she declared that his parents felt that the wedding reception would not be complete without a champagne toast to the bridal couple. Her mother said that they could not manage champagne for over a hundred guests but a bottle or two for the bridal table would be all right (an acceptable practice, by the way); the rest of the company could toast with wine or whatever they have in their hands from the open bar.

No, no, sang the generous father of the bridegroom, everyone will have champagne and he will pay for it. So to the tune of a few hundred dollars, her mother ordered the extra fine champagne which the bridegroom's father was so fond of.

Now, the bridegroom's family was well able to afford whatever they wished so it was not a matter of grandstanding. However, a few weeks after the bill was sent to the bridegroom's father, it seemed obvious that the money would not be forthcoming. The bride's mother spoke to her daughter; her son-in-law paid the tab. She has never asked her daughter if her husband went to his champagne-loving father for remuneration.

LADIES AND GENTLEMEN, when I was a little girl I overheard a conversation in which a complaining mother-in-law expressed her feeling that her son was much superior to his choice of a wife and, what was more, the girl came from a poor family. The remark that stuck in my mind was the woman's "crowning" comment: "Besides, she waited to marry my son and then had her teeth fixed!" And that reminds me of an ongoing *Amos 'n' Andy* skit from the golden age of radio.

Amos was in love but the lady wouldn't marry him until she had some dental work done. You can imagine what Amos, Andy, and Kingfish did with those episodes. Because Amos's heart's desire simply did not have the money to pay for it, he managed to find the wherewithal. Alas, as soon as she sported a fine mouth of teeth she told him she belonged to somebody else. It might be that young people will not see the humor or the sense of the "teeth" bit, especially if they carry health insurance that includes dental coverage—unheard of in the days of *Amos 'n' Andy*.

Clothing

When the bride's dress has a long train and a headdress holding the bridal veil, the bridegroom wears formal dress and all that goes with it to complement her. The bridal ensemble determines what everyone else wears.

Through the centuries brides have looked distinctive. Some

of the features of the bridal outfit have become symbolic; other aspects are merely custom and no one really knows the background. Rebekah veiled herself out of modesty when she was taken to meet Isaac for the first time. A peasant bride in Poland wore a wreath—a symbol of her maidenhood—and after the wedding night she clipped a lock of her hair and donned the white cap worn by married women. In ancient Rome, layers of artificial hair were wrapped around the bride's head and were held by a short orange veil that covered her eyes. A crown of flowers entwined with herbs secured the veil in place. A thick rope encircled the waist of her bridal tunic, over which was thrown a flowing robe. Ceremonial dress has always eloquently dramatized the significance of marriage rites.

Lucky is the bride for whom the "something old" in the old rhyme is going to be an heirloom wedding dress handed down from one generation to the other. One photo sent to the Bridal Desk was of a bride, a vision, in a most exquisite dress. It had been worn on *her* wedding day by her great-grandmother, who had sewn it by hand.

If "something new" is going to be the dress the bride wears on her wedding day then she should start the search early—six months ahead—because so much depends on delivery and on what the rest of her color scheme will be. She might choose white but there are varying hues of white such as ecru or eggshell. It could be that the first frock in the first store is the one she has been dreaming of, but it is likely to take more of an effort than that.

It is a good idea to attend the bridal shows that are so popular nowadays. January is bridal-show month but, since they are well attended by the public, some firms have them in the summer as well. Magazines are also excellent sources for what is currently shown, as well as giving an idea of costs. Also, keep in mind that the bridal gown is the most expensive part of the regalia but that the total outlay will have to include the veil and accessories.

The bride can be good to her pocketbook by finding out when wedding dresses go on sale—they do, but she should shop only in stores of good reputation. There are two major worries when buying a dress on sale: the material has to be compatible with the time of year the wedding is to take place—no one wants to be in heavy satin in the summertime; and the garment must be in good condition—it may look shopworn if it has been tried on by too many brides. It could be that all the dress needs is a cleaning by professionals specializing in wedding dresses—the salesperson should be able to advise if it can be restored.

Custom-ordering is quite another matter. The bridal shop takes the bride's measurements and orders the gown from the manufacturer. She will be required to go for a fitting at a later date for alterations since the manufacturer will send her dress size but it will not be to the bride's exact measurements; the store does the rest.

Since department stores and bridal shops have varying policies regarding the purchase of wedding gowns, it is important to know the ground rules of the establishment before signing on the dotted line and handing over the deposit, which is legally binding. The store may have a limited cancellation period—which means the bride will be obligated to buy the dress should she change her mind about it after the time limit is up; sometimes she has only five days from the date on the receipt. She should find out whether alterations are included in the cost of the dress. If not, the estimate should be added to the budget.

The delivery date should be noted on the deposit receipt. To avoid a harrowing last-minute experience, some brides request delivery several weeks earlier than the actual date of the wedding.

By the way, if the bride's weight fluctuates, she should not have the first fitting too early.

The length of the train on the dress is measured from the floor out. The sweep length is half a foot (six inches); the chapel length is almost two feet and the elegant cathedral length over two feet.

After six P.M. the ceremony is considered an evening wedding.

A *very formal daytime* or *evening* wedding in a large church, synagogue, or hall can lend itself to the cathedral-length train and a long veil, if the bride can carry it off. When she looks in the mirror she should ask herself whether the dress wears her or she wears it. Don't forget that during trying-on sessions shoes should be the approximate height of those to be worn on the wedding day. An important part of that perfect look is the way the bride's lingerie fits; the store might suggest sewing bra cups to the underbodice if the back of the dress is cut very low. More than one pair of light-colored stockings to go with the bridal gown should be packed along with the makeup and emergency kit of needles, thread, pins, safety pins, hairbrush, hair spray, etc.

Sleeves can be long or short. If the bride wishes to wear short sleeves in a house of worship there may be an objection to bare arms, so the clergyman should be asked whether elbow-length gloves are required; they are worn at evening weddings.

The veil can be sweep, chapel, or cathedral length. A separate face veil may be needed if the ceremony requires it. It is attached to the headpiece and can either be carefully lifted over the cap or removed for the reception. A headpiece should be tried on before a three-way mirror so it can be viewed from all angles. The bride might have thought a Juliet cap would suit her best but the mantilla turned out to be the most flattering.

Formal daytime and *evening* wedding frocks are usually floor length and less elaborate; the train is generally shorter and the veil can be full or a length that suits the gown. A shorter dress with a short veil can be worn for daytime, if preferred, and the bouquet should complement the ensemble.

Semiformal daytime and *evening* dresses can be floor length but should not have a train. For other lengths—ankle, princess (which is a mite above ankle length), ballerina, or cocktail—the veil should suit the outfit. Daytime choice could be a shorter-length dress with a short veil; the bouquet would also be smaller.

As with everything to do with *informal* weddings, clothing is not only a simpler choice but more practical—an afternoon frock or suit with matching shoes and a hat. A small cluster or nosegay of flowers can be held or a corsage may be preferred.

Remember, these are general guidelines. They do not mean that the bride must be locked into a format that cannot be rearranged to suit her needs.

ENTER THE BRIDEGROOM

Now, gentlemen, the lady has chosen her regalia and the bridegroom and male members in the wedding party are required to dress according to the time of day, the time of year, and the formality of the bride's outfit.

When the bridegroom and his bride start looking for his attire they will discover there are other choices, more contemporary styles, beyond the ones suggested below. Also, he and his grooms-men can rent their outfits. If the bridegroom is going to wear a tuxedo—which is suitable formal wear all year round—it might be more practical to buy one for future occasions. Whether rent-ing or buying, the bridegroom should give himself at least two months before the wedding to choose his outfit as well as those worn by the groomsmen and both fathers. Go to a store with a good reputation and knowledgeable salespeople.

Very formal daytime wedding attire requires what is known traditionally as morning dress, which translates to a black or gray cutaway, gray trousers with black stripes, gray waistcoat, winged-collar shirt, ascot or striped tie, and plain black shoes and socks. If the bridal couple will be kneeling during the ceremony the soles of the bridegroom's shoes should be blackened. Gray gloves are optional.

For a *very formal evening* wedding "white tie" is worn: this traditionally consists of a black tailcoat, matching satin-striped trousers, and white waistcoat. Studs will be needed for the stiff front-winged collar shirt and cuff links for the French cuffs; white bow tie, black socks, and black patent-leather or kid shoes—white gloves and top hats are optional.

A *formal evening* "black tie" wedding requires a black tuxedo (black dinner jacket with matching trousers), white dress shirt with a turned-down collar and French cuffs, black vest or cum-merbund, black bow tie, and black shoes. In the summer, the bridegroom might want to wear a white dinner jacket and cum-merbund. Gloves are optional.

Formal daytime wedding wear consists of a black or charcoal-gray sack coat or stroller, which is a long jacket, waistcoat, striped trousers, turned-down-collar dress shirt with French cuffs, black-and-gray-striped tie, and black socks and shoes. Gloves and hom-burg are optional.

For *day* and *evening semiformal* weddings the bridegroom can wear a dark blue suit, white shirt, and tie.

For *informal* or *civil marriages,* a dark blue or dark gray suit, white soft shirt, conservative-stripe or small-pattern tie, black socks and oxfords, white boutonnière; no gloves.

The bridegroom, best man, and ushers can be dressed alike. Or it might be more interesting for the best man to wear a boutonnière or tie different from the bridegroom's and the ushers to have boutonnières or ascots different from both.

HERE COME THE BRIDESMAIDS

Honor attendants and bridesmaids wear long or short dresses with shoes dyed to match and can have short veils or headdresses. Gloves are optional. The elaborateness and length of the frocks depend on the formality of the wedding and the bride's taste. The matron and maid of honor can be gowned in slightly different styles and shades from those of the bridesmaids, who are generally in identical outfits, or all attendants can be dressed the same with different bouquets.

For a *semiformal day* or *evening* wedding, which generally has no more than one attendant, the matron or maid of honor would wear an elaborate afternoon frock with shoes to match, and would carry a small bouquet. But at an *informal* wedding the matron or maid of honor wears a dress and flowers to go with the bride's outfit.

Junior bridesmaids' bouquets, headwear, and dresses conform in style and color to those of the older bridesmaids, though they are less sophisticated. Slippers should be a height suitable to the wearers' ages, and if the bridesmaids have gloves the juniors should wear them also. Junior ushers wear the same formal wear as ushers.

Flower girls are also dressed in a manner suited to their ages. They wear ribbons or flowered wreaths in their hair and carry baskets of flowers. Navy Eton suits with knee-high navy socks and black shoes, or white suits, white knee socks, and white shoes are what ring bearers, pages, or train bearers wear. If very young, they can wear velvet suits.

Mothers of the bridal couple wear harmonizing shades and must be careful that their gowns are the same length. The style should be different from those of the attendants.

For a *very formal evening* wedding mothers can choose elegant full-length gowns or cocktail dresses (according to fashion) with shoes to match, head covering, and gloves. But for *formal evening* weddings their gowns should be less elaborate.

At a *very formal daytime* wedding mothers wear long but

less elaborate gowns. Flowers can be wrist corsages. For *formal* daytime weddings, they can have cocktail or street-length frocks.

Semiformal evening wedding wear should be dressy cocktail or street length but *semiformal daytime* clothing is toned down a bit.

For *informal* weddings mothers should wear suits or frocks, like the bride and maid of honor.

MILITARY DRESS

A woman in the armed forces can be arrayed as a bride or she can be married in uniform. When in uniform she refrains from putting on a corsage and carries a bouquet instead.

SECOND WEDDING

Until recently etiquette dictated that a woman marrying for the second time was simply dressed. Conservative brides still follow those guidelines.

The conservative bride can choose a wedding dress that comes in shades of off-white, ecru, or cream; some have the palest pastel tints and the lengths vary. Silk suits or afternoon frocks are also appropriate. Materials range from the almost bridey-looking to soft sophisticated. Headdresses follow the same mode. She generally wants to achieve the look of a bride but does not want to imitate the first time she was married, when she was in her early twenties. She asks herself the same questions when choosing a bridal outfit as she does when she chooses any article of clothing—is it suitable for the occasion? and does it fit?

Some second-time brides, however, have taken a less conservative position, wanting a traditional formal wedding including the bridal gown, headdress, and orange blossoms (which have been considered a symbol of innocence and fertility since ancient Greece). The affair has all the trimmings of the first time from beginning to end, though the bride and her future husband may foot the bill, realizing that two elaborate functions for one daughter are more than most parents can afford.

This second-time bride reasons that a wedding dress is uniquely a bride's outfit and can be worn by a bride no matter how many times she has been married before. As for white standing for purity (virginity), this is no longer true for first-time brides. White in some countries symbolizes joy; in Asia it is worn as a sign of mourning. The Asian bride wears bright colors—predominantly red.

JUNE IN JANUARY

Q: *We are planning my daughter's wedding. She and I found a beautiful parasol which, when opened, picks up the color scheme of the wedding. Since she is short we've decided that a wreath headdress would suit her better than a veil. Now for my question. When she had on the bridal gown and opened the parasol she looked lovely. But we are not sure it is appropriate. What do you think?*

What time of year is the wedding and is it to be held in a garden?

Q: *December, so it will naturally be indoors.*

My first reaction is that it would not be suitable. I associate a parasol with the outdoors and sunshine. As with an umbrella that shields from the rain, a parasol is used as a portable shade from the sun. Though I think it nonsense, some people are superstitious and would not open an umbrella indoors. It may also be hard to handle. As you explained to me, the parasol would be held so that it frames the bride's back rather than covering her head. That would mean that as she walked with her father she would have to be careful to hold the parasol still so as not to make him uncomfortable. When the walk is completed, the maid of honor would have to carefully take the parasol and furl it without poking anyone's eyes out. Seems a bit awkward to me.

Q: *The bridegroom's father gleefully refuses to wear a formal suit, saying that he is not in the wedding party and doesn't have to stand in the receiving line. Please say he is wrong!*

Um, he's right and yet, er, he's sort of wrong.
Well, what I mean is that in a Christian wedding the bride-

groom's father is not directly involved in the ceremony, unless he serves as the bridegroom's best man or is asked to be in the receiving line. If he has no function other than circulating among the guests then he can wear the same attire as a guest, except that he should have a boutonnière in his buttonhole.

However, the fathers should dress alike if the bride would like to achieve a unified look distinguishing them from the rest of the company. If it is a black-tie affair then he dresses accordingly.

In some Jewish wedding ceremonies, when both sets of parents escort their children to the altar, the fathers dress in the same manner as the bridegroom and best man.

RING BEARER'S TEMPEST

Q: *My husband's twenty-one-year-old sister is being married. She asked my five-year-old to be the ring bearer, but when I heard she wanted him to wear a tuxedo, I said I'd never heard of anything so ridiculous; he would wear an Eton suit or nothing. She said nothing it was. I became angry and told her I would not come to the wedding. My husband is very angry with me and wants me to apologize. Am I so wrong?*

Wait a minute! Are you really not going to the wedding? Picture a teapot and try to create a tempest in it . . . that is what you and the bride are doing. If you can't meet her requirements, then okay, your little one won't be the ring bearer. But saying you aren't going to the wedding is involving not only your husband but his entire family. You are chancing a split of long duration—and over the outfit of a five-year-old!

You may not agree with the bride's taste or decision but she does have a right to state what she wishes those in her bridal party to wear. If you had expressed your opinion to the bride without getting angry, she might have thought it over and not responded in such a defensive manner. Calm down and get a brave soul to play mediator. Remember, the only person allowed to have nervous palpitations is the bride.

LADIES AND GENTLEMEN, I know of a little five-year-old who absolutely refused to wear a short-panted Eton suit.

Though the men wore black tuxedos, the compromise suggested was a cream or beige tuxedo, which the bride said worked out beautifully with his shock of red hair, his happy, smiling face, and her lovely bridal dress.

Q: *At my son's wedding should his brothers, who are not in the wedding party, dress in formal clothes?*

Brothers and sisters not in the wedding party are guests and should dress accordingly.

Q: *My wedding is in two weeks. The maid of honor, who is a large size and hard to fit, had difficulty finding a dress in lavender to go with the maids' outfits. At last we found one in a mail-order catalog but when it arrived it was the color of cream. We called; they do not have lavender in her size. Well, I felt the dress would be fine; it fit and we could add a splash of lavender to tie in with the color scheme. My future in-laws are having a fit. No one but the bride wears white, they insist. My friend cannot afford another dress. I am so upset because I feel that if it's all right with me, it should be all right with them. I don't want to do the wrong thing. Do you think it will look right?*

Since when is cream the same shade as white? The dress sounds fine to me provided the style is suitable. You can tie in the color scheme by choosing a lavender bouquet with cascading lavender ribbons. Placate your future in-laws by saying that both you and your maid are looking for something else but that since it was so hard to find an appropriate shade and style before, there is no reason to suppose you will have better results now.

It is true that wedding-dress white should not be worn by anyone but the bride. By wedding-dress white I mean satin and lace, cathedral train and flowing veil; in other words, the bride has to look different from everyone else—separately, wonder-fully, glowingly special. Okay? Now picture your maid of honor on your wedding day in cream with a touch of lavender; in no way will she be mistaken for you. What is more, to distinguish the maid or matron of honor from the bridesmaids, the bride often gowns her in a different hue that blends with those in the bridal party.

"Snowball" weddings, so called because all the members of the wedding party, including the bridegroom and attendants, are in white, are a splendid sight. So, my friends, the bride is not always the only person wearing white at weddings.

Q: *The bridegroom's mother has bought a dress practically the same color as mine, the bride's mother. I don't mind, neither does the bride. Is it incorrect? We want everything to be just so.*

It is not incorrect, but I am glad you said her dress was *almost* the same shade. Traditionally, the mother of the bride has first choice as to style and shade of outfit. When her selection has been made she notifies the mother of the bridegroom, who then picks a dress of the same length but in a different style. Shades are not necessarily the same but should go nicely with those in the bridal party. Mothers should never wear the same style as the bridal party.

IMPETUOUS MOM-IN-LAW

Q: *My future mother-in-law, when told her son and I were planning to marry, bought her dress for the wedding because she was traveling abroad and found something she liked. There has been no discussion as to the type of wedding we will have. I don't know if the dress will go with the type of wedding or with the color scheme. What shall I do if it clashes?*

Your fiancé's mother has let her enthusiasm overcome her good judgment. But why not wait and see? It might be a color that will go well with any other shade. Of course, the formality of the wedding is another thing, for if she has chosen a plain daytime style and you are having a formal wedding, she has a problem.

DE GUSTIBUS
NON EST DISPUTANDUM

Q: *You will think this is a silly problem but it is just annoying me into a temper.*

As mother of the bridegroom I picked an expensive and perfectly appropriate dress to wear to the wedding. Well, when my future daughter-in-law and her mother saw it they expressed displeasure. Then, when I saw her wedding gown, the maids' dresses, and what her mother was going to wear, I knew why. I've never seen outfits so tacky-looking and never have I had a dress like theirs on my back—styleless, formless, eighty-dollar dresses that hang loosely on the body. They reminded me of a Li'l Abner wedding, the two-dollar kind. I am astounded by my son, who tells me that I'm trying to outshine the bride and I should wear something that goes with their "taste." What should I do? Do I wear what I bought or buy a dress in which I will feel ashamed to be seen? My family will wonder what came over me. What are the ground rules?

As they say in Latin: where taste is concerned there is no arguing. Actually, the ground rules are: after the mother of the bride chooses her dress, the bridegroom's mother buys one that suits her taste but tries to follow the color scheme and length set by the bride. Her family, if the shade blends nicely, has no right to dictate the quality of choice.

To suggest that you look for another dress doesn't seem to be the solution since, obviously, your taste is so different from theirs. I would be hard put to wear something so alien to my taste and I am tempted to say go with what you have chosen. The only hesitation I have is over your son's reaction—'tis a dilemma.

LADIES AND GENTLEMEN, after the wedding, when Mrs. In-Law called to place the wedding announcement, she told me how she solved the dress problem. She *rented* a mother-of-the-bridegroom dress in an appropriate length and shade for forty dollars and change—the bridal rental shop even altered it to fit. But because she didn't want future generations to see her so adorned, she stood sideways during the photo session with the bride and bridegroom, and the table-hopping shots showed her head popped up between two people. She said her son had no reason to complain.

Good show! Mrs. In-Law has won my undying admiration for her sportswomanship. I wished I had thought of the idea, though there are not many of us who would compromise like that.

Privately, I wondered what they would have said if it had been the other way around. What if Mrs. In-Law, as the mother of the bride, and the bride herself had chosen expensive ensembles and objected to the rest of the wedding party's dull, cheap, and tasteless dresses, insisting that they go beyond their means to buy outfits that suited the bride?

Will you wear white, oh, my dear, oh, my dear
Oh, will you wear white, charming guest?
No, I won't wear white, 'cause the bride will have my life,
Oh, I will buy me . . . Ah, you'll have to wait and see

Oh, will you wear black, oh, my dear, oh, my dear
Oh, will you wear black, charming guest?
No, I won't wear black 'cause you'll all be on my back,
Oh, I'll buy me . . . Ah, why don't you wait and see

But, will you wear gray, oh, my future ma-in-law
Oh, will you wear gray, charming lady?
Gray? Gray? In that you have no say.
I've bought me a dress!

Q: *I have attended a few weddings recently, both formal and informal, and there is always a woman or two in white or black. Isn't that a "no-no"?*

Although some women will try to avoid wearing either color to a wedding, the rule about white is that in no way should it resemble the bride's wedding dress. Some brides couldn't care less, but some stand on the theory that they should have no equal in look or shade on their day of days.

It would be most unsuitable for mothers of the bridal couple to wear either black or white (unless white is chosen by the bride for the entire bridal party), and neither should they wear extremely bright hues.

For wedding guests, I see nothing wrong with a white or cream-colored suit and a colorful blouse or scarf or even a white dress with a splash of color.

A severely styled stark black dress is, of course, inappropriate.

But our young people today do not associate black with sadness and wonder why a black suit with a blouse of another color is not proper.

Q: *I have chosen a gray mother-of-bridegroom dress that suits me perfectly and goes with the bride's lavender color scheme. Her mother said gray is only worn by women in mourning (for a moment I thought she said "in the morning," because her statement made no sense to me). I was stunned. Is that true?*

Gray is considered a lovely shade for all occasions and it comes in varying hues from dove to hints of blue, lavender, and mauve. Now to the mystery of why your son's future mother-in-law has a prejudice about gray. Don't tell her I said so, but she's revealing her age. In times past, bereaved women did not go to public functions but were allowed to attend family gatherings such as weddings. Since black was a constant sad reminder to the celebrants, the mourner was allowed to appear in colors ranging from dove gray to mauve and purple.

Wear the dress, if you wish, for her reason is simply passé and I don't think anyone at the wedding would interpret gray, mauve, or purple in such a light.

Q: *My stepdaughter is getting married. I would like to wear a street-length dress but the bride tells me her mother is wearing a full-length dress. When I spoke to the bridegroom's mother, she said she was going to wear full length but would prefer short. Why can't we wear what we want?*

The bride apparently did not disagree with her mother when the decision to wear full length was made so the bridegroom's mother, according to wedding etiquette, wears the same length. You can wear whatever length you wish. If, however, you and the bride's father are host and hostess, it would be nice if you wore full length also. It is not an absolute must, though it might please the bride.

You see, the bridegroom's mother is next to the last to be seated; when the bride's mother walks to her place in the first pew, that signals that the ceremony is about to begin. That is why they wear the same length.

GARB-GUESSING GUESTS

Q: *My sister's daughter is getting married this summer. My sons, of course, are invited. Do you think they can go to church in shirt sleeves? Since they are growing so fast and will get so little wear from them, I am reluctant to buy them jackets.*

I think it is appropriate for them to have jackets on during the ceremony, though little children who are not in the bridal party are not always noticed for their attire. By the way, how old are they?

Q: *Thirteen and fifteen.*

Please! I thought, from the way you were talking about them, that they were little ones. It would be inappropriate for two young men to come to church and to their cousin's wedding in shirt sleeves.

Q: *Oh, I was hoping I could tell my sister that Mrs. Gruen said it would be all right and that would be that.*

Mrs. Gruen says that's not fair!

Q: *(Laughing.) I know.*

LADIES AND GENTLEMEN, one has to know the right questions to ask!

Q: *Why, when one calls the bride's family about appropriate attire for guests, won't they give a straight answer? Surely they are not giving away any state secrets.*

What to wear at a certain type of wedding is such a frequent question. I think the family is reluctant to dictate the dress of their guests but there should be no hesitation in doing so. The rule of thumb is that guests wear attire suited to the time of day and the formality of the occasion.

At a *daytime informal* wedding in a house of worship women guests wear smart street clothes and the men wear dark business suits—even though the bridal party and family might be dressed more formally.

For *very formal daytime* and *semiformal* weddings women guests can wear cocktail length or smart street-length dresses; hats are back in style and gloves are appropriate. Dresses should not be too dramatic nor the material too glittering. The men wear dark business suits.

After six o'clock, at a *formal* wedding, guests can be formally dressed in styles suited to the fashion of the day. If his lady has chosen to wear a long dress then he is expected to wear a tuxedo; if she is attired in a cocktail dress then he can wear a business suit. However, as with our wayward father of the bridegroom, men often do not wish to wear a formal suit even though they are going to attend a *very formal* wedding and so they show up in business suits. If the invitation says "black tie" or "white tie," male guests should dress accordingly.

Sometimes the formality of dress depends on the part of the country where one lives. So if you live in the south, where evening weddings are more formal, and the wedding is up north, telephone the bride's family and ask what attire is generally customary for that area. If you don't fancy being so direct, call that town's department store or hotel for advice.

LADIES AND GENTLEMEN, it is not correct for men to wear tuxedos before six o'clock, though people will tell you it is done all the time. They also tell me that it is hard to remember the "black tie" rule. Maybe this little ditty will help:

A tuxedo during the day—no way.
Cutaway and gray striped trousers—okay.

Attendants

A friend may well be reckoned the masterpiece of nature.
—Emerson

Should the bride and bridegroom have such friends as Emerson described, they will try to find ways of bringing them into the wedding party. But should the couple be unable to give them any special honors, Emersonian friends will understand. If there are many close young relatives and the wedding is small, it may be that only family members can be included. It's the difference between wedding dreams and life's reality. Sensitivity will be the most important asset on which the betrothed, relatives, and friends will have to rely.

Traditionally, the bride and bridegroom choose brothers and sisters as attendants. After all, who but siblings have known the bridal couple all their lives, and aren't most weddings family affairs? Parents tell their children—at least I have mine, many times over—that they can travel the world and make wonderful friends but none can claim the same parents or have similar memories. In most families, when an event such as a wedding or a funeral occurs, the joy and hurt are shared without explanation.

The same tradition is extended by the bridal couple toward each other's brothers and sisters. Including one's future sisters- and brothers-in-law in the proceedings establishes a foundation for good relationships. At the very least it recognizes everyone's special status within the family circle. There is no guarantee that all will go well throughout married life but, in the beginning, every effort should be made to see that it does.

Of course, it all depends on what has happened within the family structure way before a new person is brought into its fold. Not every family can elicit the goodwill and reasonable approach my friend has achieved these past few years.

She and her husband have three sons, A, B, and C. Though they all have good friends of their own, there was no question that one brother would stand up for the other. When the oldest son was married he asked B to be his best man and C to be an usher. A year afterward B and his lovely lady set the date. The problem was that if the older brother was best man, the youngest would not have the chance of being a best man to either brother. So it was arranged among them that C would be B's best man and the youngest would ask his oldest brother to be his best man when he was married—an event that took place the next year. So friends can truly be nature's masterpieces, for they can be brothers.

This does not mean that close friends cannot be selected as attendants. The field is wide open, for if the bride does not have a sister, she can ask someone close to her. The bridegroom can choose in similar fashion and many times a son has asked his father to act as his best man, bringing the father of the bridegroom into the wedding party.

One of the fascinating things about the Washington, D.C., area is that so many people who live there were born elsewhere in the United States, not to mention overseas. I have asked many of them about their methods of choosing wedding-party members. Though the general practice and published advice center on siblings, for some regional areas there is no set pattern and the final decision depends largely on cultural outlook.

It could be that traditionally the bridegroom's side has chosen family before friends but that the bride's custom is to ask friends even though there are brothers and sisters in both families.

When the bride and bridegroom know what type of wedding they will be having they should select the number of attendants they want and whom they will ask to perform those duties. Careful thought should be given the matter before asking someone to be a member of the wedding party. The person should be more than an acquaintance, because there is time and expense involved. As I have explained in the chapter on expenses, attendants are required to pay for their own clothing and transportation, whether that means by plane, train, or car, though their lodgings are the responsibility of the bride and bridegroom. Aside from the affection of the family circle, the practical aspect of asking family members into the bridal party is that they will have expenses and an obligation to the bride and bridegroom anyway.

Maids are responsible for the cost of the dresses the bride chooses for them along with the accessories such as shoes, headpieces, jewelry, and gloves, if worn. The bouquet is the expense of the family. A mother of two with a talent for sewing told me that when she was married she made her bridesmaids' dresses and they bought the accessories. Her family was comfortably off and she wanted to save her friends the expense. She and her husband chose friends to be members of the wedding party and did not feel any obligation to select family members.

Though the bridegroom pays for the ushers' wedding ties and gloves, they must supply their own clothing. Then there are shower and wedding presents, whether given individually or jointly.

The number of attendants waiting on both the bride and bridegroom depends on the size of the wedding. An *ultra-formal* wedding held in a large place of worship can have up to twelve bridesmaids, including flower girl and junior bridesmaids, and twelve groomsmen, including the ring bearer. Less formal affairs generally have from one to six. It is recommended that there should be one usher for every fifty guests. The number of maids depends on the wishes of the bride, and there can be more ushers than maids.

The role of attendant carries a commitment: a promise to the bride and bridegroom. The maid and groomsman should be wholeheartedly part of the prenuptial events, on time for the rehearsal, and at the ceremony site at least half an hour early.

The bride selects her maid of honor from those who are young and have never been married before. The matron of honor can be a married woman, a divorcée, or a widow.

Q: *There are so many unforeseen abstruse questions I have had to face during the planning of my wedding. Who takes precedence, the maid or matron of honor?*

It depends on their relationship to you. If the matron of honor is your sister, she is first attendant. However, if both are equally related to you or are equally close to you as friends, then the maid precedes the matron. Why? I really don't know but I think it is based on the original tradition that virgins attend the bride. Nevertheless, should you be having a hard time choosing, let Lady Luck decide by tossing a coin in front of both.

HIS SISTER, HER BROTHERS

Q: *My daughter has asked two close friends to be matron and maid of honor respectively. Her fiancé invited his closest friend to be best man and his sister's husband, who is also a business associate, to be the usher. She would like to hold firm on the amount of attendants. However, does she have to ask her fiancé's sister to be in the wedding party? Also, her two married brothers have not been asked to serve. If they are asked, what about their wives?*

So many times planning a wedding starts out simply. The bride and bridegroom state the terms of the event, but soon find they do not stand alone. Those shadowy figures in the other's family, and suddenly in their own as well, start a prenuptial dance known as protocol and etiquette.

The couple have two choices: remain with a small wedding party, since its composition is their decision, or offer a trade-off: his sister and her brothers. There can be more ushers than bridesmaids, since bridesmaids are decorative but ushers have specific functions. The bride is under no obligation to invite her brother's wives to be members of the wedding.

HOW YOUNG IS YOUNG?

LADIES AND GENTLEMEN, the two queries below are the same; only the reason for asking is different.

Q: *My only sister is twelve years old. Since our mother died we have been very close and now that I am being married her life is being disrupted again. I would like her to be my maid of honor and only attendant. I've mentioned it confidentially to a few people and they have never heard of someone so young performing those duties. Have you?*

You're the bride and the choice is yours. I bet if you had approached your confidants by saying that you want only one attendant and that you are going to ask your little sister to be your *maiden* of honor they would have received it differently. Your main concerns should be that your sister is mature enough to handle the excitement and that you have more than one rehearsal privately with her.

Q: *I'm having a formal wedding but I don't want a lot of bridesmaids, just my fiancé's adorable five-year-old niece as flower girl. Must I please everyone? I've explained to my future husband that it is hard for me to be constantly surrounded by hosts of people and I abhor the struggling and pulling on both sides. I feel like a politician forming a cabinet in a banana republic.*

Even if you are having a large wedding you can have only one attendant if you wish. Sometimes that decision solves many problems when there are many conflicting expectations. The choice is yours. There is nothing quite so touching as a little one in a bridal party but be sure she is a mature little one. Also, she should not be burdened by too many duties.

You should, however, consider the practical reasons for a maid of honor and you will see that role is not for show only.

At the ceremony itself, she holds your bouquet during the ring ceremony; lifts your veil at the appropriate moment; and holds the bridegroom's ring if it is a double-ring ceremony. Also, throughout the ceremony the maid is supposed to be aware of any unexpected help the bride may need, such as straightening her train. Before the ceremony and during the preceding days she is supposed to be your handmaiden, to help you in any way possible. If you wish, your bridegroom can lift the veil and his ring can be held by the best man. The little one can manage the bouquet.

By the way, in Sweden the bride walks down the aisle by herself and has only two flower girls, no bridesmaids. In England, maids walk behind the bride.

Q: *I was maid of honor for my best friend, who has no sisters. Now that I am being married, she expects me to ask her to be matron of honor, but I have a married sister. I don't want to hurt my friend, but what can I do?*

Your sister should be your first choice. I think your friend will understand when you explain how torn you are about having to choose between her and your sister. Is it possible to invite her to be your bridesmaid? That is your best solution. But, remember, since each wedding and family require different decisions, you are not obliged to return the exact compliment.

Q: *Can a married woman be a bridesmaid?*

Of course.

YES, YES, LADIES AND GENTLEMEN, let me quickly explain that I do know that the origin of maids in the rock-throwing stage of man was to provide a virginal circle around the bride and that they helped her dress and prepare for the loss of maidenhood held so important in our not-too-distant past. But, please, nowadays? Diogenes, whose ancient quest was to find an honest man, had it easy!

Q: *Can a married man be a best man?*

Yes.

GOLD AND THE RULES

Q: *I am so upset. I have one question to ask you. Who chooses the bridal attendants?*

Why, the bride, of course. It is her day and her choice.

Q: *But my grandfather won't come to the wedding because I don't want to ask my cousin, his favorite grandchild, to be maid of honor. I've already asked my best friend.*

LADIES AND GENTLEMEN, what does the bride do when her paternal grandfather will not come to the wedding because his demands are not met? Everyone will agree that Grandfather is interfering in an outrageous manner. The bride should choose her own maids and if Grandfather doesn't like it then he can stay home. Right?

That might be the spontaneous reaction, but not necessarily the best advice, and it did not take me long to realize why Grandfather thought he could act that way and why the bride and her family were so upset.

Wealthy patriarchs and matriarchs get a special kind of respect. It is part of the unique golden rule—which you will not find in the Bible—that says that he who holds the gold makes the rules. Apparently, Grandfather presented no idle threat, as other hapless family members had learned when they didn't meet his standards. The bride even blames her overbearing grandfather for her parents' divorce.

It may sound melodramatic, but it has been my experience that the type of person who holds the gold and has a tendency to make all the rules does not generally back down, so the bride is in a no-win situation. If she gives in, she will feel aggrieved. If she can't give in she must be strong enough to withstand the possibility of Grandfather and entourage boycotting the wedding.

One suggestion is to have two maids of honor. Another is for the bride to explain the predicament to her friend and ask her to be first bridesmaid. Or she could discreetly approach her cousin, who may be feeling embarrassed about being forced into such a position by her grandfather.

I've always wondered what course the bride decided to take. This query was one of the first asked at the Bridal Desk and set me on the road to *Your Wedding*. Now, when the phone rings with a question, I ask the caller to let me know the result of our conversation—some people do and others forget.

TWO MAIDS

Q: *Is it possible to have two maids of honor? My daughter is being married and wants her best friend—they have been together through good times and rough—to be her honor attendant. She also lives nearby. My youngest daughter, who attends college out of town, will be hurt if her sister chooses someone else over her. Though the bride has agreed to both, if it is considered proper, she has stated to me frankly that her friend will be more supportive and more dependable.*

Having two honor attendants, whether two maids or a maid and matron of honor, is not that unusual. It serves no good purpose for the bride to hurt her sister's feelings. Sometimes these situations have a way of compounding themselves, and an action followed by a reaction followed by a counterreaction gets lost in a maze of misunderstanding. Most of the chores beforehand will fall to the bride's friend, who, being the person she is, will understand and be available to the bride.

Duties on the wedding day should be divided between both honor attendants.

Q: *My daughter has asked me to be her matron of honor. It is her way of showing love and saying that I am special to her.*

*However, I feel a little uneasy wondering if it is really the proper
thing to do.*

*Yes, my husband will escort her to the altar and give her in
marriage. Her sister, who is married and will be a bridesmaid,
understands, though she says that if a friend had been picked
over her then she would have been hurt.*

If the family has discussed it and the bride wants you to be
her matron of honor, there is no reason you should not, especially
since the only one who might have felt sensitive about it, her
sister, said that she understands.

It is important, though, to realize that next to the bride and
bridegroom, the bride's mother has the most important job. It is
an extremely taxing one, since the responsibilities of the wedding
arrangements are mainly hers and her role at the wedding includes
being hostess at the reception. Your daughter is placing the part
of matron of honor—a function more suitable to her sister—
over that of mother of the bride. There is no one in this world
who can take mother's place on that special day. But the maid
and matron can be picked from the breadth of the bride's acquaintance. What is more, once the father has escorted their
daughter to the altar, he and his wife will not be sitting together
watching the exchange of vows.

A friend of mine, whose daughter's wedding was a great
success, told me she was left with one lingering regret. She was
so involved with looking after a houseful of guests on the wedding
day that by the time she was able to rush upstairs to help her
daughter dress, the process was over; there stood the bride looking absolutely lovely in her formal wedding dress and headdress.
It did not dawn on her until the wedding was over and her
daughter had left for her honeymoon that she had let that special
time between mother and daughter slip by her.

IS THE MAID OF HONOR THE BEST MAN?

LADIES AND GENTLEMEN, with the permission of my
daughter-in-law, Ruth, below is a repeat of conversations held
before she and my son, who were planning a small wedding, were
married.

But first I will set the scene. Ruth has a small family whom she loves dearly—just her mother, father, and brother. One day she said to me: "Mom, I'm thinking of asking my brother, Steve, to be my only attendant. What do you think?"

"That's a fine idea," I answered.

Ruth on the phone to Steven: "Steve, I have a great idea. I would like you to be my maid of honor."

Steve: "You've got to be kidding!"

A day or two later Ruth is telephoning Steve again.

Ruth: "Steve, I've got a great idea!"

Steve: "I can't possibly be your handmaiden."

Ruth: "Look. Richard's brother, Mark, is going to be his best man. There's no reason you can't be my best man. You could both walk down the aisle together."

Steve: "Now you're talking."

'Twas a lovely wedding.

SANS BEST MAN

Q: *My daughter is marrying a colonel in the United States Army. It is a formal wedding in a military chapel. He tells me he is not having a best man. My daughter will have an honor attendant, but if there is no counterpart won't it look awkward? By the way, his father is deceased; he has no brothers.*

It is unusual not to have a best man since his support to the bridegroom on his wedding day is invaluable. I am terribly curious to know the reason. The tradition, so it is told, stems from the time a caveman needed the strong arm of a friend to help drag the lady of his choice to his abode. Still, it is your future son-in-law's decision.

You can, however, run a smooth wedding ceremony without one. List all the most important duties of a best man on the wedding day. He generally witnesses the signing of the marriage license, hands the ring to the bridegroom during the ceremony, and gives the first toast. A close relative or your husband can offer the toast, anyone attending the wedding can be a witness, and the bridegroom can produce the wedding ring on cue. But you will need ushers to do exactly what the word implies—escort people to the proper seats and be helpful during the whole wedding process. They can perform some of the duties expected of a best man, such as driving the newlyweds to the reception if a limousine has not been hired for the purpose. If the bridegroom does not want to select ushers from his acquaintance, you must do so from yours.

BEST MAN AND USHERS

The bridegroom relies on the best man for support and direction, so the person chosen should know and memorize as much about the plans for the wedding as possible. The bridegroom, for his part, understands that if he has asked someone who lives out of town, the help and support given before the wedding day will of necessity be less. There will be many telephone calls and notes going back and forth.

Since the best man is the one closest to the bridegroom his role is to anticipate the events and take an active part. His responsibilities include overseeing the ushers: he and the bridegroom designate a head usher, preferably a family member who knows many of the guests, to help achieve a smooth and well-organized event. It is a good idea to give each a list of what is expected of them, viz.:

- The type of clothing they should rent if they do not own the proper outfits for the wedding
- That they appear on time for fitting
- Request ushers write down their glove sizes, if a formal wedding.
- Every effort should be made to attend pre-wedding parties.
- Detail their functions during rehearsal and the importance not only of showing up but of being there on time.
- Punctuality is essential on the wedding day; arrive at house of worship an hour early.
- Their duties during the seating of guests before the wedding ceremony
- Invite suggestions for the joint wedding present.

On the wedding day, the best man arrives early at the bride-groom's home with a checklist of reminders to prevent any last-minute delays or panic. He sees to it that the bridegroom is organized and appropriately attired *and appears on time for the ceremony.* One by one, he goes over the checklist:

- Marriage license
- Ring
- Checkbook, money, driver's license, car keys, as well as enough gasoline
- Passport and travel tickets if the couple is going abroad
- Check hotel reservations
- Luggage for the honeymoon trip and the overnight bag
- Envelope with fee for clergyman and house of worship
- Boutonnières for bridegroom, best man, and ushers
- The bride's bouquet (if it has been arranged that way)
- Transporting arrangements for the bride and bridegroom after the ceremony to the reception
- A few taxicab telephone numbers for emergency purposes
- The return of the bridegroom's rented suit to the shop, especially if his parents live out of town and are leaving the next day

The best man and the bridegroom arrive at the house of worship at least fifteen to thirty minutes before the time set for the ceremony, and both wait in the vestry until it is time to walk together to the chancel. The best man holds the ring in his vest pocket or on his own finger until it is time to hand it to the bridegroom or clergyman, and he can act as witness to the signing of the marriage certificate after the ceremony is over. In a Jewish wedding a relative by blood or marriage cannot act as a witness even if he performs the duties of best man.

Traditionally, the best man will propose the first toast to the newly married couple at the reception and, if the family wishes, read the telegrams and mailgrams that have been received. When the family stands in the receiving line, he is expected to mix with the company.

The best man needs to know, among other things, if there will be a photo session directly after the ceremony and how the bride and bridegroom are to be transported after the ceremony and for the wedding party in general. He might be needed to drive the couple to the reception and later to the airport or train station. No one should know where the bridal couple's car is parked so that it will not be decorated by those fond of mischievous pranks.

When the bridal couple are ready to leave, the best man should ask the bridegroom's parents to the dressing room so they can wish him and his bride a safe trip.

USHERS

Since it is estimated that at a large wedding one usher is needed for every fifty people, the main duty of an usher is to lead guests to the correct pews.

It is customary for him to be attired—at his own expense—in the same manner as other male members of the wedding party. Wearing his boutonnière, and possibly gloves, he stands to the left of the portal of the house of worship and greets guests as they arrive. He asks which side of the family they know, extends his right arm to the lady, and, with her husband walking behind, guides them to the correct pew. Some couples prefer to walk together rather than be conducted by this formal method, but the usher still leads the way.

In England, the ushers place themselves along the aisle and direct guests to their seats, but only unaccompanied ladies are escorted. If there is more than one unaccompanied lady, the usher escorts the oldest and asks the others to follow. Men are guided, not escorted.

When the wedding is extremely large there may be more reserved pews than the first two that seat close family. The head usher should have a list of names of those who will sit in the reserved rows, which are designated with white ribbons.

It is an obligation to arrive on time for the rehearsal and for the ceremony. The rehearsal is extremely important, for everyone should know just what to do during the processional and recessional. Two ushers are assigned to lay the canvas runner if there will be one.

Ushers should participate in the prewedding festivities. They are participants in the processional and recessional. Ushers do not stand in the receiving line, but make themselves as pleasant as possible by dancing and being amiable to guests and bridesmaids.

It is customary for the ushers and best man to join in giving a gift to the bridegroom.

MAID/MATRON OF HONOR

Though the bride and her family, along with the bridegroom, make most of the arrangements, the honor attendant should make herself available to the bride as much as she can. There are so many ways before the actual wedding day to be of help, perhaps by addressing wedding invitations or organizing the bride's list and index cards.

As with the best man, the honor attendant should know what the procedures will be so that, on her part, the wedding ceremony will go well.

The honor attendant organizes the bridesmaids and together they discuss entertaining for the bride.

She assists the bride by seeing that bridesmaids go for their dress fittings and that their outfits are coordinated to suit the bride.

She and the bridesmaids must attend the rehearsal and the function that takes place before or after it.

On the wedding day, she calmly assists the bride.

It is a good idea for the honor attendant to dress before the bride so that she can be helpful to her and her mother as they get ready.

She prepares a list of what is to be done and checks items off as they are accomplished.

The honor attendant must know time and transportation schedules.

She arrives at the house of worship at least fifteen to thirty minutes before the ceremony is to start.

If it is to be a double-ring ceremony, the maid or matron of honor carries the bridegroom's ring (unless there is a ring bearer), and wears it on her finger until it is time to hand it to the bride or the clergyman.

During the processional, she is the last to walk down the aisle before the bride.

Her main duties to the bride during the ceremony are to hold the bride's flowers, see to her veil, and produce the bridegroom's ring at the appropriate time. She must be sure to adjust the bride's train for the recessional, return her bouquet to the bride, and, most of all, be alert to the bride's needs during the proceedings.

At the rehearsal she will know on which side of the bride she is to stand during the ceremony, whether she will be the one to keep an eye on the flower girl, and whether to walk with the best man during the recessional.

She stands in the receiving line and sits at the bride's table, as well as joining in the festivities, and also signs the marriage certificate.

When it is time for the bride and bridegroom to leave, she assists the bride into her going-away costume, takes care of the bridal gown and veil, if necessary, and notifies the bride's parents that their daughter is ready to leave.

BRIDESMAIDS

The bride, when she invites her relatives or friends to attend her, is saying that they are special to her. They, in turn, form a warm circle of friendship around the bride by cooperating as much as they can. Their responsibilities to her are not as demanding as those of the maid of honor but they should try to offer help.

Their outfits are chosen by the bride, and if she asks maids to wear silver chains around their necks and shoes that match their dresses, all the maids do so. If one bridesmaid does not own a silver chain she should tell the bride so that one can be borrowed.

Bridesmaids should be on time for fittings and participate in as many of the prewedding functions as possible. One of the most important is the rehearsal—an event that helps make a large formal wedding a smooth operation. Tardiness can put everyone on edge and spoil what should be a lovely time.

Among the various prewedding parties is a shower. If maids are in town they should make every effort to attend and give a present. However, if there is more than one shower to which maids are invited there is no obligation to produce unending gifts, but, nevertheless, their attendance is appreciated. If possible, maids give a party for the bride and take that opportunity to give a joint wedding present. The bride in turn honors them with some sort of function and at that time gives them presents of appreciation for their support of her.

Looking as lovely as they can, bridesmaids walk gracefully down the aisle, completing the circle of friendship for the bride.

Prewedding Parties

Whatever one's age, being a prospective bride or bridegroom is an exciting and unique experience whether for the first or for the second time.

There is the delight in telling family and friends of the betrothal, along with sharing the news in the paper. There is the excitement of the round of parties that serve to introduce one to the other's world. All this can be very tiring. The ring-around-the-eyes look, so deftly touched up by clever photographers in pictures for the newspapers, can be avoided if some of the parties can be combined.

REHEARSAL DINNER

Of all the questions that have to do with entertaining during the prenuptial events, one is perennial: who hosts the rehearsal dinner?

The voice on the phone can be from the bride's side or the bridegroom's. To say that the offer generally comes from the bridgroom's family is not enough. Just give me the facts, ma'am, is implied in the urgent tones of the person on the other end of Bell's invention.

Most books on the etiquette of weddings are in agreement. Anyone can offer to entertain at the rehearsal dinner: the bride's parents, the bridegroom's parents, a member of the clan on either side, or a good, good friend who wants to help the family at this busy time.

The reasons for the queries are varied. Having waited for their daughter's future in-laws to do their "duty," the bride's parents are now wondering if the offer will be made at all.

The futures have a problem also. Only a handful of people from their side will be attending the wedding. They might have a limited acquaintance, a small family, and have to travel almost three thousand miles to the event. Her side has a large guest list with many people coming from faraway places. The rehearsal dinner would almost be the size of the wedding reception.

It might be that in the bridegroom's area the rehearsal dinner is not customarily an expense of his family. Or, let's face it, some people reason that the wedding is the bride's parents' responsibility. Who asked for a big shindig, anyway?

To be sporting about it, if all things are equal—an almost balanced guest list—and if the bride's parents are footing the cost of the entire wedding, it is a gracious way for the bridegroom's family to assume a small part of the expense. However, if the wedding is a joint venture, then the rehearsal dinner, as with the rest of the arrangements, should be discussed by all and included within the total expenses.

WHEN IS A BRIDAL DINNER A REHEARSAL DINNER?

Q: *I am told the bridal dinner is really the rehearsal dinner. When is it held and what sort of function is it? Who gives it, and is it obligatory?*

When the bride's family hosts the rehearsal dinner, or a dinner, whether or not there is a rehearsal, a day or two before the wedding, some people use the term "bridal dinner." When the bridegroom's family act as hosts at that time then it is called a "rehearsal dinner."

I think the rehearsal dinner is one of the nicest of all prenuptial gatherings because it brings together the bridal party, guests from out of town, and close family members. It is an intimate time, when toasts are proposed by anyone who wishes and all are at ease. It can occur a day or two ahead of the wedding day and be held before rehearsal or afterward.

Q: *My son is being married in our town. Most of our family and the bride's family live at least 250 miles away, which means a great proportion of the guest list will be out-of-towners. Due to circumstances beyond our control, the rehearsal has to take place two days before the wedding, which means out-of-towners will not be able to attend the rehearsal dinner. Besides, if they do arrive earlier than expected, the guest list will be almost the equivalent of the wedding reception itself. Still, I am in a dilemma and feel obligated to do some entertaining.*

Why not have an "infare" the morning after the wedding, an American custom going back to the 1800s? In those days, when the bride's parents hosted the wedding-day feast, the bridegroom's parents gave an infare the following day that was essentially another feast.

Have a breakfast—not a wedding breakfast, which is really a luncheon served after the wedding ceremony. Serve eggs, fresh fruits, rolls and butter, coffee, tea, orange juice, and little pastries. The bridal couple can attend if they have not yet left for their honeymoon. It is a relaxed time when the company exchanges memories of the previous day, conversations you would not be privy to when guests are going straight home after the wedding. You will be sending your company on the road with the warmth of your hospitality.

If your home is not large enough to accommodate so many people, arrange for the breakfast to be held at the hotel where most of your guests will be staying. There will be the same wonderful conversations and you will have time to enjoy the congeniality of your guests before they go their separate ways.

Q: *As parents of the groom, we are hosting the rehearsal dinner for the bridal party and including those guests coming from out of town. The bride's mother insists that the invitations to this dinner go out at the same time as the wedding invitations. I want to wait until responses start coming in. It seems pointless to send an invitation to a rehearsal dinner if the recipient is declining the wedding invitation. My question is, when are these mailed?*

Rehearsal-dinner invitations are mailed about two weeks before the wedding and after acceptances have been received. They are not included with the wedding invitations, since those who sponsor the wedding might not necessarily be the same people hosting the rehearsal dinner.

Q: *I am to be married in a few weeks' time. My parents are hosting the rehearsal dinner, intending to invite only those in the bridal party and immediate family members. My bride's parents want us to invite those coming to the wedding from out of town, but my parents are reluctant and say they do not have to do so. Are they right?*

It is true that the host and hostess decide what type of function they wish to give and where it will take place, which may be at home, a restaurant, or a country club. They decide what to serve—hot or cold food, a sit-down or buffet dinner, a light or a heavy meal, as they would when hosting any affair—except they must invite all members of the wedding party with their spouses, both sets of parents, and, if they are family friends, the officiant and spouse.

However, it is becoming customary though, again, not obligatory, to invite people coming from long distances and it is a most gracious thing to do. These guests have the added expenses of motels, traveling, and some may have to take time off from work.

On the other hand, I hear complaints from the bridegroom's family that they are a small group and the wedding is a large affair that comprises the bride's family and friends. If this is the case it might be unrealistic to expect a minor wedding reception.

The bride's parents are being put in an awkward situation at having to leave their guests to fend for themselves. I suggest that the dinner not be elaborate—a buffet table with cold cuts and condiments would be fine—and that the bride's parents offer to contribute to the expense of their overflow.

LADIES AND GENTLEMEN, the young man has been put in a very uncomfortable position and I wonder how he solved it. However, it was a brief phone call and I did not ask what type of entertaining his parents planned for the rehearsal dinner or where it would be. One's decision in these matters depends on the number of out-of-town guests and the size of the bridal party.

If a home party is planned, there simply might not be enough space to accommodate the crowd. In that case, perhaps someone with a large home might lend it for the occasion, although the entertainment costs would still be assumed by the bridegroom's parents. If the dinner is to be held in a restaurant or the like, his parents might not be able to afford a larger guest list. Then, as I mentioned to the young man, her parents could offer to contribute to the expense of the overflow. However, that must be handled with delicacy.

Q: *Do we have to invite both clergymen to the rehearsal dinner? We are having two officiants, one of whom we do not know.*

Does the clergyman know the people who invited him to officiate?

Q: *Yes.*

Then both should be invited.

Q: *What type of invitation is appropriate for a rehearsal dinner? Also, since the wedding is taking place out of town (we are the groom's parents), all arrangements for the function have to be made by phone. Do we request R.S.V.P.s, and should the invitations be engraved?*

The rehearsal-dinner invitation should request a response, especially if it is held in a restaurant or a rented place, since the hostess must notify the caterer how many guests are expected. It cannot be taken for granted that all the attendants and out-of-town guests will arrive early enough to attend; depending on the time of the wedding, they may even arrive the day of the wedding.

If it is a small gathering it might be more convenient to telephone; however, think of the expense that long-distance calls entail today. Engraved invitations would be appropriate for a formal dinner and dance. Handwritten invitations are charming for less formal events but if the guest list is large it might be a time-saver to have them printed. You could use at-home cards. Above your name, write:

Rehearsal dinner for Jill and Frederick
YOUR NAMES
Thursday, May 28th at 6 P.M.
The Montpelier
Concord, Mass.
Please reply   [Telephone number]

If you wish you can add your address along with your telephone number.

Handwritten notes on blank informals are also fine:

Dear Mrs. Herman [or use her given name],

 Harold and I do hope you and John can attend the dinner we are planning for Jill and Frederick after the wedding rehearsal. Our house on Thursday, May 28th, at 6 P.M. Please phone or write whether you can come.

        Sincerely [or affectionately],
        Sonia Hampenstance

LADIES AND GENTLEMEN, after accepting an invitation to a formal wedding from a family living out of town, we received another invitation listing the various functions being planned. The festivities included parties given by the bride's parents and the bridegroom's mother. There was also a hospitality room at the hotel where guests gathered, where the hosts were to be the bride's aunts and uncles. Our response was that we would be in town on Friday and would be leaving Sunday afternoon and would be pleased to attend the functions during that period.

Q: *I am hosting the rehearsal dinner as mother of the groom. My husband is deceased and I am not sure if I should give the toast that the father of the groom generally offers. Do I, or should I ask a male relative? And when is it appropriate?*

There is no rule that says only men can give a toast, or a speech for that matter. As hostess you should be the first to offer a toast to the young couple, with possibly a special word to her parents and a welcome to the rest of the company.

If the rehearsal takes place before the dinner, the bridal party might be hungry, so you could eat first. Toasts could be offered just before dessert. Once you have spoken, the bride's father will probably follow, then the best man, and anyone else who feels so inclined, including the bride and bridegroom. This is a fun, relaxed, informal time, and most offerings can be amusing.

- The rehearsal dinner can be hosted by anyone who feels like doing it, but it is sometimes given by the bridegroom's parents.
- The hosts decide what type of event they will give—from a buffet in a private home to a seated dinner at a club. It is not necessarily considered a formal occasion.
- Rehearsal-dinner invitations are issued after acceptances have been received. Wedding-invitation responses go to the bride's home but prompt replies go to the hostess of the dinner.
- Invitations can be phoned, handwritten, or engraved, depending on the formality of the party planned.
- The entire wedding party is invited including the clergyman, if a friend, and spouses and fiancé(e)s but not casual dates. Also included are the younger attendants, if they can take the excitement, along with their parents.
- Seating is informal, though the bride and bridegroom sit next to each other. At a more formal occasion the best man sits on the bride's right and the maid or matron of honor on the bridegroom's left. The host is at one end, with the bride's mother on his right, and the hostess at the other end with the bride's father to her right.
- The first toast is offered by the host. Others, including the ladies, follow if they wish.
- The wedding party can present their gifts to the bridal couple and they, in turn, can give the maids and men their tokens of appreciation if there has not been another appropriate time to do so.

BRIDAL SHOWERS

A book written in the 1920s waxed condescending about showers but admitted that they were "kindly meant." So many etiquette books were written for city or town people, but country people, various ethnic groups, and a strong middle class in this country have held to the practice and now showers are accepted.

The purpose of a shower is to have a group of intimates bring gifts to help the young bride gather "little" items for her household and her trousseau. The tone of some showers and the number of them sometimes overwhelm the original idea.

First, if the bride requests no showers and you are sure she meant it, that wish should be honored. If the signal is not clear, telephone her mother for advice. (Mother, please be direct in your answer.) Or discuss it again with the bride. If she is firm and you still want to entertain for her, have a tea or a luncheon that does not require presents from those attending.

It is recorded that in rural areas of England impoverished newlyweds went from household to household receiving whatever could be spared. Though British rules and customs have been a great influence on American culture and law, the original custom of the bridal shower came from continental Europe. The bride visited each household with her honor attendant to personally invite dwellers to the wedding. Bowing low, and starting with the head of the house, she went to every person in turn saying, "Please attend my wedding." The recipients of the invitation gave her small gifts for the home she and her betrothed were establishing.

BRIDAL SHOWER

Q: *For the bridal shower, is it true that one only invites those on the wedding list?*

Well, yes. Since bridal showers and presents are almost synonymous, it is usual to ask only the people you expect to invite to the wedding. I have heard that some people give the wedding present at the time of the shower, but this defeats the idea. Showers are mainly for "fill-in" items.

Q: *As mother of the future groom, I was asked for a list of those to be invited to the bridal shower. Well, now I discover that the guest list for the wedding has been drastically cut. What shall I do now? It is so embarrassing.*

You have a tough decision to make and three alternatives. The first is not to do anything immediately and later, if necessary, say the guest list had to be cut, much to your disappointment.

The second is to obtain permission from the bride to add the shower guests to the wedding list at your expense, provided those people would have been on the second guest list and closer people have not been omitted.

If you decide that the second suggestion is not possible because a small wedding is being planned and her family are holding close to the guest estimate, then you have to find a way of telling those people that they are invited to the shower but not the wedding. Explain the embarrassing situation in which you find yourself.

If it is feasible, you could add that you are having a reception in honor of your son and his wife after the wedding for those you were, sadly, unable to ask.

LADIES AND GENTLEMEN, it has occurred to me that Mrs. Faux Pas might have caused her own embarrassment without the help of a restricted guest list.

Showers take place after wedding invitations are received and within a month to two weeks before the wedding. Surely she knew who and how many guests were invited on her side of the family, unless the blunder was caused by a bridal shower taking place earlier than it should—before wedding plans were completed. In that case, his mother is the victim of her own and someone else's lack of knowledge on wedding etiquette.

Did I hear someone say, "What's the big deal? Recipients of the invitation have a free choice to decline or accept. The present won't send them to the poorhouse."

But that is not the point. Inviting people to a shower without their being invited to the wedding is confusing; they are being sent a wrong signal. The recipients might think that an invitation to the wedding is forthcoming. It is also unflattering, to say the least, to those people who think that the only thing wanted from them is a present.

Q: *Last week I sent out invitations to a "recipe" bridal shower I am giving for my friend. Someone else has decided to give one on the exact same date and time for the same person, inviting the same people, even though I had sent her an invitation that she had to have received before she mailed hers. That twit will not change the date. Shall I give my party anyway? I'm afraid people won't come. What are the ground rules?*

LADIES AND GENTLEMEN, I offered a few suggestions.

Since neither the bride nor the guests can be in two placcs at the same time, the most sensible thing to do is for the hostesses to combine their efforts, which might be difficult since they are obviously not on good terms.

Another proposal is for the more gracious one to back down, saying she wants to relieve the bride and company from an awkward situation. Ms. Gracious can then give a tea on another day and, since no presents are required, she will have spared guests the expense of buying gifts for both occasions. If time does not permit, she could give a "welcome home" tea or luncheon after the bride comes back from her honeymoon.

What can be gained by involving everyone in spite work? All it does is inflict bad feeling on everyone, especially the bride, whose prewedding time is supposed to be full of lovely memories. I could not have a good time at a party knowing I was being used as a weapon in someone else's vendetta. All that can be hoped is that most guests do not know that the conflicting dates were a deliberate act intending to embarrass.

Revealing the above allows me to say that when people behave themselves showers are lots of fun. Good friends should combine their efforts so showers do not become a burden on both finances and time.

Only those who host the shower are asked to contribute to the cost of the refreshments. Guests are not expected to foot the bill: they bring presents.

YES, LADIES AND GENTLEMEN, that is another sticky situation in which people find themselves. I have had calls, not only from those planning or attending showers, but from adult children giving an anniversary dinner for their parents asking where on the invitation do they list the cost to each guest. You simply do not, unless everyone got together and decided to have a joint party for the celebrants.

- Immediate family members on either side do not host bridal showers. It gives the appearance of asking for presents. By immediate family members I mean parents, sisters, brothers, and grandmothers.
- Aunts, cousins, neighbors, and friends in general can host showers.
- It is customary for the maid or matron of honor and the bridesmaids, if they are not immediate family, to give a joint shower the week of the wedding.
- When the bride does not know many people, an immediate family member might enlist a trusted outsider to host the event, with the family contributing to the refreshments. Discretion is imperative.
- Only family and close friends are invited. Both mothers are invited to those showers that are concerned with family and should try to attend; they take gifts.
- However, fellow workers sometime surprise the bride with a shower. Invitations are limited to those at work, unless the bride's co-workers are also social friends.
- It is not a good idea to invite those who live a distance away. They cannot possibly accept and would feel obligated to send a gift. The only exceptions would be the bridegroom's mother, grandmothers, or godmothers who might want to send presents in lieu of being there in person.
- Combined gifts can be given, but not too many, since the idea of a shower is to unwrap lovely packages and to comment on the originality of the purchases, adding a few oohs and aahs on the way.
- There is no obligation to send a present if you cannot attend the shower, though close family and friends might want to.
- Showers can take place any time after the wedding invitations have been sent, and only those invited to the entire event should be asked. Some people say those invited only to the ceremony can also be included, but that negates the idea that only intimates are asked.
- Showers are generally held during the evening or on weekends, day or evening.
- Guests should arrive at the scheduled time, since most showers are supposed to be a surprise to the bride. Often, the sur-

prise part of the party is not practical because of the busy schedule of today's bride and of the host or hostess.

- Both men and women can participate.
- Some showers have a theme, or the party can be a "bring-whatever-you-wish shower."
- Theme ideas:

> Bring your favorite recipe and a kitchen gadget.
> Liquor-bar utensils
> Bottles of wine and liquor
> Gourmet delicacies—packaged
> Garden tools for new homeowners
> Lingerie—the bride's size must be indicated
> Sports items
> Linens—tablecloths, table or cocktail napkins, towels, and bed linen

Do some detective work at the bridal registry, maybe, to gather ideas and to determine color schemes for bathroom items, bed linen, blankets (check sizes), and kitchen towels. Great fill-ins are sewing baskets and "how-to" books on gardening, cooking, and etiquette.

- Remember, shower gifts need not be expensive.
- Phone or write invitations, or buy printed shower cards that indicate the time, date, location, and whether it is to be a tea, luncheon, or cocktail party. Don't forget to ask for a response by telephone or note.
- Presents, along with a note from the giver, are brought to the party and placed together out of sight until the bride's arrival, especially if it is a surprise shower.
- The hostess decides when the presents should be opened, though generally this is done before the refreshments are served.
- Seated on a chair which is sometimes decorated with white ribbon, the bride opens each present. The cards accompanying the presents can be read out loud. Someone is assigned to keep cards and gifts together and also to make a written list of the item and giver so the bride has a record.
- As presents are opened, have someone make a bouquet from ribbons and bows. Use a strong paper plate in which slits

are made and insert the bows one by one, allowing the ribbons to fall loosely. This makes a charming centerpiece on the buffet table afterward and is also used at the rehearsal dinner.

- At some showers games are played and small prizes offered to the winners. One popular game is the word-scramble game using wedding-related clues.
- The bride's thank-you note(s) to her hostess(es) are a must.

MISSING GUEST OF HONOR

Make sure the bride is somewhere in the area. Years ago a surprise party for a star celebrating her ninety-fifth spring as an ingenue of screen, stage, radio, and television was being held at the Waldorf Astoria in New York City. But the real surprise was for the guests, who were informed by the master of ceremonies that the actress had just left for Hollywood, not knowing, of course, that she was being honored.

THANK-YOUS

LADIES AND GENTLEMEN, now a ticklish question about thank-you notes to shower gift givers.

There are two schools of thought. One says that if each person was thanked individually at the shower, there is no need to send notes of thanks, since the bride has so many other chores before the wedding. Thank-you notes would be sent only to those who sent gifts but did not attend. (Wedding-present thank-you notes are a must, of course.)

Some feel that no matter whether thanks were offered in person, a note of thanks is due. But often a shower is given a day or two before the wedding and there is no time to write notes. The only writing the bride has time for is for checks for services.

A friend of mine lives away from her large family and is often invited to her nieces' bridal showers, though she is not always able to attend. She sends a shower gift and later a wedding present. Since the shower comes so close to the wedding, she often receives a combination wedding and shower present thank-you letter on the bride's stationery.

No matter what the question, local custom is important and so it must be with thank-you notes.

Q: *My husband is going to be an usher and we are invited to a party in honor of the future bride and bridegroom given by a friend of the bride's mother. Do we have to take a present?*

No, I do not think it an occasion to take a present. If the party was going to be a shower, then it would say so on the invitation.

BRIDE, BRIDESMAID, AND BACHELOR PARTIES

Entertaining for the bridal couple, or the bride alone, can be done in many different ways and does not require presents. Today's life style makes it difficult to have the type of gala balls of yesteryear. But reaching into the past for ways of entertaining that will not burden everyone's time is a good idea. Keep in mind that any function will be as stiff and formal as you allow it to be.

Don't let prejudice stand in the way of a Saturday- or Sunday-afternoon tea. It is a simple and elegant way of bringing people together. Coffee and tea are served, with quartered, triangular-shaped sandwiches and finger pastries. Mimosas (a combination of champagne and orange juice) or cocktails are perfect optional accompaniments.

You could ask people in for evening cocktails at eight any evening of the week. Drinks and nibbles go well with fruit and ice-cream cake.

Another option is a buffet lunch at twelve noon, or, if the group is small, you can have a sit-down affair with wine to toast the bridal couple.

In Sweden, a day or two before the wedding, the bride's girl-friends bedeck her in a pseudo-wedding dress and a veil topped with a funny wreath of fruit. Around her neck they place a lei of vegetables. Thus attired, they take her to a restaurant where they blithely have dinner.

A SPINSTER'S FAREWELL LUNCHEON!

Did you know that the bride's party was once known as the spinster's farewell dinner? Apparently it was given not to say good-bye forever to one's friends but to one's spinsterhood.

It is not always feasible to follow the forms laid out for who hosts what for whom. The bride may be marrying from her parents' home but she and her attendants are scattered from one end of the country to the other and everyone will arrive within a day or two of the wedding. That is why the bridal or rehearsal dinner has taken on so much importance.

Remember, the larger the wedding, the more complicated things get. The approach to these functions should be sensible and should not tax everyone's time and finances.

Having said that, I will go on to say that it is customary for the bride to entertain her bridesmaids or for them to entertain her or both.

If out-of-town guests are expected, the maid or matron of honor and bridesmaids sometimes decide to have a shower for the bride within the week of the wedding. It is more than likely that the bride will hold some sort of party to thank her attendants.

BRIDE AND BRIDESMAID PARTY

Should the bride decide to entertain, about two weeks before the wedding she might choose to have a morning coffee, a luncheon, a tea, or a dinner for her maids. It is an ideal time to present them with gifts of appreciation. If the party is held at home, then maids have a chance to see some of the wedding presents, unless the bride doesn't wish to show them.

BACHELOR DINNER

Well, ladies, if you can have a spinster's farewell party, surely the gentlemen can have a party—now what is the term for an unmarried man? Ah, a bachelor party. Why does the spinster's farewell have such a tragic ring to it, whereas a bachelor party is just that—a party? I'll tell you why. Picture the young maidens weeping for their maidenhood while bachelors go out on the town living it up, trying to do everything in that one evening so they can behave themselves the rest of their lives. Gracious, could they too be weeping for their bachelorhood? Ah, the nonsense of it all.

The same problems of distance go into the holding of a bachelor party, which is given either by the bridegroom, a male member of his family, or by his friends. The list comprises the best man, ushers, and close male family members and friends.

Arrangements vary, but the party should be timed so that it takes place a few days before the wedding, sometimes on the same evening as the bride's party.

The celebration can take the form of a dinner in a restaurant that has some entertainment. When the bridegroom is the guest of honor, everyone orders for himself, but the check is divided among the company except the bridegroom. When the festivities are at someone's home or apartment the fare can be as simple as sandwiches and pizza along with liquor, wine, and beer, or a catered meal can be served. Or a dinner party can be held at a club. It is traditional for the bridegroom to propose a toast to his bride. That might be the only serious toast of the evening: the others offer witticisms.

Sometimes bachelor's and spinster's farewell parties are not planned at all. The bride and bridegroom might decide to have a joint "maids and men" party. At that time they can distribute the gifts, and other guests might be invited as well. It can be an informal get-together or a splendid cocktail party. At these functions, attendants can take the opportunity to give the bridal couple their joint wedding present.

Often, when there are out-of-town guests, relatives and friends in the area help with the entertaining by inviting the visitors to lunch, afternoon tea, or dinner. It is a most gracious way of relieving the host family of some of the responsibility, especially for elderly visitors.

Not every family can elicit that kind of aid, so visitors must understand the family's involvement with last-minute details—

the wedding is the reason guests are in town in the first place.

It helps a great deal when the area in which the wedding celebrants live has enticing spots for sightseers and theatergoers, but it may not be possible for the family to provide escorts. Apart from attending functions specifically organized as prewedding entertainment, guests find their own ways of amusing themselves during their free time and make their own reservations, possibly through their hotel.

Florist

Composition is what makes a successful flower arrangement, whether one is forming a bouquet or a table display. Knowing what elements go into a composition for a painting, a photograph, or a floral arrangement is what makes an artist.

Flowers create warmth and beauty. Harmonizing a floral arrangement with a setting or the bouquet with its bride is as important as achieving the proper composition in a photograph—both need an artistic eye.

There is a difference between a designer and a florist. Florists generally have a shop full of plants and flowers, along with sundry items such as planters and plant foods. Naturally, they also do different social occasions. Some shops have designers on staff.

Flower designers do not necessarily have retail shops but go directly to markets and wholesalers for supplies. Their time goes into making arrangements for various functions, and, like clothes designers, they are expensive.

If you want to go it alone, work with a local florist or a designer, but first familiarize yourself with the subject. There are excellent books and magazines at the library on both flowers and brides. A horticulturist with care of a public area in your town or city is also a good source of advice. Discuss with a local florist what blossoms and leaves show to best advantage and what flowers will be in season at the time of your wedding. Such a discussion can result in a lifetime of appreciation that will enable you to arrange centerpieces on your dinner table for entertaining and vases full of flowers for everyday enjoyment.

Finding a talented florist is like finding a good caterer or photographer. Get to know the person's work, either by attending a function he has provided the flowers for or through personal recommendations.

When hired a year ahead, the florist can only estimate charges based on today's prices because, as with the caterer, prices fluctuate depending on inflation. If your taste leans to unusual, imported, or out-of-season flowers you must expect prices to be higher. Shop for price, try both designers and store florists, and make your decision accordingly.

Whether on the telephone or in person, your first talk with the florist will indicate what type of interest and imagination will go into the floral designs for your wedding.

A floral designer can weave seasonal flowers into lovely displays, whether decorating a house of worship or forming blossoms carried by the bride and her attendants. Bud roses with sprays of baby's breath or lilies of the valley in tiny vases on cocktail tables can be just the right touch to achieve an inviting setting at an informal reception. Stately flowers at a lavish reception give the room elegance. Greenery and flowers in a house of worship bring warmth to a large area. Though large formal weddings require an abundance of flowers, like everything else they should not be overwhelming.

Flowers decorating the wedding and reception places and those carried or worn by the bride and bridal party should follow the general color scheme. That does not mean you must have the exact hues, but blends that go with the colors in the wedding and in the bride's wedding gown.

Size and style are also important. For instance, a full, dramatic bouquet cascading down the front of a dress may hide the splendor of the wedding gown. Yet that very bouquet might set off a simple but elegant line to perfection. Tall centerpieces in the dining room might be impressive but only if they are designed so that guests can see one another across the table.

When you look at a successful arrangement, whether it is a bridal bouquet, a centerpiece for the table, or a chapel banked with plants and decorated with flowers, note that the contrast of even a small sprig of greenery breaks up the excessive beauty of the principal flowers and allows the secondary group to offset the entire presentation.

Suppose the bride has sentimental reasons for wanting to

carry three long-stemmed roses. The florist's function is to understand the client's wishes and work the rest of the plan around the symbolic flowers.

The main concern with flowers is that they should be delivered on time and retain their fresh look throughout the proceedings. They generally last a week. The bouquet should be put together so that there is no chance of its coming apart, even when it is thrown during the bridal toss. Some brides have a separate bouquet made up for this purpose by the florist, or the center can be fixed for the bride to save while she throws the outer part.

Walk with me through a formal wedding done by a flower designer in consultation with the bride and her mother. Marriage vows were exchanged at noon one day in May in a chapel on the grounds of a well-known university. Four ficus trees in white lattice boxes flanked the altar. Because the carpet runner had been secured to the floor before the ceremony the center aisle was cordoned off with wide white ribbons. White lace, entwined with miniature and bud roses centered by baby's breath, was tied together with white ribbons on the posts on both sides of the center aisle.

The sun shone through the stained-glass windows. Its rays fell on the bride's wedding dress of white tulle overlay, accented by Venice lace roses on the English net bodice, and fashioned with slightly puffed sleeves, a hem edged with lace, and a cathedral train. Attached to the banded lace headdress was a fingertip veil trimmed with matching lace. Her bouquet consisted of tiny white and eggshell roses.

The bridegroom and his entourage wore gray tuxedos that set off the bridegroom's white rose and the ushers' eggshell rose boutonnières.

The bridesmaids, dressed in long silver moiré, carried colorful bouquets.

The reception following was held at a posh hotel and included a cocktail hour, dinner, and dancing. Earlier, the designer had arranged low centerpieces of pink and burgundy flowers with a touch of lavender here and there in two-inch-tall containers. She centered each arrangement on the mirrored dining-room tables set with burgundy cloths, pink napkins, and glass dishes. The ballroom was filled with reflected light and colors that danced back and forth from the chandeliers to the tables.

The bill, including the cost of the flowers at the rehearsal dinner, the chapel, and the reception, was expected to fall between $1,300 and $1,500.

There are so many interesting combinations that can be made using candelabra, tapers, candles, flowers, and greenery. One is not supposed to be overwhelmed by one aspect; as in a needlepoint tapestry, the colors should subtly blend.

I received this call from California:

Q: *On festive or special occasions my fiancé gives me a corsage, and he insists on doing the same when we attend a friend's wedding next month. I feel uneasy about wearing one, though I am not certain why.*

Only members of the bridal party and grandparents carry or wear floral arrangements, to distinguish them from other guests. Explain to your fiancé the impression it will have on the other guests and suggest he give you a lace handkerchief as an alternative keepsake.

Q: *I have chosen the most beautiful centerpieces for tables at our seated dinner. How do I let people know that the flowers are reserved and not for them to take home, as I've been told has happened at some wedding receptions? There is a good reason. It would give me so much pleasure to take them to special people who will not be able to attend my wedding, such as the mother of my maid of honor, who is sick in the hospital, my grandmother, who is not able to come though she lives nearby, and certain close elderly relatives who would enjoy them for the time the flowers remain fresh.*

It is unusual for guests to take the flower centerpieces without being invited. The only suggestion I can make is to tag the flowers with the names of the people with whom you want to share them. Generally, both sets of parents like to have some as a reminder of the wedding and certain guests are told by the family to take the flowers home.

Sometimes, when the flowers are not designated for special purposes, they serve as a source of entertainment. With the permission of the hosts, a card is placed under a dessert plate at each table. The drummer rat-a-tat-tats and the band leader announces that whoever finds the card gives it to the third person on the left or it may be the second person on the right, who is then directed to give it back to the second person on the left. That person is the lucky winner of the flowers.

Music, Music, Music

"Do I know Slava? I danced at his wedding!" In this old European phrase is the key to sharing the festivities of a happy event and the memory of it. The quiet hush of the ceremony and the burst of well-wishers afterward are a study in contrast—solemnity alongside joyful celebration.

The choice of wedding music depends largely on the setting and, if held in a house of worship, on the policy of the religious institution. Some have set requirements based on the traditional wedding ceremony of that particular denomination.

Perhaps only the church organist and possibly a vocalist are allowed to perform certain approved selections. Or there might be a chanter or a choir accompaniment available. The bridal couple should discuss their preferences with the music director if they wish for pieces different from those which are usually offered. The music director or organist needs to know what musical selections to play and if there is to be a soloist.

The number of selections, both classical and semiclassical, is so vast that sometimes it takes professional advice to decide whether or not the choice suits the type of ceremony. Some pieces I know well and others I recognize only when I hear them played. The music director may only be capable of performing pieces from his or her repertoire. While this limits the selection, it also serves the purpose of narrowing the options, making it easier to choose. It has been said that any piece of music is suitable if the professional is a good arranger.

For the processional the music should be slow and dignified, though not necessarily a march nor a lengthy piece. Most of the time the music director will take a short segment from the couple's favorite selection and repeat it until the wedding party has walked down the aisle. For instance, if they choose the slow movement of Beethoven's Pathétique Sonata, chances are that not more than a page and a half will be played; the first thirty-two measures of that piece take almost two minutes to perform. If more time is needed the musician will simply go back to the beginning. Music for the recessional should be more vivacious but still dignified, signifying the conclusion of the wedding ceremony.

A traditional Protestant wedding ceremony might go like this: before the processional, as guests are being seated, the soft refrains of Bach, Liszt, or Beethoven fill the church. While the wedding party walks down the aisle the choice might possibly be the second segment of Wagner's Bridal Chorus from *Lohengrin* ("Here Comes the Bride"). When the organist glides into the first measure, the company rises and the bride comes into view on the arm of her father. A choir could be used intermittently throughout the service and the exchange of vows might be followed by the triumphant tones of Mendelssohn's Wedding March from *A Midsummer Night's Dream*. However, regardless of tradition, the couple may want to use some of their own, less popular, favorite pieces.

Eastern Orthodox wedding hymns are sung by a choir accompanied by the organ.

In Roman Catholic ceremonies Gounod's or Schubert's "Ave Maria" is sung during the offertory and a quiet piece is played while the congregation prays.

There may be some background music for silent prayer at the midpoint of a Jewish ceremony. Classical composers are popular at Jewish weddings so the choice is very broad. Jewish couples might find it fruitful to explore works by Ernst Bloch, who has composed much original music based on Jewish themes, such as "From Jewish Life" and "Schelomo." Musical segments from one's own culture provide a familiarity that gives comfort, strength, and a sense of unity.

The choice of music Richard and Ruth decided on when they were married in a hotel before a small company might have suited other situations too but was perfect for a small wedding. About thirty minutes before the ceremony, while guests were being seated, Richard and Ruth asked for love songs, medleys of show tunes, and light classical music. For the short procession, Ruth chose the slow movement of Beethoven's Pathétique piano sonata and, for her walk to the altar, the slow movement of Chopin's Fantasy Impromptu. Their first walk as husband and wife was to Grieg's

"Wedding Day at Troldhaugen," a piano piece Ruth was particularly fond of playing. At the reception, after the toast and just before the cutting of the cake, Mark, Richard's brother and best man—who is a professional performer and composer—sang a song he wrote as a surprise for the newlyweds.

If a couple is uncertain about the list of selections given by the music director, they should do some research at the local library or university. I am told that unless there are definite preferences, the musicians should be allowed to do the guiding, since music is suggested by their repertoires. It stands to reason that the renditions will be played to the best of their abilities.

MUSIC FOR THE RECEPTION

Not every couple wants the type of reception that has a lively band. Not every place for a reception—the bride's home, for example—can accommodate an area for dancing. But generally some sort of music adds to the texture of a gathering as it weaves gently through the room, filling the spaces.

The couple can hire a set group, a band that performs together without changes in personnel. Of prime importance is suiting the size of the orchestra to that of the room and the number of guests. It is estimated that for a party of 100 to 150 people, a four- or five-piece band is sufficient. Trios, duos, or soloists are best for fewer people. Instruments such as harp, viola, violin, and piano or a combination of two or more, depending on the size of the premises, work well when there is to be no dancing.

There is music to be found for most combinations of instruments but the largest classical repertoire is for the string quartet, which generally consists of two violins, viola, and cello; a string trio uses one violin instead of two; and a piano quartet can include piano, violin, viola, and cello.

Though there are many combinations, a woodwind trio might consist of flute, clarinet, and bassoon; flute, oboe, and bassoon; or oboe, clarinet, and French horn.

Most musical groups are "combos" that play popular music and usually consist of a rhythm section, brass or woodwind, and a vocalist. The rhythm section generally comprises piano, drums, bass, and possibly a guitar, which can, if necessary, replace the piano. The brass and woodwind section can include saxophone (a saxophonist can often also play clarinet or flute), trumpet, and trombone. Frequently one or several of the instrumentalists will also perform vocals and vocal harmony. Versatile groups such as these are very much in demand.

Some people prefer to hire a string quartet or other classical combination for the ceremony, cocktails, and dinner, and then to bring in a dance band for lively after-dinner dancing.

Since a wedding consists of a variety of age levels, an experienced ensemble should be able to offer music of the big-band era, show and love tunes, old rock and roll, and contemporary rock and pop, as well as the appropriate ethnic tunes. The ideal is to have a band that can play all those styles authentically, with good taste and common sense.

One hopes that the bride and bridegroom have similar tastes but if not, that can be handled by combining both preferences while keeping in mind the type of wedding planned and guests expected. Care should be taken when considering a group that specializes in one style. If, for example, the couple are fans of traditional jazz and hire a Dixieland band, they run the risk of leaving out part of their company. As wonderful a musical expression as jazz is, one style of music throughout a three- or four-hour party can get monotonous.

Choosing an ensemble takes time—time to audition the band and bandleader by attending a function. Some organizations play tapes or show videotapes of their group, which doesn't tell the couple anything about how the band performs on the job. Smart groups are now making videotapes of their live performances, because observing the effect the band has on the crowd is important, especially seeing how the audience responds and hearing how loud the band plays.

When hosts are gracious enough to allow visitors in to hear the orchestra, visitors must take care to be as inconspicuous as possible. It is distressing to both musicians and the hosts if they show up in jeans and risk the chance of being refused admission.

Each bandleader has his or her own way of running an affair. Some will take an active hand by conducting the rehearsal for the ceremony, acting as master of ceremonies for the reception, and helping coordinate events between the caterer, photographer, and band. This is a great service and can cost more. Others take a less visible role, preferring to limit their duties to selecting the right music as the party progresses. It depends on the kind of help required—parties need some guidance. Either way, the talent of a good bandleader, as with any performer, is in sensing the crowd and in the selection of music that will keep the rhythm of the party flowing. That vital function will create a happy and convivial atmosphere.

The maestro needs a list of the music the couple desires at least a month before the wedding day, including a selection for their first dance and possibly another for the bride and her father. Do not assume that musicians know all the tunes ever written. If new songs have to be learned, time is needed to make preparations for a musical arrangement to be written and rehearsals may have to take place. Keeping the couple's preferences in mind, a competent professional must be allowed to do the job. But once the party starts the leader needs to program the music according to his or her best judgment and, as I have mentioned before, by sensing the mood of the crowd and knowing how to use that rhythm to best advantage.

Though groups work with slight differences, they generally play for a given number of minutes per hour and then take a rest period. For instance, they might play for forty-five minutes with a fifteen-minute break; other leaders work the twenty-minute set with a five-minute pause. Both ways work well for the musicians and guests. Unless there is a definite preference, accept the professional's advice.

The orchestra can be hired to play continuous music, which means the only pauses are when the maestro changes styles or during the cake cutting, and for the toast offering. Naturally, the cost will increase. Though this might not have been contracted for initially, with the flush of a successful party the hosts may want the group not only to play continuously but to play overtime as well. Hosts should be aware of the extra expense they are letting themselves in for this way.

If in the back of their minds hosts contemplate overtime but do not want it in the contract, it is wise to check with the leader beforehand, since the group might have another function right afterward.

Some hosts invite the musicians to partake of the hors d'oeuvres and other food, especially if there is a buffet table. Performers should have the good taste to wait until all the guests have been served before they help themselves. The code of conduct for musicians includes never eating, drinking, or smoking while on stage. Singers might have to take a sip of water now and then to keep in good voice but this should be done discreetly. When playing the group should always look interested and as if they are enjoying it. Most of all, musicians should remember they are not playing for themselves but to make the event "happen." The sound system should be well placed and the volume level controlled; guests should not be blasted out of the room.

The person who arranges the room should leave enough space for the band to set up, and musicians should have a place to leave their cases and coats.

The maestro has to be a charming presence on stage and also needs the ability to handle all kinds of emotions exhibited by the family. Again, as with anyone in the entertainment business, the leader has to be able to deal with a relative who has had too much to drink. Thinking he or she is an undiscovered Sinatra or Streisand, that guest sings inanely out of tune, forgetting there is a music group trying to back up the rendition. Remember, some of these antics embarrass the family as well, but they do not want hurt feelings, so a leader has to keep calm. At the same time, if the bride invites her Uncle Thomas to sing, convince her that the perfect time would be during dinner. This avoids the possibility that the wonderful cadence and conviviality building up will be interrupted during dancing. Such control benefits the entire affair, because once someone acts the clown or breaks up the mood in some way, it is hard to build the momentum again.

As with other services, the couple will be asked to sign a contract mutually agreeable to both them and the performer(s). The information should be checked very carefully: wedding date, time, and place(s) of the ceremony and reception. As the day nears, touch base with the leader.

Contracts differ from area to area and city to city and according to whether union or nonunion musicians are involved. Some reception sites require union musicians and a minimum number of hours for which they must be hired.

As with the photographer, if the couple is booking through a contracting firm and likes a particular leader or ensemble, they should stipulate the person(s) by name in the agreement. It might be that the group, or the individual, is booked so the couple would need to rely on the agent to find other musicians. Not all groups consist of the same people every booking, but professional local musicians with experience should be able to, and do, play with most other musicians in town.

Again, as with a photographer, find the most professional group that can be afforded. A friend's amateur musician son who is paying his way through school may show off his skill as a talented dilettante, but it takes a mature professional to successfully lead and control a complex event such as a wedding.

Not everyone realizes what a special mood live music creates at a wedding celebration, but then not everyone can afford the cost. Another option is taped music—but the couple will have to spend some time gathering the appropriate selections, and they might need the advice of a musicologist.

Disc jockeys bring stereo equipment with amplifiers and speakers designed to fill a large room without distortion. The DJ's selections, whether on records or cassette tapes, are organized in some way so that he or she can quickly select any tune. Some disc jockeys supply mood lighting and may or may not act as a master of ceremonies.

The difference between live and taped music is that live music touches a spontaneous chord with listeners. A DJ costs less. A lot depends on whether or not the DJ knows how to pace a party or can suggest the appropriate music for the ceremony . . . Imagine having Itzhak Perlman play at a wedding!

Photographs

Unlike the wedding dress, which is packed away in a box to gather dust in the attic, the wedding album can be enjoyed for many years. Photographs of the most significant day of the couple's life take on an even greater meaning as time passes—both in the sweetness of life and in the sadness of it. At the very least, those faces that look back at us are living remembrances in which future generations can take pleasure. I recently came across a photograph of my great-grandmother that fascinated my entire family—my children's great-great-grandmother, flanked by two of her grandchildren, looked out matter-of-factly from the print.

Peering through the magnifier we tried to glean from her face, clothes, jewelry, and bearing how life had treated her. Ah, the mystery of it all—she was as silent as the two youngsters, now also a memory.

One of the pitfalls one should avoid is hiring a friend who is a once-in-a-while photographer with some nice shots of swans gliding on the water in Manhattan's Central Park one Sunday afternoon. The offer may be made, but accepting it because feelings might be hurt is a mistake. If an amateur photographer does not know how to shoot a wedding the bridal couple will not have a true picture record of the event.

Even if the photographer is excellent, the most important question is whether he or she has a portfolio of weddings to display. If not, that person might just be branching out into the wedding specialty business and one takes a chance that some important phase of the wedding will be missed. Or the wedding album might be incomplete, even though a professional did the work. It takes experience and knowledge to successfully shoot all the phases of the wedding day from beginning to end.

Going to an established business is fine, but the couple must ask to see the work of the particular photographer who will shoot the wedding. If they are satisfied, then that name should be written into the contract as the only one hired for the job; some photographers take the formal stills and then leave, allowing someone else to finish the job. This might be an equitable arrangement, but it should be clarified beforehand. Let us suppose a Mr. Simon, who has a fine reputation in his field, has a staff of photographers. Viewing *his* work will not answer questions about the talent of the person he will send if he himself is not free to do the wedding.

I have seen some impressive wedding albums, containing both formal wedding portraits and candid shots, that show the photographer's excellent knowledge of composition, an important element, as well as the clarity of the print. Good composition means that the background does not clash with or detract from the subject and that there is nothing in the photograph that does not belong. When a photo is in focus it means the lines are clear, not fuzzy, and the principals are sharply defined. Poses should be natural and pleasing. Color tones should be lifelike and true.

Most photographers do their best to provide a fair contract, with everything spelled out, and then present fine albums for families to treasure. There is, however, a down side to picture-taking that must be discussed.

When my husband and I were married, the photographer shot every guest table at the dinner but there is not one decent photograph of the two of us. What is more, every picture is awkward looking. We had a beautiful wedding but that cannot be seen in our album. Those moments are over, never to be recaptured.

Recently, an irate mother of the bride told me of her experience with the photographer at the wedding. He was too much in evidence throughout the ceremony and reception. Without the family's authorization he took pictures of the guests and handed his cards to everyone. Instead of taking shots of the guests at the dinner tables, he sat down uninvited to eat as leisurely as they. The man worked for a well-known photo studio in the Washington area. If that story has reached me then rest assured the offended client has spoken to family and friends who, in turn, have repeated it to others. It does not take many jobs handled like that to ruin the reputation of a company that depends on word-of-mouth recommendations.

Some unforeseen events can interfere with the picture-taking process. A careless guest once toppled a photographer's camera. Though the camera was replaced the photographer was still upset, not only because she couldn't use her best camera but because the work she had done up to that point was lost. Another absentminded type forgot to remove the lens cover so that although the photographer worked hard, there was not one photograph taken of the entire proceedings. These events are the exception.

GUIDELINES

- A photographer should be able to do a job as unobtrusively as possible.
- Check with the clergy about the rules governing the taking of photographs during the ceremony. Some houses of worship do not allow shooting during certain parts of the proceedings.
- Question the photographer about his or her portfolio; study more than one album to learn about the sequence of events

at a wedding. Take notes so that you will have a clear idea of just what is wanted in the memory book.

- Some photographers like to take the formal portrait of the bride at the time she goes for the fitting of her bridal gown. Other photographers will not consider formals until the wedding because there is no look that can match the radiance of a bride on that day.
- Prepare a list of the type of pictures wanted during each phase of the wedding, including both formal and informal shots. The photographer needs to know what the couple expects.
- Have formal shots of the wedding party taken before the bridal couple are tired and wilted.
- Some brides prefer exciting candid shots of the wedding party arriving at the ceremony site; others like the formal photographs taken before or after the ceremony but before the reception. Have a balanced picture story of the event from beginning to end, including both the bride and bridegroom's families and friends.
- If the family does not wish photographs to be taken of guests other than those specified, that fact should be listed. The couple might rightly be nervous at the possibility that an important part of the festivities will be missed because the photographer was elsewhere taking unauthorized shots.
- The photographer should be told that only a couple of people, mainly the mother of the bride and the bride—if she has a level head at this exciting time—can give instructions. Too many cooks spoil the broth.
- To engage the services of a studio, a contract will be drawn up and signed by both parties. Take it home and look it over carefully. First check the time and date of wedding. Pencil in the changes needed and send it back to the photographer. There may be a clause that says that the photographer must be allowed to eat or rest after a certain number of hours of work. This is a reasonable request. Remember, the photographer comes early to the wedding; the job starts immediately and he goes almost nonstop until the wedding is over.
- Sometime after the wedding the photographer will telephone to say the proofs are ready. He might show all the

successful shots on a contact sheet, from which the couple makes their selection for the final album. I prefer the proof method, because each photograph is about three inches by four inches and clear to the naked eye. Although contact sheets are less expensive, the prints can only be seen through a magnifying glass and it is still very hard to evaluate details.

- It might be a good idea for the three albums, one for the bridal couple and the other two for their parents, to be different so that a more complete record can be had of the wedding. Also, list the names of the guests on the back of each page, so that as the years go by others can identify them.

VIDEOTAPING

At this writing videotaping is in its infancy. Firms keep developing more sophisticated equipment both in cameras and in sound, so I can only write what is going on at the moment. The danger is that anyone can buy the most elementary equipment, put an ad in the paper, and be in business. It's not always safe to assume that the results will be as pleasing as good photography.

Videotaping is becoming popular and although it is somewhat similar to photography, in no way does it take the place of those beautiful stills that capture a particular moment.

If allowed, the video photographer can tape the entire ceremony and also interview guests who talk into a microphone—possibly editing those imbibing too many drinks. When viewed later, the event is seen as it really happened, rather than just as highlights. Videotaping services can frequently be provided by the photography studio, which would more than likely engage a talent equal to the standards of their firm.

Since the video camera has a microphone attached to it, don't surprise anybody with videotaping equipment at the wedding ceremony. Discuss with the clergy whether audio recording and picture-taking are permitted during the service. It is against the religious code of some denominations.

Nor should this equipment be used at the reception without touching base with the music contractor. Some union musicians will refuse to allow sound recordings of their performances unless an arrangement has been made with their union.

Professional videotapers should have good cameras, light-enhancing devices, and recording equipment. As with a photographer, a video recorder is required to unobtrusively tape various scenes to make three hours of festivities into a living memory. The shooting should be done so subtly that people are not aware they are being filmed, except during interviews with guests.

Because good natural light is needed for video filming, there has to be cooperation between the bandleader, the video technician, and the wedding party. People like to dance under dim lighting; videotaping is impossible without floodlights or natural light. Blinding lights that make people uncomfortable can kill a party, and avoiding electrical wires is a nuisance, to say the least. Battery-powered lights eliminate the need for trailing wires but the batteries drain very quickly, which makes them impractical for a long party.

Then there is the end product, which should be tastefully edited—not even Uncle Thomas wants to see Uncle Thomas standing on his ear. Guests must be discreet when being interviewed. A videotaper told me that the mother of the bride made a derogatory remark about her ex-husband. When she realized the remark was there for posterity she asked that it be deleted from the tape. The sound can be recorded; if a tape is too dark it can be made lighter; a tape can be unsuccessful in many ways, but there are companies that can restore or doctor a tape so that it looks highly professional—all of which, of course, increases the cost.

Because video equipment is hard to move about, someone should be assigned to notify the operator if there is a change of plan for a segment of the party. As with the photographer, a missed scene can never be repeated.

The two home formats of video recorders are VHS and Beta. The sizes of the tapes are different, so the firm that does the video work must be able to make copies in either format.

Copies can be made from the original without losing too much color and depth. It is also possible to make a copy from another copy, but with each generation the pictures fade a bit more.

The Wedding Ceremony

$\backsim$ There is something comforting about the familiar, and so we stick to customs and tradition often without knowing how or why they began. This is particularly true of weddings—the reception as well as the ceremony. Tradition sets weddings apart from any other function. The marrying couple, while looking forward to the future, become enwrapped by the wedding customs of the past; for many their marriage becomes the first step in their recognition of their place in the scheme of things.

My walk through the different religious and nonreligious wedding ceremonies has been a special experience—the poetic words that reach the very depth of our cultures . . . Dearly beloved . . . Thou art consecrated unto me . . . I take thee to be my lawfully wedded wife . . . and so I invite readers to look into the window, not only of their own backgrounds, but also of others.

In most marriage ceremonies there are traditional components without which we would be bewildered, however small or simple the event; the wedding ring for the bride and the exchange of vows, for instance. Yet wedding rings are not part of the marriage ceremony of the Seventh-day Adventists, since they wear no jewelry.

It is fortunate that some customs have disappeared. In ancient Rome the bridal couple just stood next to each other in their wedding clothes and silently pledged their vows in front of witnesses and before an augur, who divined the signs for the success of the marriage by sacrificing an animal to the gods. The augur examined the poor creature's entrails and pronounced the gods' approval, or, in some cases, their disapproval.

As recently as the fourteenth century, English marriage rites were viewed very casually. If the betrothal, which included the contract, was followed by consummation, it was considered binding by the church and the community. Children born before the actual marriage but after the betrothal were considered legitimate.

247

But there were no formal guidelines and bigamy was rampant, due to the absence of any kind of registry or formal ceremony.

At one time most marriages were not entered into through the couple's own free will but by pressure from other sources. They were arranged between families for political and financial gain. Not all parents felt their children had to bend to their will but they viewed romantic love with one's spouse as a development that came after marriage (the same philosophy holds in many countries—such as India—today). So marrying into a family at the same social level was of prime importance. A mismatched couple could displease the Crown and completely ruin a family's connections, which might spell financial disaster.

Despite the possibility of putting their families in jeopardy, children from affluent families did sometimes elope to escape their parents' choice of a marriage partner. Often they ended up with fortune hunters or worse, and were married by clergymen of dubious reputation. The church tried to control these renegade clergymen but with little success.

Though teachings on marriage are found in the New Testament, it was not until the middle of the fifteenth century that marriage came to be viewed by the church as a sacrament. It took another century for vows to be said before a Catholic priest. Laws were passed requiring the registration of births, marriages, and deaths.

By the seventeenth century the laws governing marriage had tightened and banns had to be posted as part of the betrothal ritual. But marriages were still arranged by parents, contracts were signed, and verbal promises given both at the betrothal and in the church. It was not until 1753 that the British Parliament passed the Marriage Act that affected the entire country. For those with means, a written financial contract had to be drawn up between the marrying families, generally to give the bride some protection if her husband died or deserted her. Witnesses had to be present and verbal promises exchanged, banns were posted three consecutive times, a religious ceremony took place, and, finally, consummation . . . and before they knew it, the couple were married!

Nowadays a civil marriage ceremony can be arranged in a week, or a formal wedding can take as much as a year to arrange.

The time of day or evening the wedding occurs often depends on the part of the country in which one lives. Evening weddings are more popular in the south and southwestern states, a custom that owes its existence, of course, to the sultry climate before the advent of air-conditioning. The northern and eastern states tend to favor afternoon weddings between four and five o'clock.

It is important to check with the clergyman for the appropriate times and dates for a wedding for all Christian and Jewish weddings or for any religious group with which you are not completely familiar.

Roman Catholic weddings are held at various times during the day. The very formal wedding is celebrated before noon or at noon during High Mass, when there is a choir to offer liturgical music. Others might have the ceremony at Low Mass as early as eight or nine o'clock in the morning. Catholics can be married on Sunday before six in the evening. Marriages during Lent or Advent must be cleared with the priest.

Jewish weddings can be held any day of the week except during the Sabbath, between sundown on Friday and sundown on Saturday. They generally take place Saturday evening, Sunday noon, or Sunday evening. There are specific dates during the Jewish calendar year when a rabbi is not permitted to perform a marriage. The Hebrew calendar, unlike the Gregorian, is based on the lunar month of twenty-eight and a half days.

In most Christian churches women wear a headcovering.

The kiss at the end of the nuptial service is usually up to the bride and bridegroom, but in some houses of worship it is not allowed and in some it is up to the clergy.

In most states and in most religious ceremonies two witnesses must be present.

PROGRAMS

Programs for weddings, as for regular church services, are a custom in some areas. They serve as guides to the schedule of the marriage ceremony and are handed by ushers to guests as they enter the church. They can be printed on inexpensive paper but many are handsomely designed to match the color and quality of the wedding invitation. The cover might be elegantly embossed with the words OUR WEDDING PROGRAM.

The inside wording guides people through the proceedings:

THE MARRIAGE SERVICE OF
Jill Candace Ode
and
Frederick Eldon Hampenstance
Saturday, June 6th, 1987
1:00 P.M.
Trinity Church
Washington, District of Columbia

ORGAN PRELUDE . . . Medley of Nuptial Selections

SOLO
Wedding Song . . . . Paul Stookey
One Hand, One Heart . . . . Stephen Sondheim
and Leonard Bernstein

LIGHTING OF CANDLES

PROCESSIONAL
Trumpet Voluntary in D . . . . Purcell
Wedding March from *Lohengrin* . . . . Wagner

INVOCATION . . . . Genesis 2:18–24
Scriptures: I Corinthians 13: 1–4

ACT OF WEDDING
Purpose of Marriage
Charge to the Bride and Groom
Commitment
Consent and Blessing of Parents
Wedding Vows
Giving of Rings
Pronouncement of Marriage
Blessing of the Couple

PRAYER

THE LORD'S PRAYER . . . the people united and bowed in prayer

BLESSING

RECESSIONAL
Wedding March . . . . Mendelssohn

[On the facing page:]

THE BRIDAL PARTY

Maid of Honor	Ms. _____
Bridesmaids	Ms. _____
Best Man	Mr. _____
Groomsmen	Mr. _____
Acolyte	Miss _____
Flower Girl	Miss _____
Ring Bearer	Master _____
Officiating Minister	Rev. _____
Organist	Mr. _____
Soloist	Ms. _____
Wedding Coordinator	Mrs. _____

PEW CARDS

The first few pews left and right of the aisle in the church are cordoned off with ribbons so that family and intimate friends can view the proceedings comfortably.

When a lot of people are expected at the church, the rows fill rapidly with people and the ushers may have a difficult time figuring out who sits where. This is why pew cards are so practical. They ensure that the front rows are taken by those closest to both families.

The mothers of the bride and bridegroom draw up for the ushers lists only of those who will sit within the ribbons. When they enter the church, those who have pew cards show them to escorting ushers. These cards are enclosed with the invitations. Sometimes, when the church is expected to be full, pew numbers are assigned to those within the ribbons, and notice of this has to be mailed separately to those who have accepted. This is when one needs an efficient social secretary.

The phrase "within the ribbon" can be handwritten by the bridal pair's mothers on their named printed cards, although some people go the expensive way by having pew cards printed:

Within the ribbon [handwritten]
printed name of hostess or host and hostess

Protestant

The Protestant marriage ceremony is taken from the Episcopal Book of Common Prayer and can vary slightly from one denomination to the other. I have included the first section verbatim, since it is the basis and the very depth of the philosophy of marriage; I quote from the rest of the ceremony.

THE ORDER FOR THE
SOLEMNIZATION OF MARRIAGE

The Persons to be married shall present themselves before the Minister, the Man standing on the right hand of the Woman. Then, all present reverently standing, the Minister shall say:

Dearly beloved, we are assembled here in the presence of God, to join this Man and this Woman in holy marriage; which is instituted of God, regulated by His commandments, blessed by our Lord Jesus Christ, and to be held in honor among all men. Let us, therefore, reverently remember that God has established and sanctified marriage, for the welfare and happiness of mankind. Our Saviour has declared that man shall leave his father and mother and cleave unto his wife. By His apostles, He has instructed those who enter this relation to cherish a mutual esteem and love; to bear with each other's infirmities and weaknesses; to comfort each other in sickness, trouble, and sorrow; in honesty and industry to provide for each other, and for their household, in temporal things; to pray for and encourage each other in the things which pertain to God; and to live together as the heirs of the grace of life.

For as much as these two persons have come hither to be made one in this holy estate, if there be any here present who knows any just cause why they may not lawfully be joined in marriage, I require him now to make it known, or ever after to hold his peace.

Then, speaking unto the Persons who are to be married, the Minister shall say:

. . . if either of you know any reason ye may not be lawfully joined together in marriage, ye now confess it . . .

Then if no impediment appears, the Minister shall offer a prayer:

... We beseech Thee to be present and favorable unto these Thy servants, that they may be truly joined in the honorable estate of marriage, in the covenant of their God ...

Then the Minister, calling first on the Man and then on the Woman by their Christian names, shall say:

_____, will thou have this Woman (Man) to be thy wife (husband), and wilt thou pledge thy troth to her (him) in all love and honor, in all duty and service, in all faith and tenderness, to live with her (him), and cherish her (him), according to the ordinance of God, in the holy bond of marriage?

The Man (Woman) shall answer:

I will.

Minister asks:

Who giveth this Woman to be married to this Man?

Then the Father, or Guardian, or Friend, of the Woman shall put her right hand in the hand of the Minister, who shall cause the Man with his right hand to take the Woman by her right hand and to say after the Minister as follows:

I, _____, take thee, _____, To be my wedded wife (husband); And I do promise and covenant; Before God and these witnesses; To be thy loving and faithful husband (wife); In plenty and in want; In joy and in sorrow; In sickness and in health; As long as we both shall live.

Then if a ring (rings) be provided, it shall be given to the Minister, who shall return it to the Man (Woman), who shall then put it upon the fourth finger of the Woman's (Man's) left hand, saying after the Minister

This ring I give thee; In token and pledge; Of our constant faith; And abiding love.

Or,

With this ring I thee wed; In the name of the Father, And of the Son; And of the Holy Spirit. Amen.

Before giving the ring, the Minister blesses the ring.

Let us pray.
Our Father, who art in Heaven; Hallowed be Thy Name. Thy kingdom come. Thy will be done; On earth as it is in

heaven. Give us this day our daily bread. And forgive us our debts; As we forgive our debtors. And lead us not into temptation; But deliver us from evil; For Thine is the kingdom, and the power, and the glory, for ever. Amen.

Then shall the Minister say unto all who are present:

By the authority committed unto me as a Minister of the Church of Christ, I declare that _____ and _____ are now Husband and Wife, according to the ordinance of God, and the law of the State: in the name of the Father, and of the Son, and of the Holy Spirit. Amen.

Then, causing the Husband and Wife to join their right hands, the Minister shall say:

Whom therefore God hath joined together, let no man put asunder.

It is fitting that the Bride and Groom kneel to receive this benediction.

The Lord bless you, and keep you: the Lord make His face to shine on you, and be gracious unto you; the Lord lift up His countenance upon you, and give you peace: both now and the life everlasting. Amen.

Or,

God the Father, God the Son, God the Holy Spirit, bless, preserve, and keep you; the Lord mercifully with His favor look upon you, and fill you with all spiritual benedictions and grace; that ye may so live together in this life that in the world to come ye may have life everlasting. Amen.

Though the substance of the marriage ceremony remains the same, there are minor changes in method incorporated within the ceremony that indicate the preferences of the particular church and each individual minister.

And now on to the arrangements and suggested patterns of the wedding day.

Guests arrive at the church or ceremony site at least twenty to thirty minutes before the wedding is scheduled to begin.

It is important for the ushers to be at church an hour beforehand so that they can meet guests at the entrance.

Candelabra are lit, possibly by the ushers, fifteen minutes before the start of the ceremony. Ribbons should be in place.

Especially in cities where a traffic tie-up could occur, the entire bridal party, the bride and bridegroom, and parents should give themselves ample time to be at the church. The bride arrives five minutes ahead of time if the wedding takes place in a quiet area.

Traditionally, the bride's guests sit on the left of the aisle and the bridegroom's on the right. However, it looks much better to have random seating on either side of the aisle if the guest list is heavily one-sided.

Ushers stand at the entrance of the church to guide ladies and escorts to their seats after asking which side of the family they know. Usually, an usher extends his right arm, the lady links her left arm lightly in his, her husband or escort keeps two paces behind, and children follow a pace behind their parents. Or a couple might prefer to walk together just a pace behind the usher who leads them to their seats.

It is considered polite for ushers to make some sort of comment since, though the occasion is solemn, it should not be rigid.

Sometimes when guests arrive all at once and time is short, the usher should extend his arm to the senior lady, asking the others to follow.

While the soloist is singing guests should stand at the entrance until the song is concluded.

No one is escorted when the bride's mother is being taken to her place.

At military weddings when the bridal couple's families are not able to attend, the commanding officer and spouse may be asked to sit in the first pew. Though weddings do not have the same protocol as other social occasions, high-ranking officers might be seated with the couple's immediate family.

Some houses of worship have a center aisle and two side aisles. The center aisle is used by both families—the bride's side sits left and bridegroom's on the right. Immediate family—brothers, sisters, grandparents, aunts, and uncles—sit in the second row. Depending on the size of the guest list, guests sit behind in the center row, divided by families the same way. Or they can sit in the side pews.

For *very formal* weddings, large white bows are attached to the aisle posts, and ribbons or ropes indicate that the first few pews are reserved for the family. Those guests to be seated within the ribbons should be told to mention this to the usher.

The bridegroom's parents should arrive at the latest about ten minutes before the ceremony is scheduled to start. Sometimes, however, they may arrive earlier and wait with their guests. They are next to the last to be seated, and so should be aware of the time to enter the church.

The ceremony is about to begin when the bridegroom's mother, on the arm of the head usher and followed by the bridegroom's father, is led to the first pew and sits down on the aisle side. When the bride's mother, also escorted by the head usher, is seated in the first pew, the door to the church closes and the ceremony begins. Latecomers wait until the bride's mother is seated, then go discreetly to the side aisles in the back.

Guests who are seated early get the choicest seats and those who arrive afterward should not expect them to move.

If the bride's parents are divorced and her mother has remarried, her stepfather is seated in the first pew. Her father goes in the third pew, where his wife—if he has remarried—is waiting. The same applies for the bridegroom's parents.

The bridegroom and the best man arrive at the church about half an hour early and sit in the vestry until the head usher warns them that they should be ready to take their places.

If there is to be a canvas runner, it should be rolled out by two ushers immediately after the bride's mother has been seated. Ushers walk to the foot of the chancel and unroll it to lie flat in the center of the aisle. Some people have the runner nailed down beforehand and cordon off the center aisle so guests are seated from the side aisles. Supposedly used to protect the hem of the bride's wedding dress, the runner is not as popular as it once was and, unless it is laid properly, can be a nuisance. However, if romance appeals to you, ask yourself how many times in your life will a carpet be spread before you as if you were royalty?

The processional starts with the music chosen for the occasion. The minister enters the sanctuary, goes up the steps to the chancel, and faces the congregation. The bridegroom enters from the sacristy, followed two paces behind by his best man, and stands at the right foot of the chancel with the best man slightly behind and to the right of him when they are facing the clergyman. They then turn at right angles to the company as the procession starts so that the bridegroom can watch his bride come toward him.

Though it depends on the size of the house of worship, the ushers usually walk in pairs according to height—the shortest first. During the rehearsal the organist can give a musical clue to the first attendants so they arrive at their appointed place on time. At a steady gait, they start with the left foot, each pair about four paces ahead of the next. (The space between attendants depends on the length of the church and the number of attendants.) As they arrive at the foot of the aisle they separate, left and right; or they can be all on one side in front of the choir stands. Maids can proceed singly or in pairs. Following the formation of the ushers, they either separate left and right in front of the ushers or stand next to one another on the left. All face the minister and turn in the direction of the bride as she enters the church.

There are a great many possible variations in these arrangements; the clergyman and the verger know best how the procession should run.

The maid of honor is next. She stands opposite the best man on the left of the chancel; if there is to be a matron of honor, she places herself slightly back from the maid. Or they can walk together.

Flower girl(s) stand alongside or slightly behind the maid of honor. The ring bearer stands by the best man. Should there be one flower girl and a ring bearer, they could walk together, separating as they reach the chancel.

Now the bride and her father stand at the entrance for a moment while the chords of the nuptial march fill the sanctuary. The company stands as the bride takes her father's right arm and holds her flowers in her other hand. Discuss which arm the bride should take. It might be more comfortable to take the left, since it will be easier for her father to hand the bride over to the bridegroom and then make his way to the pew.

Left feet first, they proceed down the aisle and halt a few paces from the foot of the chancel. Now the bride might give her father a kiss as he releases her arm. If the father is to give the bride in marriage, he remains where he is. If not, he goes to the first pew and sits next to his wife. Meantime, the bridegroom steps forward and holds out his right arm to aid the bride, who places her bouquet in her right hand. Together they face the minister. During the rehearsal they will be told whether to hold hands before the minister places the bride's hand in the bridegroom's—it depends on the custom of the house of worship.

In most denominations it is up to the bride and the minister whether the company stands or sits for the ceremony. If she wishes guests to be seated, then the clergyman makes the announcement. As the actual service begins the bride can hand her bouquet to the maid of honor so her hands are free to receive the ring. If the maid is holding the bridegroom's ring, she should have a convenient stand on which to place the bouquet. Of course, if there is a matron of honor she would hold the bridal bouquet.

When the minister asks the question "Who giveth this woman to be married to this man?" the father steps forward, takes his daughter's hand, places it in the minister's, and says, "I do," or "Her mother and I do."

When the minister asks for the bride's ring, the best man gives it to the bridegroom, who then gives it to the minister for the blessing.

The minister declares, "I now pronounce you husband and wife." If the bride has chosen to wear a veil, the maid of honor lifts it for the bridal kiss, but this depends both on the feelings of the bride and bridegrooom and on the custom of the denomination within which they marry. Sometimes the couple shake hands with the clergyman.

Before turning to the company, the bride is given her bouquet by the maid of honor. Then the bridal couple, with the bride on the right arm of her husband, lead the recessional to the joyful music of the recessional march. The flower girl follows. It is optional whether the best man and maid of honor, and the other male and female attendants, walk couple by couple or in pairs according to gender.

At this point in a military wedding there might be the Arch of Swords ceremony. (See Military Wedding, p. 279.)

The ushers return swiftly to complete their duties. First the head usher escorts the bride's mother, followed by her husband; then the bridegroom's mother takes the arm of the usher, who walks her up the aisle, with father pacing himself a little behind.

I prefer to see either set of parents walking together. To me it equates the steps of nurturing parents and the first steps their children take as husband and wife.

All the ladies who were part of the procession are escorted again unless it is decided that they too will walk with their husbands.

Ushers are on hand to direct guests discreetly to wait until the entire wedding party has reached the vestibule. Only then do guests leave in turn—row by row, the front pews first.

The photographer's role is determined by the policy of the house of worship. It is up to the clergyman to give permission for photographs to be taken during the ceremony, but they can certainly be shot during the recessional. The couple might wait with the bridal party and parents in the vestry until the entire church empties. Then the photographer snaps them retracing the steps of the ceremony; sometimes the clergyman consents to participate. This is a photo session, with just the main parts of the service reenacted. Shots should also be taken of the couple leaving the church. Careful arrangements should be made beforehand with the photographer for the formal pictures.

The best man sees the bride and bridegroom to the limousine or to their car, which he may also drive.

In the meantime, the bridesmaids and the parents of the bride and bridegroom all meet at the place where the reception will be held.

Lutheran

In the Lutheran tradition those attending a marriage ceremony are not just invited guests; they are participants in a service of worship, one of the joyous occasions declared "very good" by the Creator. Marriage is a social contract of commitment. It is the couple who perform the marriage, since they marry each other; the minister represents both the church and the state, attesting that they have made their religious and legal statements in both areas. The basic ingredients of Lutheran philosophy regarding marriage are the fidelity and "steadfast love" on which marriage is founded, not passion.

A notice of the forthcoming marriage may be published in the church bulletins, its purpose being to ask for the congregation's prayers.

In many areas of the country, Holy Week (Easter) is the only time when Lutheran weddings are not performed, and in a few churches the time span also includes Lent.

The music is selected for its appropriateness.

"Giving away" is not part of the tradition. Parents may be invited to accompany their children in the procession, exchange the peace with them, read the lessons, stand behind them as vows are exchanged, and take part in the blessing.

The procession may be arranged in various ways.

An appropriate hymn may signal the congregation that they should stand for the entrance. It can begin with the carrying of the cross and torches. The minister(s) and the bridegroom enter from the sacristy, as is the case in most Protestant services. Or the assistant minister, presiding minister, attendants, parents, bride, and bridegroom walk down the aisle in that order.

The marriage ceremony may be celebrated with or without Holy Communion. According to the Reverend Doctor Arnold F. Keller of the Church of the Reformation in Washington, D.C., most couples have a simple wedding service, but if the larger Holy Communion service is preferred, then the ceremony precedes Holy Communion.

During the rehearsal, the minister instructs the couple where to stand for the exchange of vows. The assistant minister addresses the couple, after which the presiding minister charges them with the commitment of marriage based in the vows and the ring ceremony.

At the marriage ceremony the officiant asks the couple:

_____ and _____, if it is your intention to share with each other your joys and sorrows and all that the years will bring, with your promises bind yourselves to each other as husband and wife.

The bride and the bridegroom face each other, join hands, and exchange vows that can be of their own composition, with the guidance of the minister, who ensures that the necessary wording reflects promises of marriage fidelity. If they write their own vows they are instructed not to promise too much but to hope and pray that the gifts of marriage can be sustained.

A sample of the vows that can be offered is:

I take you, _____, to be my wife from this day forward, to join with you and share all that is to come, and I promise to be faithful to you until death parts us.

After vows are declared, at which point the couple are now married, a single- or double-ring exchange takes place. When the traditional single-ring ceremony is preferred, the man slips the ring on the woman's fourth finger and says:

I give you this ring as a sign of my love and faithfulness.

In a double-ring ceremnony, the bride does the same. Then the officiant places his hand over those of the bridal couple and announces the marriage. The company joins in praising God and the Holy Trinity, and the clergyman quotes from Matthew 19:6.

Quaker

There are four branches of Friends or Quakers in the United States: the Friends General Conference—Hicksite; the Evangelical Friends Alliance; the Friends United Meeting—organization of the Orthodox branch; and the Conservative Friends—Wilburite, as well as some other nonaffiliated groups. Each group conducts meetings somewhat differently. Contrary to general belief, some branches do have ministers and use the standard Protestant form of marriage rites.

The Friends General Conference and Conservative branch conduct weddings in the classical tradition of Quakers, since each member is looked on as a minister and their signatures are recognized in the United States as legally binding on a marriage certificate.

To be married within the Friends Meeting, petitioners must be known to the Community of Friends. Their union has to be investigated by the Clearness Committee and approved by the whole meeting, for they come under the care of Friends, as the

name denotes, who assume an obligation for that couple throughout their lives, as that couple will for other Friends.

After notification in writing stating their wish to marry has
been received from the engaged couple, a committee is appointed
to meet with them to determine if the young people are ready to
take the step in a spirit of sincerity and dedication. Once they
are assured of the couple's intent, another committee is formed
at the monthly business meeting to ensure that all the requirements are met.

A Friend can marry a non-Friend, and the meeting can be
held at home or in the regular Friends meeting place.

The simplicity of the meeting site matches the simplicity of
the way members come together in silent contemplation until
someone speaks out of the silence; it is free-form witnessing.
When there is a wedding it is incorporated into the events of the
meeting especially called for that purpose.

On the wedding day benches are patterned in the round or
in a square, leaving an aisle for the bridal couple to enter alone
or with their families. Dressed either in a white wedding gown
or in everyday clothes, the bride enters holding the bridegroom's
hand and they seat themselves in assigned places. All is quiet for
a while until the bridal couple stand and "speak out of the silence"
to exchange marriage vows and wedding rings before the company.

The original phrasing of the pledge is still the one most chosen
by marrying couples:

> In the presence of God and these our friends, I take thee,
> _____, to be my wedded wife, promising with Divine assistance
> to be unto thee a loving and faithful husband as long as we
> both shall live.

The bride makes a similar pledge and they then exchange rings.
Some couples, because they wish to carry through their feelings of equality, choose to pledge in unison:

> In the presence of God and these our friends, we take each
> other, promising with Divine assistance to be loving and faithful
> as long as we both shall live.

After making the pledge they sit down. Relatives are often assigned to carry in a table bearing the marriage certificate and place it in front of the newlyweds. They sign their names and the document is read out loud. Worship resumes and those who are so moved say something about the bride and bridegroom. The meeting is over when one person turns to another and shakes hands, then as many as wish to are welcome to sign the marriage certificate.

A celebration with music generally follows. Sometimes the couple will ask friends to bring a potluck dish instead of a gift; others might have a catered reception at home.

Mormon

To be married in a temple of the Church of Jesus Christ of Latter-Day Saints, the betrothed must be members in good standing, which means they have to have met the religious qualifications, to have paid tithes, and to have served within the Church for two years.

Because temple ordinances are not discussed and the teachings are implicative, the written material available to outsiders does not specify what constitutes the actual wedding ceremony or the wording of the exchange of vows. Dressed in white temple clothing, the ceremony takes the form of a sealing ordinance and is held in the "sealing" room, where the bridal couple are joined symbolically for "time and for eternity"—time on earth and after death.

The Mormons view temple marriage as "a covenant that bridges death, transcends time, stretches unbreakable into eternity."

Though the process is private, the bridal couple can choose to invite the relatives and friends closest to them. The "good standing" rule applies to those guests as well. One or both sets of parents may not be qualified to witness the temple marriage (the sealing) of their children, but they can be invited to be part of the festivities afterward.

The Church has no objection to either the bride or the bridegroom's having been married before, provided they are members in good standing. I am told that the divorce rate among those married in the temple is low, though not unheard of. Grounds for such an action are adultery and gross misconduct.

Mormons who are not in good standing can be married in a "civil" ceremony—which is still considered a religious event, despite its name—by bishops of the church in a room in the visitor's center that welcomes all.

Being married outside the temple does not preclude marriage rites within it later on should a couple decide to meet the requirements.

Bishops can marry a Mormon to a non-Mormon.

Seventh-day Adventist

Rarely do Seventh-day Adventists marry on Saturday, since that is their Sabbath. The wedding ceremony itself is viewed as a religious event, so it could be arranged on Saturday as part of the basic worship services. If the reception takes place afterward, however, the event is considered to be a secular one and not acceptable, so most weddings are held on Sunday.

Rites are based on the Protestant wording, but there is no prescribed ceremony as such. The church encourages simple weddings in keeping with the meaning of marriage. The ring is not part of the marriage ceremony of the North American Adventist church; most Adventists outside the United States do wear wedding bands, however. Wearing jewelry, though not forbidden, is rare among Adventists, few of whom owned any in the nineteenth century when the church was formed.

As guests enter the church, they are asked to sign the guest book.

The bride is escorted by her father.

The *Manual for Ministers* gives a choice of several sermonettes, one of which is read by the pastor, after which he asks the couple to clasp right hands, sometimes suggesting all husbands and wives in the congregation do the same. Then he pronounces one of four possible vows given by the *Manual* or those written by the couple themselves. The pastor asks:

Who gives their blessing to this marriage?

Sometimes her parents respond:

We, her parents.

On other occasions, every member of the family, on both sides, stands and says:

We, the families.

There are some pastors who will not take part in an ecumenical ceremony. Others might participate in a limited way, possibly administering a blessing and directing a personal talk to the bridal couple, but the minister for the other religion would perform the actual ceremony.

Roman Catholic

When a couple is to be married in the Catholic Church, banns announcing the forthcoming event are published in the church bulletin three weeks in a row starting one month before the wedding date, viz.: "Jill Candace Ode, of St. Mary's Church, and Frederick Eldon Hampenstance, of St. Joseph's Church . . ." Banns give the community a chance to state an objection should there be one and are the equivalent of the Episcopal "speak now or hold his peace."

Banns hark back to the days before marriages were registered. They were posted at the church door for all to see. It was the duty of those who knew of an impediment to the marriage to speak up for the protection of either marrying party.

A Catholic can be married, with the permission of the Catholic church, to a non-Catholic in the church of another denomination. The Catholic Archdiocese of the area in which the Catholic lives must be petitioned by application for Matrimonial Dispensation. When this is granted, the Catholic priest will be allowed to participate in an ecumenical ceremony, if desired. With the knowledge of the non-Catholic partner, the Catholic partner must promise the priest, either verbally or in writing, to bring up their children as Catholics. The marrying Catholic has then met form and consent: "form" means that the priest has been involved and may have also witnessed or concelebrated the marriage; "consent" means that the marriage was not entered out of fear, coercion, or immaturity. Reasons for improper consent would be, for example, marrying when severely emotionally unstable or telling a priest that no children were desired from the marriage.

A traditional Catholic marriage ceremony requires the bride's home church, a priest, and the sacrament. It is advisable to start planning early, especially during those months that are popular times for weddings.

Marriage rites generally take place in the bride's parish, and if for any reason the groom's parish or one away from both hometowns is preferred, special permission has to be obtained.

The Catholic couple are interviewed by the priest, who instructs them on proper procedure and also counsels them during several meetings on the importance of being married in the Church and of the meaning of the foundation of marriage. They are also required to attend the Catholic Engaged Encounter—a weekend designed to help betrothed couples recognize the seriousness of the steps they are taking (which the church prefers), *or* Pre-Cana—an afternoon session among engaged couples and sponsors who lead a discussion on marriage. Most couples choose the Pre-Cana, since it takes less time. (John 2:1–11 tells of the Marriage Feast of Cana: the first sign given by Jesus—the first miracle—was at a wedding where there was no wine. Jesus told the servants to fill the jars with water and the water turned to wine.)

The priest's guidance on the ceremony itself is of the utmost importance, since each church has its own guidelines within the bounds of the Rite of Marriage. The bride and the bridegroom can express their preferences among a list of approved prayers and blessings that can be used during the ceremony. Though it is rare, couples can compose their own vows for the Prayer of the Faithful. According to Father Hughes at St. Mary's Catholic Church in Rockville, Maryland, most couples prefer not to do so.

Because the conduct of the ceremony may differ from one church to another, the priest will advise where attendants will stand during the marriage rites, and on the suitability of musical selections, the taking of photographs, and floral arrangements. (Costs for floral decorations can be shared by couples being married in the church during the same weekend.) Some priests, when marrying a Catholic and a non-Catholic, do not require the couple to kneel for the Blessing of the Rings and the Exchange of Rings.

The Mass is the center of the Catholic Church and the Sacrament of Marriage can take place within the Mass; the combination of both together is known as the Nuptial Mass. The ceremony, performed only between two Catholics, takes about fifty minutes. It can be held anytime during the day, with the Mass or not, except during the times for confession. Weddings sometimes take place on Saturday evening.

A marriage between a Catholic and a non-Catholic can be held in the church. However, the Mass is not performed during the traditional marriage rites.

The priest and the bridegroom walk from the sacristy to the altar, and the bride comes down the aisle escorted by her father. The couple meet within the sanctuary or before it and join hands; they are coming together, from their single state, in a blessed union to form their lives together in the Church.

Attendants follow the bride; the maid or matron of honor stands to the left of and slightly behind the bride, and opposite the best man. Other bridesmaids stand behind and to the left of the bride, opposite the ushers. The celebrant stands at the center of the altar, with the bridegroom to his left; the best man and the ushers stand to the left of the bridegroom.

When the father has escorted his daughter, he genuflects and sits next to his wife in the first pew.

First the priest offers prayers in which the bridal pair's names are mentioned, followed by readings from Scripture. If the ceremony is a Mass, one of the readings must be from the Gospels, while the others can be from the Old or the New Testament. The first two readings are given by close family members. After a five-minute sermon there is the exchange of vows.

In a Catholic ceremony the sacrament of matrimony consists of the couple's exchange of vows. The priest acts as a witness who asks questions of them separately on their freedom of choice and feelings and conduct in the future:

> Since it is your intention to enter into marriage, join your right hands, and declare your consent before God and his Church.

The exchange of vows may vary slightly but below are two of the traditional versions:

I, Frederick, take you, Jill, to be my wife. I promise to be true to you in good times and in bad, in sickness and in health. I will love you and honor you all the days of my life.

or

I, Jill, take you, Frederick, for my lawful husband, to have and to hold from this day forward, for better, for worse, for richer, for poorer, in sickness and in health, until death do us part.

The celebrant blesses their pronouncements and declares:

You have declared your consent before the Church. May the Lord in his goodness strengthen your consent and fill you both with his blessings.
What God has joined, men must not divide.

The couple face each other and kneel for the Blessing of the Rings and the Exchange of Rings. The best man hands the ring to the acolyte to be blessed by the priest and given to the bridegroom. The bridegroom takes the ring and places it on the bride's left ring finger, saying:

Jill, take this ring as a sign of my love and fidelity, in the name of the Father, the Son and the Holy Spirit.

The bride does the same. The priest performs the Blessing and the Sign of the Cross.
Then comes the Prayer of the Faithful, followed by the Receiving of the Eucharist, which can include an offertory procession with family and friends.
A Nuptial Blessing is said after the "Our Father," with the Sign of Peace and Communion optional.
After a final blessing the recessional takes place.

CIVIL CEREMONY AND ELOPEMENT

Sometimes a couple marry in a civil ceremony. Later they may decide or perhaps are encouraged by their families to receive the Sacrament of Marriage. Many parents do not really feel their children are married until a Catholic priest or deacon has performed the rites according to the Church's teachings.

Eastern Orthodox

The Orthodox Church does not allow any changes in the Sacrament of Marriage. Some churches have an organ and a chanter to accompany the ritual music, prayers, and hymns. At the discretion of the priest, secular classical music may be played as guests arrive at the church and for both the processional and the recessional.

A license to marry must be obtained from the Church itself as well as the usual license from the state.

Orthodox churches outside the United States do not have pews; everyone stands. Led by the priest, the bridal party and immediate family form a circle around a portable altar or table where the ceremony takes place. Their guests encircle them in widening rings.

In the United States, rows of benches or seats face the altar, so the processional is fairly similar to any other Christian denomination's. The best man leads the bridegroom to the portable altar, where he awaits his bride. After the traditional stream of attendants, the bride is escorted by her father, to be presented to the bridegroom. The father then joins his wife.

Nuptial rites in the Eastern Orthodox Church are dramatic. The first part is known as the Betrothal Service. Lighted candles are held by the bride and bridegroom as the priest invokes the four blessings, asking salvation for the betrothed; perfect and peaceful love; an honorable marriage and undefiled fellowship; deliverance from affliction, wrath, danger, and want.

The ceremony continues with the blessing, in which references to the Old and New Testaments are made, and the rings are exchanged with the aid of the "koumbari," or sponsor. The bridegroom's ring symbolizes the sun and the bride's ring the moon.

The sponsor must be a member of the Church in good standing, and by assuming the role takes a silent pledge to give moral support to the bridal couple throughout their married lives.

The ceremony can be conducted in both English and the

native tongue of the church of origin, which could be Greece, Russia, Rumania, or Bulgaria.

As the priest blesses the rings and betrothes the bride and bridegroom to each other, he touches first the bridegroom's forehead and then the bride's with the bridegroom's wedding band, and reverses the process using the bride's wedding band. Because the right hand is the symbolic one in the Orthodox Church, he places the rings on the third fingers of their right hands. The koumbari switches the rings, first placing the bridegroom's ring on the bride's finger and the bride's ring on the bridegroom's finger, then returning them. The exchange of rings completes the bond of betrothal. It is customary for the bride to continue to wear her wedding ring on the third finger of her right hand.

The Sacrament of Marriage begins with the invocation, then the Prayers, Blessings, and Exchange of Crowns, in which the priest crowns the bride and the bridegroom. The crowns are made of white beads and joined in the back by a white ribbon, symbolizing the kingdom that is the couple's marriage. Next, the couple drink wine from the Common Cup, which symbolizes both the cup of life and Holy Communion—since Holy Communion is not taken in Orthodox weddings. Then, while hymns are being sung, the priest leads the bridal couple—their right hands tied together—the sponsor, the best man, and the maid or matron of honor three times around the portable altar, leading them back to their original places, where he removes the crowns.

The ceremony ends with the invocation of the Holy Trinity.

The bridal couple can choose as many attendants as they wish, including a flower girl and ring and crown bearers.

Weddings can take place any day of the week. The periods in which weddings cannot be performed are from December 13 through Christmas Day; Epiphany Day and the day before it; August 1 through 15 (Fast of the Holy Theotokos); during Great Lent, Holy Week, and Easter Sunday; and on Pentecost and major feast days.

MIXED MARRIAGES

The Orthodox Church views the marriage of its members outside the Church very seriously. If the Sacrament of Marriage is not performed in the Church, the Orthodox Christian excommunicates himself or herself. Grace can be restored if the Sacrament of Marriage takes place later.

The marriage of an Eastern Orthodox Christian to a baptized non-Orthodox Christian is considered "mixed." It cannot take place in the Orthodox Church if that person has not been baptized within the Church. Nor would a baptized Christian be recognized in the Orthodox Church unless he or she had been instructed.

The Orthodox Church, headed by its own Archbishop and separate from the Roman Catholic Church, recognizes only divorces or annulments obtained under its auspices.

Jewish

There are three disciplines in the practice of Judaism in America: Orthodox, Reform, and Conservative. The first follows the most traditional path, the second is most influenced by Western society, and the third is a bridge between the other two. There are cultural differences within the Jewish tradition as well as varying degrees of Orthodoxy. The wedding traditions of the Sephardic Jews are similar to but not the same as those of the Ashkenazim. Some marriage customs are based on four thousand years of Jewish history combined with customs of the country the family live in.

On either the Sabbath, the Monday, or the Thursday before the wedding, the bridegroom goes to synagogue for the "Aufruf," a prewedding honor at which he reads the Torah. In many congregations the future bride can take part in the Aufruf by accompanying her fiancé to the bimah (the altar).

In an Orthodox synagogue, men and women sit in separate sections and women wear long sleeves. Both Orthodox and Conservative synagogues require women to cover their heads and men to wear skull caps (yarmulkes) or hats. Men and women sit together in some Conservative synagogues and in all Reform temples. Head coverings are not usually worn in the Reform temple. All guests should follow whichever dress code applies.

The bride's family sits on the right of the aisle and the bridegroom's family on the left, but many Jewish weddings leave the other guests to sit where they please.

The superstition against the bride being seen in her wedding gown by the bridegroom does not seem to be part of Jewish folklore. In fact, the Veiling of the Bride (badeken) takes place in Orthodox and some Conservative ceremonies in an anteroom before the public service, with only the bridegroom and close family members present. The bride is veiled, following the Biblical custom of Rebekah, and the bridegroom lowers the bride's veil after he has seen that she really is his beloved—unlike Jacob, who worked seven years so he could marry Rachel only to discover the next morning that the heavily veiled bride was her older sister, Leah.

The bride sometimes receives guests in an anteroom before the ceremony, but she may prefer not to have the badeken and wait in seclusion until her husband-to-be sees her for the first time as a bride.

There is no set rule for the processional and there are many variations, depending on what the rabbi advises, the size of the wedding party, the possible complication of divorced parents, and the preferences of the couple.

Processional music and the appearance of the rabbi signal the start of the proceedings.

The rabbi and the cantor might come from the side entrance or walk to the bimah, which is the raised platform before the Ark; but if the wedding is not held in a synagogue, they walk to an estrade where the ceremony will be performed under the traditional marriage canopy (huppah). In front of or behind the rabbi is a wedding table covered with a cloth on which are set glasses for the ritual wine, the wrapped glass for breaking, and the ketubah (the marriage contract).

The canopy can be made of a square of satin or velvet and finished with a fringe or covered with flowers and leaves. Its four corners are attached to poles fitted into supports on the floor, or four men (preferably of the same height) can be given the honor of holding them.

The bride's grandparents, followed by the bridegroom's, are the next to walk and seat themselves in the first row. Some families are fortunate enough to have great-grandparents or great-aunts and uncles and wish them to be honored in this way. Single grandmothers should be escorted by a male member of their family but the single grandfather may choose to walk alone if he wishes.

If there are several ushers they should be in pairs; if only a few, they may walk singly and stand along the right and left of the aisle.

The best man follows and waits for the bridegroom at the left of the marriage canopy.

The bridegroom walks with his mother on his right and his father on his left and awaits the bride on the rabbi's right. His parents stand nearby or under the huppah.

Walking in pairs, or singly, the bridesmaids stand on either side of the aisle.

The maid or matron of honor follows and stands under the canopy, on the right side, to await the arrival of the bride.

The flower girl precedes the ring bearer and both sit with their parents after they have performed their parts.

There is no moment quite like the first step the bride takes toward her waiting bridegroom. The entire company turns to watch her progress. Dressed in white, with her face covered by a bridal veil, she holds the bouquet in her right hand. Her father offers his right arm and her mother walks next to her on the opposite side. At the huppah she takes her place on her bridegroom's right while her parents stand to the right of the honor attendant(s).

In some Orthodox ceremonies the fathers escort the bridegroom and stand together near him under the canopy; the mothers accompany the bride and stand with her.

Some Conservatives follow the American custom for the procession. The bridegroom comes from the side with his best man and the bride is escorted by her father to the estrade. As the bridegroom steps from the canopy he offers his hand and waits for the bride's father to place her hand in his. The father then seats himself next to his wife.

According to the Old Testament Tuesday is a "good omen" day to take an important step in one's life, but a wedding can take place any day of the week except Saturday or during a religious observance.

Be sure to check with a rabbi about the dates when marriage is prohibited. There are certain days when neither Orthodox nor

Conservative rabbis will perform a marriage ceremony; the longest period, which lasts forty-nine days except for one or two days within that span, is from Passover to the Feast of Weeks (Shavuot).

Recently, an Orthodox family who were planning their daughter's wedding more than a year ahead were told after arranging the entire wedding—signing contracts for service and placing deposits—that there had been a mistake in calculating the date. It was the rabbi who discovered that the chosen date fell within the forty-nine prohibited days. Luckily the wedding was scheduled far enough in advance for those under contract to accommodate the family when a new wedding date was decided upon. But what would have happened if the invitations had been engraved and mailed and all the services and deposits had been tied up?

Most Jewish weddings take place Saturday evening or Sunday afternoon or evening. Because the Sabbath begins at sundown on Friday evening and ends at sundown on Saturday, a Saturday-evening wedding in the summertime starts quite late.

Neither Orthodox, Conservative, nor Reform rabbis will marry a Jew to a non-Jew. At this writing, it is possible to find a rabbi who will participate in an interfaith ceremony, but most rabbis refuse.

Although divorce is accepted by all disciplines, all Orthodox and most Conservative rabbis will not marry anyone who has not obtained a Jewish divorce, called a "get." A man who is of the priestly tribe known as Kohane cannot marry a divorced woman or someone of another religion without losing the special honors reserved for a descendant of Aaron, brother of Moses.

Reform rabbis recognize a civil divorce decree and do not insist on a "get" (Jewish divorce).

Should a couple wish to have a religious ceremony after being married in a civil one, a rabbi will gladly perform the rites. There are two parts to the ceremony: legal and religious. Since the legal part has been fulfilled by the civil authorities, only the religious side is performed, including the signing of the ketubah, the giving of the ring, and the seven blessings.

At least ten men (the minyan) must be present at the ceremony.

The Orthodox and more stringent Conservative bridal couple

fast on the day of the wedding. One source says it is in remembrance of the destruction of the temple of Solomon in Jerusalem by the Babylonians and then again when the Romans tore down the walls of the temple in 70 A.D.; others think it a symbolic act of purification—the bride and bridegroom come to each other free of the past. There are those who view the day a man and woman marry as so important that they compare it with the Day of Atonement (Yom Kippur), the holiest day of the year. After the wedding ceremony, while the company gathers at the reception, the couple are left alone in a small anteroom for a short time to eat a light repast.

The breaking of the glass by the bridegroom is also thought to commemorate the fall of the temple; some say it is done as a reminder to the couple that even at this happiest of times there will be sad moments in their lives.

Some Orthodox couples do not see each other from one to seven days before the wedding ceremony, depending on custom. When the Orthodox bride reaches the huppah she might walk from one to seven times around the bridegroom, according to local custom. Sometimes she is accompanied by her mother and the bridegroom's mother.

The ceremony is traditionally conducted in Hebrew, the language of the Bible. Many rabbis chant the prayers in Hebrew and read them in English. The exchange of vows is optional and is included in some Conservative services.

The ceremony has two parts: the betrothal and the marriage ceremony. The betrothal includes the signing of the Jewish marriage contract (the ketubah), which takes place before the ceremony in a private room and is attended by the rabbi, the bridegroom, sometimes the bride, both sets of parents, and two men not related to the family. The men also serve as witnesses to the public marriage ceremony in which the bride is given the wedding ring.

The reading of the marriage contract is included in Orthodox and Conservative wedding ceremonies and the bridegroom presents the contract to the bride during the ceremony.

The ketubah is written in Aramaic, the ancient language of commerce. Though today the wedding ceremony is a religious one, in the Jewish tradition marriage is considered a civil arrangement between two families, not a sacrament. Since, in ancient times, divorce was easily obtained by husbands and death was no stranger, the woman was often left unprotected. The governing bodies drew up a marriage contract guaranteeing that if the marriage ended, the woman's dowry and property she brought with her to the marriage would be returned to her.

To return to the ceremony: the first invocation is given, followed by a prayer over the first cup of wine from which both the bride and bridegroom drink.

The best man hands the wedding ring to the rabbi, who gives it to the bridegroom and asks him to recite:

Thou art consecrated unto me with this ring as my wife, according to the law of Moses and of Israel.

The ring, which should be of plain unadorned metal and purchased by the bridegroom, is put on the forefinger of the bride's right hand. Later, if she wishes, she can remove it and place it on the third finger of her left hand.

Ultra Orthodox Jews do not have a double-ring ceremony, since the plain gold ring symbolizes the ancient tradition of giving something of value to the bride.

The rabbi reads the ketubah in Aramaic and in English.

Holding the second cup of wine, the rabbi offers the Seven Benedictions:

Blessed art Thou, O Lord our God, King of the universe, who createst the fruit of the vine, symbol of joy.

Blessed art Thou, O Lord our God, King of the universe, who has created all things to Thy glory.

Blessed art Thou, O Lord our God, King of the universe, Creator of man.

Blessed art Thou, O Lord our God, King of the universe, who has made man in Thine image after Thy likeness, and has fashioned woman from man as his mate, that together they may perpetuate life.

Blessed art Thou, O Lord, Creator of man.

May Zion rejoice as her children are restored to her in joy.

Blessed art Thou, O Lord our God, King of the universe, who has created joy and gladness, bridegroom and bride, mirth and exultation, pleasure and delight, love, brotherhood, peace and fellowship. Soon may there be heard in the cities of Judah, and in the streets of Jerusalem, the voice of joy and gladness, the voice of the bridegroom and the voice of the bride, the jubilant voices of those joined in marriage under the bridal canopy, and of youths feasting and singing. Blessed art Thou, O Lord, who makest the bridegroom rejoice with the bride.

The bridal couple then drink from the wine goblet.

The ceremony is concluded when the rabbi hands the glass to the best man, who places it on the floor so that the bridegroom can crush it with his right foot, hoping it will shatter the first time. The congregation responds with "Mazel tov," which means "Good luck" or "Congratulations."

Though there is no set point in the ceremony for the rabbi to express some personal words to the bridal couple on their role as husband and wife and their relationship to the outer world, they are usually forthcoming just before or just after the Seven Blessings and before the breaking of the glass.

The bride and bridegroom walk up the aisle followed by her parents, then his parents, the maid of honor and best man, and then pairs of maids and ushers. Grandparents should be worked into the recession, possibly assigning two ushers to see that they follow the wedding party before guests start exiting. The ushers tactfully hold guests in place while the first row empties, then the second, and so on—row by row in orderly process.

Rabbis, while following the guidelines their discipline sets, have their own preferences about the manner in which they conduct the ceremony. Rabbi Tzvi H. Porath of Chevy Chase, Maryland, Rabbi Emeritus of Ohr Kodesh Congregation, Conservative, uses the phrase "according to the law of Moses and the traditions of our people" during the ceremony instead of "the law of Moses and of Israel." He makes the distinction because to many people "Israel" means the existing country of Israel, although the actual meaning of this word in the prayer refers to Jewish traditions going back centuries, traditions that are followed by Jews all over the world as well as those in the state of Israel.

The marriage contract below follows the traditional wording:

Be thou my wife according to the law of Moses and of Israel. I faithfully promise that I will be a true husband unto thee. I will honor and cherish thee; I will work for thee; I will protect and support thee, and will provide all that is necessary for thy due sustenance, even as it becomes a Jewish husband to do. I also take upon myself all such further obligations for thy maintenance as are prescribed by our religious statute.

And the said Bride has plighted her troth unto him, in affection and sincerity and has thus taken upon herself the fulfillment of all the duties incumbent upon a Jewish wife.

The language can be slightly rephrased so that both man and woman "work for, protect, and support each other . . ."

There also might be included in the marriage contract a mention of the dissolution of the marriage. This can seem very strange but it has its practical aspects, since under Orthodox Jewish law only the man can petition for a divorce. If an Orthodox Jewish woman wants a religious divorce—and indeed has been divorced according to civil law—but her ex-husband refuses to give her a Jewish divorce, she will not be able to remarry in a Jewish ceremony.

Today some Conservative couples, in order to avoid strife, include wording in the marriage contract that permits either the man or the woman to ask the Beth Din (the Jewish court) for a divorce. This has been approved by the Rabbinical Assembly and the Jewish Theological Seminary of America. Couples can, of course, seek other avenues rather than including provision for divorce in a marriage contract. For some this approach resembles the drawing up of a premarital contract—it is discouraging and rather unromantic.

REFORM

The more liberal Reform Jewish ceremony follows the American tradition, though the rites take place under the canopy. The rabbi comes from the side, followed by the bridegroom walking with the best man, or they may all walk down the aisle together. The bridegroom receives his bride from her father at the foot of the canopy.

The service is mainly in English, though the rabbi generally chants the prayers in Hebrew and then says them in English.

The rabbi starts the ceremony with the blessings and delivers an address to the couple. Then he says:

Do you, ———, take ——— to be your wife, promising to cherish and protect her, whether in good fortune or in adversity, and to seek together with her a life hallowed by the faith of Israel?

The same is asked of the bride.

After the benedictions, wine is offered to the bridegroom and to the bride.

The exchange of rings follows as the rabbi instructs the bridegroom and then the bride:

As you, ———, place this ring upon the finger of your bride (bridegroom), speak to her (him) these words:

With this ring be thou consecrated unto me as my wife (husband) according to the law of God and the faith of Israel.

The Reform wording of this prayer uses the phrase "according to the law of God and of Israel." The Reform philosophy interprets "of Moses" as too confining for present-day living. To quote Rabbi Joshua Haberman of the Washington Hebrew Congregation in Washington, D.C., a Reform temple: "We recognize the law of Moses as a valid foundation but we do not live in the structure that has been erected upon it and therefore we claim the right to interpret."

After declaring the couple husband and wife, the rabbi asks for a silent prayer and then raises his hands in blessing:

May the Lord bless thee and keep thee. May the Lord cause His countenance to shine upon thee and be gracious unto thee. May the Lord lift up His countenance unto thee and give thee peace. Amen.

Then follows the traditional breaking of the glass.

Military Wedding

There is no difference between a military and civilian wedding ceremony; Christians are married by a chaplain of their own-denomination and Jews by a Jewish chaplain. Chaplains of all faiths follow the rules, customs, and rituals of their particular religious orders.

Those in the military, like civilians, have to make arrangements for a house of worship, decide whether to have a formal or informal wedding, what type of reception to have, and how many and whom to invite.

It is essential, as in civilian life, that as soon as the engagement takes place there is a meeting with the chaplain, who will ask the same questions as a civilian clergyman would; i.e., whether either has been married before, whether both are of the same denomination and, if applicable, whether both have baptismal papers. The chaplain will not only meet with the betrothed for counseling but will also advise on the steps and requirements necessary for the preparation of a military wedding, such as medical tests, a marriage license, and the signing of the Marriage Register.

Also as in civilian life, the chaplain sets the style of both the ceremony and processional. Any changes have to be approved by him.

If the couple want to be married on base in the chapel then written application has to be made through the chaplain's office. Planning a year ahead is not unusual.

Because June is a popular month for marriages at educational military sites, reservations for the chapel are allotted on a first-come basis. Many wedding ceremonies can be held on a single day, the time of day being determined by the luck of the draw.

Permission to invite one's hometown clergyman to assist in the wedding rites has to be obtained from the chaplain.

The chaplain is paid by the military and will not accept a fee for officiating, but the visiting clergyman should be offered an honorarium. If the organist is also a member of the armed forces there is no fee involved. However, a musician hired from outside would obviously have to be paid.

A donation toward the upkeep of the chapel is advisable. The suggested donation, at the time of writing, is forty dollars for a chapel in an academy. It is drafted to the chapel fund and used for decorations in the chapel and expenses toward the marriage ceremony. Since, at busy times, one wedding ceremony follows another, it is not possible to have one's own preferences in floral arrangements, and the music is chosen from a prepared list.

The base chapel may not supply decorations at all, so the couple may have to make their own arrangements.

A betrothed couple in the armed forces, like anyone else, have to arrive at a date that suits them both. The date depends on where each is stationed and whether they can coordinate leave, and both sides have to consider out-of-town family.

The couple must notify the branch of service in which they serve of their impending change of status. A servicewoman has the choice of keeping her own name or of assuming her husband's.

The marriage ceremony is essentially the same, with two differences. One is the dress code: the bride has the option of wearing a wedding dress or being married in uniform; the bridegroom wears the type of uniform suitable to the formality of the wedding. The other difference is the impressive Arch of Swords or Sabers ceremony.

The Arch of Swords is formed by an honor guard. It can be held indoors, with the permission of the chaplain, or out. The Army and Air Force conduct the Saber ceremony in the same manner; the Navy has its own Sword tradition, but the components are similar and the meaning the same.

In a military wedding, an outdoor Arch of Swords ceremony takes place at the completion of the nuptial ceremony and is part of the recessional. The bride and bridegroom go into an anteroom to wait for the best man to announce that the officers have formed the arch.

In the meantime, the attendants line up on either side of the chapel's main doors. Guests are asked to leave the chapel and place themselves on the steps and beyond to view the impressive display. Six to eight officers, who may also have served as ushers, dressed in appropriate uniforms, line up facing one another, swords in scabbards. Upon the command of the senior officer they draw swords in unison and raise them so the tips of the swords touch. The bride and bridegroom pass under the arch by themselves as the honored couple. As they reach the end of the arch, they stand for a moment while the head usher issues the command to sheath swords. Applauded by the company, the couple rush happily to a waiting limousine to be taken to the reception.

The indoor Arch of Swords ceremony takes place just after the last blessing. The main difference is that the ushers line up along both sides of the aisle facing one another. When the bridal couple have passed through, the sabers are returned to scabbards and only then do members of the bridal party continue with the recessional.

Double Wedding

Double weddings do not seem popular. Few of the announcements I have received from families whose daughters are engaged to be married indicate a double wedding, though the parents may want to have a joint engagement announcement in the paper. One bride will be marrying in May from her parents' home and the other chooses to exchange nuptial vows in June in the town in which she now resides. It is double the expense within a short period of time for everyone involved.

There are many reasons for this. The main one is that the bride and bridegroom wish to have a special day all their own. They do not want the complications and compromises that four people's involvement entails.

But for those who do choose a double wedding, the older of the brides is first in all phases of the proceedings, both for the ceremony and the reception. Her younger sister might not like to be in a "secondary" position, though it is a tradition going back to biblical times. In those days—and in some countries not so long ago—it was a cardinal rule that the younger sister could not marry until the older one had found a husband.

If the order of the proceedings is the only obstacle, bridal couples could take turns; the older bride would be first during the wedding ceremony and the younger one could be first at the reception. Or the elder could walk down the aisle first, and the younger would be the first to walk during the recessional, and so on. But be careful. This can be complicated. You need time to rehearse and someone, such as a competent bridal coordinator, is needed to serve as a guide and moderator.

When two brides are close—twins, cousins, or friends—a double wedding may be what they have dreamed about. Their families get along famously and all sides find it fun to plan. Expenses are shared, which reduces the cost for each family.

There is no reason brides should not have different style dresses but they should be of the same length and formality. Attendants are dressed in varying hues blending with the color scheme. The bridegrooms, as with single weddings, dress according to the formality of the wedding and the time of day. The mothers of the brides and bridegrooms wear the same length but in slightly different shades.

It is best to have the same number of attendants. Sometimes one bride is the honor attendant for the other.

Bridegrooms can each serve as best man for the other.

Double-wedding decisions must be carefully weighed by all sides and the expenses equally divided. I would think that these are the most sensitive aspects of the arrangements. For instance, if one bridegroom offered to pay for an item or two but the other did not . . .

If you are contemplating a double wedding, consider the people involved, their tastes, style, and nature.

Civil Ceremony

Marrying in a civil ceremony answers a need for those who, for various reasons, cannot or do not wish to go through a religious ceremony. Often a civil ceremony seems less complicated.

Having obtained a marriage license, off to the courthouse the couple go, just the two of them, accompanied by two witnesses, or more if they wish. They stand before the officiant to exchange vows and are pronounced husband and wife. It is a private, quiet event involving few people. Some couples have a big bash afterward, inviting relatives, friends, and business associates. Others keep the reception low-keyed by limiting the celebration to a wedding cake and champagne or a luncheon for those who witnessed the ceremony.

Policies differ from state to state on who is allowed to perform civil marriage ceremonies. In some areas only the Clerk of the Court can do so; in others judges, magistrates, and public officials can officiate. A telephone call to a county's Marriage Bureau Service will determine that jurisdiction's policy.

I am told that some couples, after contemplating marriage for a while, suddenly decide that Friday the thirteenth is just the right time to marry—perhaps it comes before a long weekend. So on Tuesday he or she applies for a marriage license and Friday they appear at the registrar's office, ready for nuptial exchanges and a three-day honeymoon.

Other couples have more involved reasons. Family interference might make it easier for the lovers just to come home after marrying and announce the fait accompli.

Couples with different religious backgrounds who cannot meet the requirements within their denominations solve the problem by skirting the issue.

Having a civil ceremony does not preclude a religious ceremony of some sort. If the couple decides to be married later according to their religious affiliations, they can ask a clergyman for advice on the course to be taken.

In this event, Protestants have what they call a "Blessing of the Marriage Service," without the exchange of rings or the bride being given away. The phrasing is similar to the formal marriage ceremony except that words such as "accept" are changed to "acknowledge."

Adherents of the Catholic and Eastern Orthodox churches can have a full ceremony because a civil ceremony is not recognized by those churches.

Civil ceremonies are recognized in Jewish law.

In the United States, to have a civil ceremony is to be married within the laws of the country, so all legalities have been met by the marrying couple. A religious wedding is also binding in the eyes of the law, since the clergy are licensed by the state to perform marriages.

In some other countries, such as France, the only recognized married state is that of a civil ceremony. Most couples, after the civil exchange of vows, go right to the church and repeat the process according to its dictates. In England, most marriages take place within the Church of England.

If you are planning to marry overseas, check beforehand on the laws of the country. Most countries have a longer waiting period than in the United States and some have residence requirements.

WORDING OF CIVIL CEREMONY
STATE OF MARYLAND

We are gathered here in the presence of these witnesses to join
this man and this woman together in matrimony. The contract is a most solemn one and not to be entered into lightly,
but thoughtfully and seriously and with a deep realization
of its obligations and responsibilities. If anyone can show
just cause why they should not be lawfully joined together
let him speak now, or else forever hold his peace.

_____, will you take _____, here present, for your lawful wife?
Answer: I will.
_____, will you take _____, here present, for your lawful hus-
band?
Answer: I will.
Bride and Groom will join right hands.
Groom:
   Repeat after me . . . I, _____, take you, _____, for my lawful
   wife, to have and to hold, from this day forward, for better,
   for worse, for richer, for poorer, in sickness and in health,
   until death do us part.
Bride:
   Repeat after me . . . I, _____, take you, _____, for my lawful
   husband, to have and to hold, from this day forward, for
   better, for worse, for richer, for poorer, in sickness and in
   health, until death do us part.
To be repeated by Groom as ring is placed on Bride's finger.
With this ring, I thee wed.
To be repeated by Bride as ring is placed on Groom's finger.
With this ring, I thee wed.

By the power and authority vested by law in me as Clerk of
the Circuit Court for Montgomery County, Maryland, I now
pronounce you husband and wife.

On the back of the Civil Marriage Ceremony pamphlet is:

Groom _____
Bride _____
Were married this _____ day of _____
in the year of _____

By: _____

Witness: _____

Witness: _____

ELOPEMENT

A marriage in secret, in either a civil or a religious ceremony, is considered an elopement. It is a legally binding union.

Questions on elopement center on what happens after the couple and family no longer want to keep the marriage a secret. If the newlyweds were married in a civil ceremony or by a clergyman they still may want to have another service conducted by their own religious leader and with their families present.

Other areas of confusion concern whether announcements should be mailed after the wedding and, if so, how much time can be allowed to elapse after the event before the announcements are sent.

Mailed printed announcements sent to relatives, friends, and acquaintances along with newspaper notices are an appropriate and efficient way of spreading the news. As for the time span, a woman is technically a bride for one whole year after her wedding day, so announcements could be mailed within that time frame. Of course, the sooner they are sent the better. Notification would have to be sent to newspapers immediately after the elopement.

The perennial question is, should we have a reception? I say, why not? At one time a no-reception-and-no-presents-if-we-can-help-it attitude permeated the air around the elopers. Nowadays, parents may or may not like the idea, but they are more accepting of their children's choices. Whose life is it, anyway?

The next inevitable query from those receiving announcements is whether they should send a present. Again, wedding announcements attach no obligation. Your relationship to the couple and their families is the determining factor.

HOST HOUSES OF WORSHIP

There are churches that accept those not directly connected with their institution to be married under their auspices: the

Ethical Culture society and the Unitarian Church, for instance. A telephone call will supply the information needed to arrange an appointment. The officiants will want to meet with the betrothed and go through counseling sessions as if they were members of the congregation.

Among the states where couples can be married on the basis of little more than their physical presence is Nevada. The couple can apply at the Marriage License Bureau and be issued a certificate within half an hour. They can reserve a private marriage chapel beforehand. The officiating minister, who is accommodating, and the couple meet to arrange the type of wording for the ceremony, be it secular or religious. If only the couple appears they use a small chapel, but there are chapels for larger wedding parties and guests. A florist and photographer are available so the couple can have flowers and a picture record of the event. Three weeks later the newlyweds receive the license in the mail.

Intermarriage

"Tradition, tradition," sang the father in *Fiddler on the Roof*. But today's children are setting the stage for their own songs. Parents are having to look for clergy of different faiths who will co-officiate the exchange of marriage vows. The clergy are performing rites together, with each trying to retain the essence and beauty of their respective religions.

If ever we need to be sensitive to and understanding of one another it is the day our child introduces a person of another denomination or faith and says: "We are going to marry." This goes for the young couple as well as for their respective parents, who need an understanding of the other side's beliefs and of their future in-laws' convictions.

It is important to define the meaning of the words *ecumenical* and *interfaith*. *Ecumenical* concerns the mingling of Christian churches of different denominations. *Interfaith* is a coming-to-gether of people of *different* faiths.

Suppose the bridegroom's side of the family cares little about religious rites and the bride's family are deep believers. Arrangements with her family's clergyman and place of worship should be virtually free of strain. But when both are strongly tied to their faiths much careful discussion and planning is necessary. Each side should have some knowledge of the religious marriage customs of the other.

I would like to share a letter from a thoughtful mother whose daughter married a Jew. Mrs. B. admitted that the arrangements seemed difficult in the beginning. She did not know much about Jewish customs and was confused by the varying degrees of orthodoxy in that faith.

The first decision discussed was the site for the ceremony. They chose a place where both the ceremony and the reception could be held. After that had been decided the matter of the day suddenly became important. It never occurred to Mrs. B. that Saturday daytime would not be suitable until the bridegroom's mother informed her as tactfully as she could that Friday after sundown to Saturday sundown was the Sabbath. All agreed on a Sunday wedding. The rehearsal dinner, hosted by his parents, was to take place Saturday evening.

The invitations read ". . . the honour of your presence is requested . . ." because Mrs. B. felt her daughter's wedding would be as religious as any other and deserved that solemn wording. She insisted, and rightly, that there can be "a dignified wedding with all the rules of formality in a place other than a church."

The processional was another first for Mrs. B. It is traditional for Orthodox and some Conservative Jewish parents to escort their sons and daughters to the altar. Their future son-in-law's parents were Conservative or Reform and did not choose to do that. But, as Mrs. B. said, his family should be consulted.

We discussed at length the symbol of candles for the ceremony. Mrs. B. thought that the Gothic-shaped wedding candelabra were not suitable for an interfaith ceremony, so she used hurricane lamps and other candlesticks. Secular music was carefully chosen and played by a string quartet.

One of the most sensitive areas of the reception was the food. Mrs. B. discussed the menu with her daughter's future mother-in-law. Even though they were Reform Jews and did not keep to a strict kosher diet, his family might have felt uneasy about being served pork or shellfish. The bill of fare included both fish and meat so that a choice could be made. If the bride's in-laws had been Orthodox Jews, of course, they would not have been able to eat anything not prepared by an authorized kosher caterer.

The meal was served after the traditional blessing over the bread. The blessing, offered by the bridegroom's uncle, is generally performed by a rabbi, or it is an honor bestowed on a venerable member of the family.

With the help of a school friend, who was to perform the ceremony, and of a rabbi, a relative of the bridegroom, the bride and her fiancé wrote their own vows in which they included elements of their respective religions.

Mrs. B's letter to me has been a source of pleasure. She showed a wealth of understanding, sensitivity, and caring when she planned that interfaith wedding. Some people find it hard to handle their feelings of emptiness when children marry out of their religion.

Q: *My fiancé, an atheist, objects to being involved in a religious ceremony and feels that vows said in this fashion are without worth. I feel that unless I am married by a man of the cloth the vows are not binding. We are very unhappy and do not know what to do.*

The obvious compromise would be that you have both a civil ceremony and a religious one. Another is to elicit the help of a clergyman in writing your own vows, incorporating what each of you considers important. Your love for each other will have to find a way.

Your differences, however, are serious. If one of you compromises totally now, it could spell trouble later in your marriage. The best chance a union has of succeeding is when two people share the same philosophy, which may not necessarily mean the same religion but the same goals and outlook.

Though *Your Wedding* can guide you through a maze of customs and wedding etiquette, one point should be made to you both. Deep philosophical differences require a knowledgeable marriage counselor or a religious adviser with experience in this area. If you do not feel free enough to go to your own clergyman there are churches and houses of worship that have counseling services. You may have to try more than one adviser, one who meets your needs and before whom you both can speak honestly.

Q: *My fiancé is Jewish, and I am willing to be married by a rabbi, but we are having a hard time finding one who will perform the ceremony. Why do we have to say I am not Jewish?*

Most rabbis, whether Orthodox, Conservative, or Reform, will not perform the marriage ceremony if one of the couple is not Jewish. But don't give up; it is possible to find a rabbi who will officiate. Telephone some of the Reform synagogues; though their rabbi may not undertake such a task, they might be able to recommend one who would. You must, however, be frank in your discussions with anyone you engage. Besides, clergy of all faiths ask questions that you would not be able to answer without some background, and they may ask for proof of religious affiliation.

THE UNINVITED

Q: *Do I have to pay for a wedding in which I will not be allowed to participate? I will not be able to escort my daughter or see her exchange marriage vows.*

Oh, I see, she's being married in the Mormon Church of Jesus Christ of Latter-day Saints. This is not the first time I've spoken to parents who have come up against this ruling. The only people allowed in the temple itself are Mormons in good standing, which means, in part, only those who donate a certain amount of time and tithe to the church—one cannot be a sometime member. So exclusion from the temple applies not only to those of a different faith, but to Mormons who have not met the standards set by the church.

What does your wife say about the position you are taking, and is your daughter being married in Utah?

Q: *Our daughter is going to school in Utah and her future husband's family lives there; they will be the ones attending the reception. My wife is a Mormon but will not be allowed into the church either. However, she still says I am wrong; I should pay for the privilege of not being present at the marriage ceremony*

of our daughter. I feel they should change this ridiculous rule.
After all, this is our daughter!

There is nothing you can do. That rule is strictly adhered to.
I am told the rites do not take long. Those who are not allowed
into the temple itself to witness the "sealing" (marriage ceremony)
of the couple can wait in rooms at the Visitors' Center. Afterward,
the company can have a reception and an exchange of rings can
take place, since the ring ceremony is not a part of the "sealing"
rites.

If you do not intend to go to Utah, you could honor the
newlyweds at a reception, inviting your family and friends to
meet your daughter's new husband. Make it at a time when they
can conveniently visit, even if you have to pay the airfare yourself.
This gesture would show caring and support. If you separate
yourself from your daughter it will be difficult for her to approach
you in the future should she need you. I am a firm believer in
leaving doors open.

Speak to the young couple. They may agree to a Blessing of
the Church (yours) in which the minister blesses their marriage,
even though the actual marriage took place elsewhere. You must
check your denomination's policy, and also ask the newlyweds.
I understand that the Mormon Church has no objection to the
Blessing provided everyone understands that it cannot be a full
marriage ceremony.

LADIES AND GENTLEMEN, Mormons are not the only
ones whose rules are strict. In the Eastern Orthodox church the
priest will conduct the ceremony even if one of the couple is not
a member of the Greek Orthodox religion, provided the person
is a baptized Christian. But the idea of an ecumenical ceremony
is not acceptable. A minister of another denomination can offer
a blessing but may not take an active part in the nuptial rites.

As with the Eastern Orthodox, the requirement for a Jewish
wedding ceremony is that both the bride and bridegroom be
Jewish.

There are some religious denominations who will co-officiate
with one another but others have firm doctrines from which they
cannot deviate.

INTERFAITH EYE-ROLLING GUESTS

Guests at an interfaith wedding should control eye move-
ments. Have you ever witnessed the eye-rolling signals one guest
can throw another when the ceremony is not performed as tradition would have it? The recipient of those looks may feel embarrassed by the performance and pretend not to notice, but
others may. Such body language is rude, hurtful, and obvious.

If, as a guest, you have never been in a particular denomination's house of worship, try not to sit too close to the front so
that you can follow the other guests. One couple told me an
amusing story about attending their nephew's wedding in
Mexico.

As members of the family they sat in the second pew. Since
they were not as proficient in Spanish as they thought, they found
themselves sitting when others stood; no sooner had they stood
up than the others sat down. Next time, they said, they would
choose a back bench and be less conspicuous.

KING SOLOMON AND THE CHILDREN

One young couple, with different religious backgrounds, set-
tled a complicated question using King Solomon as a guide. The
problem was: in whose religion would the children be brought
up? They were, however, unable to arrive at an agreeable decision. So much in love, and with the wedding date fast approaching, they compromised by dividing the potential children in half;
sons would go to their father's church and daughters would go
to their mother's church. I wondered what would happen if they
had seven daughters, or seven sons. Would the parent blessed
with such a wealth of children share them with the other? He or
she could generously say, "Look, I've got seven, today you can
borrow Elizabeth and Joan . . ."

The Reception

The menu for the reception after the wedding ceremony depends on the time of day the event takes place and whether the wedding is formal or informal, as well as on the size of the guest list and where the function will be held—your home, the house of worship, a rented hall, a restaurant, or a hotel.

Eating is a habit humankind has developed over the past several million years, so you cannot expect your company to cure themselves of this malady on your wedding day. "Breaking bread" with one another brings warmth and fellowship. Its importance is documented in sacred books. Jesus at Cana performed his first miracle at the wedding feast by bringing forth wine from vessels of water. The Old Testament is filled with examples of the gathering of kinsmen to commemorate special events.

You are not obligated to do more than you can afford but be realistic and consider the time of day of the ceremony and plan your reception accordingly. For instance, if the ceremony is to take place at eleven o'clock then some sort of wedding breakfast or luncheon should be served. However, lighter fare would be acceptable if the exchange of vows were held at two o'clock. The important thing to keep in mind is that you plan as gracious a reception as possible, according to your pocketbook.

What is a "wedding breakfast," and for that matter what is a reception? Those two expressions seem to puzzle people.

The wedding reception is the gathering of invited guests, whether attended by just a few relatives or a large company, who come together after the wedding ceremony to fete the newlyweds.

The simplest of receptions needs only a wedding cake and a drink for toasting, not necessarily alcoholic. Champagne or champagne punch is the traditional drink for toasting the couple, but wine or soda, such as ginger ale, and even fruit juice, are acceptable.

A wedding breakfast is a term used in some parts of the

country but practically unknown elsewhere. To some it means a reception held up to the noon hour and to others it refers to a wedding feast served any time during daylight hours. Though I am particularly fond of the expression, I think it confusing to use the term "wedding breakfast" for an afternoon function.

Most wedding receptions are buffet style, which means the food is placed on a large table and the company helps themselves. More guests can be invited to a stand-up buffet-style reception than to an ordinary buffet meal, where they sit at tables that take up a good deal of space. A buffet reception also cuts down on the number of waiters.

A stand-up reception can be tiring for those who find it hard to be on their feet for long periods of time. If at all possible, have a few chairs scattered about so that some relief is available; most guests rest a spell and then circulate, so you are unlikely to need many.

If the wedding is to be at home, and there is room, chairs, bridge tables, and accessories can be rented. You can put little vases of flowers on pretty bridge cloths to go with your color scheme. Or, if the reception is held elsewhere, ask the caterer or maître d' for little round cocktail tables.

The food arranged for a buffet reception should be easy to eat. Sliced meats on small rolls can be managed, but meat that has to be manipulated with a knife and fork while one is holding a drink in the other hand is nigh impossible for two-handed homo sapiens.

After a morning wedding it is traditional to serve a wedding breakfast or brunch. This might include fruit juice, quiche or eggs en cocotte, and some sort of bread such as biscuits, muffins, or rolls and butter, along with coffee, tea, milk, a wedding cake, and champagne or champagne punch. Some people add fruit or ice cream to the menu. Coffee and tea are not toasting drinks.

Luncheon, which is served after a noon ceremony, can go the gamut from seafood to chicken to meats, a salad, biscuits or rolls and butter, coffee, tea, and milk along with the wedding cake, toasting drink, and ice cream. It can be served as a seated meal or a buffet.

An afternoon function might include all the elements of a formal evening dinner and dance.

A simple afternoon tea, served between one and four o'clock, includes dainty finger sandwiches, petits fours (small iced cakes), tea, coffee, champagne, and wedding cake. Nuts and mints might be an added touch. This menu is also customary in the southwest for an evening wedding held at eight; a full dinner is seldom served.

Sometimes a later afternoon wedding, held between two and five o'clock, is followed by a cocktail reception whose fare consists of hot and cold hors d'oeuvres; wedding cake, champagne, and liquor, along with little cakes. Coffee and tea may also be included. Or the menu can be much like the buffet luncheon.

A reception held at six o'clock or after indicates a more elaborate menu, whether supper, a buffet, or a sit-down three-course meal is served. A lavish reception would include an open bar and hot and cold hors d'oeuvres after the receiving line, then a served sit-down dinner and dancing, with the open bar extended into the evening.

Make your decisions after you have calculated the entire cost of the various choices that you have been offered.

If you are having a home wedding, with good friends to help you with food preparation, chances are you can control your expenditure. However, you will have a great deal more responsibility.

First, taking one area at a time, list what you will need other than food. Close your eyes and picture how you will serve the food from beginning to end.

- Plates—both the larger size for main dishes and smaller ones for dessert

Some caterers and hostesses will tell you that smaller plates cut down on food consumption—that is up to you. A friend of mine was mortified during her home reception when she discovered that the caterer had cake plates on the buffet table. When she asked why such small plates were being used, the caterer produced the luncheon size from her van.

- Forks and spoons—even if you are having finger food
- Utensils for the wedding cake
- Napkins—both dinner and cocktail sizes
- Champagne and liquor glasses

- Cups and saucers
- Cream pitchers and sugar bowls
- Serving trays
- Bowls and casserole holders with serving spoons and forks for each
- Punch bowls
- Chairs and tables, unless your guests are expected to stand

Most of the items listed above can be rented. You can also hire servers and a bartender, which I strongly recommend.

CATERING SERVICES

Weddings generally become too complicated for mere mortals to cope with alone and are one of the reasons why caterers and hotel banquet managers came into being. Their reputation is built by word of mouth from satisfied customers and impressed guests.

If you are not sure of the professional's talent, ask for some names of recent customers and do not hesitate to telephone for recommendations. When a caterer is confident of his good name, he will gladly acquiesce. Another source is to call your county's consumer department. Without being specific they will tell you whether there have been any complaints about that particular firm.

Caterers tell us that more food is needed for a buffet meal than at a seated dinner, where guests are given a certain amount of food per person. However, the latter is more expensive because there are generally more courses served and more waiters needed.

DRINK TO ME ONLY . . .

Liquor and champagne are expensive items. Professionals can guide you on the average amount guests are expected to consume, as they can with food, taking into consideration that some drink and eat a lot and others hardly at all. People drink less wine than they do hard liquor. Young adults seem to prefer wine.

Because good champagne costs a lot more than table wine,

the latter might be a choice if expenses have to be cut. Sometimes only the bridal table is served champagne for toasts, an acceptable practice. The estimate is four bottles of champagne for twenty-five people.

An open bar is also costly and requires a bartender. The open bar, which means that guests may order whatever they want from the bartender, can be available during the whole event or only part of the time—perhaps during the receiving line, while serving only wine during the dinner. Whoever tends the bar should be given special instructions on the time to close. He or she should measure the liquor carefully, giving the standard amount, not only because of waste but also because attitudes are changing on whether liquor should flow like water in a fountain. You do not want guests to go home tipsy, let alone drunk. Another situation to be avoided: a mortified mother of the bride realized that the bartender was asking the guests to pay for their drinks; he had confused his instructions with another assignment! I hope it was the next job coming up and not the one before.

It is important to have on hand nonalcoholic beverages, such as soda and juice, for those who do not drink wine or liquor.

In some parts of the country a cash bar is acceptable. In olde England the bride's family may have been allowed to sell ale on their daughter's wedding day to meet their expenses—hence the expression "bridal" (bride's ale)—but unless it is a custom in your area do not consider it. Elsewhere, allowing guests to pay for anything at a wedding is considered improper.

If you are having a catered affair in a hotel, you pay for each bottle of liquor. Most establishments will not allow outside liquor to be brought in, though if the wedding is large enough, say three hundred people, they might permit it, since money will be made on the food. A friend of mine who was arranging her daughter's wedding reception at a hotel discussed with the maître d' the possibility of bringing her own champagne, wine, and wedding cake. He agreed to the wine and wedding cake, but charged her per serving for cutting the cake and a bottle fee for opening and serving the wine. Even with the "corkage" fee, expenses were cut and she was able to have the brand she wanted to serve. This is standard practice, but most people do not know it can be done. Find out when to deliver the cake and wine to the reception site, since that will be your responsibility.

RECEPTION SERVICES

Whether you engage a caterer for a home wedding or have a reception in a hotel, you will be given a contract to sign. The banquet manager will go over the menu with you, explain how much food and drink you will need to cover the guest list, and guide you carefully through the menu, showing you several from which to choose. Some ask you how you see your wedding reception and what type of food you prefer, to give the caterer a clue to your tastes.

At that time you will also see the layout of the banquet rooms and what the hotel's method of operations will be, enabling you to envision your reception within those walls. Make sure there are pleasant rest rooms and a checkroom for coats.

There is an important aspect to hiring services a year ahead. The costs quoted will be at current prices. The caterer must estimate that owing to inflation there will most likely be an increase of 7 to 10 percent on the bill.

Keep a cool head. I am told that some people feel intimidated at this time; the event is so important to them personally, and they find it difficult to view the arrangements as a business deal. This is an emotional and sentimental time, whether you are a parent of the bride, the bride herself, or the bridegroom. Just keep in mind that it is a business deal to the catering and hotel services you engage.

Paring costs, trying to get the best value for your money, is sensible. Make an informed decision and then get the best price you can. Some services have a small profit margin and a deal can be made within those limits. However, remember that a contractor likes to have future dates on the books and may not want to refuse business, so be sure you are not running the risk of getting inferior services—chipped dishes, for instance. Your contract should say it all.

Ask if there are any hidden charges you should know about. Make it known that the fees quoted are what you expect to pay, other than the uncertain cost of food a year hence. An ethical business establishment will give you value for your money.

Take careful notes when discussing the various aspects of the reception. You may be speaking to a salesperson rather than to the manager, who then has to review the contract offered by sales; changes might be made and you might not be aware of them until you receive the contract. After this initial visit, check your notes and send a letter stating what you understood was offered to you and the terms under which the contract would operate. Verify the day and time of the reception.

If the date and time are agreed upon and you are certain of the menu, prices, and services, the caterer or banquet manager will hold the date for a certain amount of time. If you have not made up your mind after that interval, that date may be given to someone else. There is a danger that this will happen if you have chosen a popular place in your area that has bookings as much as a year ahead of the wedding day. You can always ask for a short extension, but do so before the hold date elapses.

A few days after your visit, the firm will send a contract for you to sign and return by mail. Read it carefully. Check the wedding date and time of day first. See whether the contract agrees with your letter. If there is any discrepancy, do not hesitate to telephone the banquet manager. Reading from your letter, question the areas of doubt. Cross out the point of contention and write in the correction, which both you and the caterer must initial. A sizable deposit is required, and once you sign the contract it is binding.

WEDDING CAKE

The wedding cake dates back to antiquity. During the wedding banquet, the ancient Greek bridal couple shared a sesame cake to ensure fertility. A bride and bridegroom, during the glory of Rome, started the wedding ceremony with a solemn offering to the officiant of a cake of spelt (a kind of wheat).

In the Middle Ages, guests crumbled little wheat cakes, also symbols of fertility, over the heads of the bridal couple. In some quarters it was also considered good luck for the bridegroom's mother to break bread over the bride's head as the new wife entered her home. In sixteenth-century England, a practical soul decided there was no point in wasting those tasty morsels and made little sugared cakes for consumption. Later, it was the French who imaginatively created the layered iced wonder.

Nowadays the cake has its own unique character. Accompanied by a silver knife decorated with white bridal ribbon, it sometimes stands on the bride's table, or can be placed alone on a wheeled table.

Some couples do not want the traditional pound or sponge cake layered with the usual fillings, so imaginative bakers are creating chocolate cakes with raspberry or even more exotic fillings.

The bridegroom's cake can be placed near the bride's wedding cake. Though still delicious—usually a chocolate or fruit cake— it pales by comparison. Some hosts put slices in small white boxes tied with white ribbon or wrapped in napkins for guests to take home. There is a superstition that whispers that if an unmarried girl sleeps with the wedding cake under her pillow, she will dream of her own wedding, but there is no mention of the same thing happening with the bridegroom's confection. Gentlemen, try it! Who knows?

Sometimes the band softly plays the song the newlyweds chose for their first dance as husband and wife while they cut the wedding cake. The bride, standing on the bridegroom's right, holds the knife as her husband places his hand on hers. She cuts a slice of cake from the bottom layer which she and her husband share (sometimes the first piece has already been sliced to make it easier for the bride). Now the waiters can divide up the rest of the cake as is necessary to serve the company.

At a military wedding, the bridegroom hands his sword to his new bride, who, with her husband's hand on hers, cuts the cake.

The top layer can be frozen. Discuss the best way to store your particular wedding cake with the baker, who knows the ingredients. Serve the cake, topped by the ornament that was originally on the confection, at the celebration of your first wedding anniversary—a sign of further good luck to the happily marrieds.

SEATING ARRANGEMENTS

Large weddings with many guests need organization. At a formal sit-down dinner, arranging guest seating at tables is no mean task for the host and hostess, who can only do so successfully once all the acceptances have been received. The family may have to sit up nights going over the seating plan.

RECEPTIONS
AFTER THE WEDDING DAY

A reception given on the day of the wedding is called the wedding reception, even though it might only consist of a wedding cake and a drink for toasting. Receptions held later than this are considered to be in honor of the newly married couple. The function can be as formal or informal as wished.

The bride does not generally wear her wedding dress at a second reception. Having just written that sentence, I am reminded of an American girl who married in the States into a socially prominent British family. She told me she would wear her wedding dress and accessories to another ceremony in the chapel on his family's estate to be attended by family, friends, and neighbors who were not able to make the trip to America. So you see, it might be that the British have different customs, or just that the hard-and-fast rules are neither hard nor fast.

There may be special reasons for wearing the wedding dress again, but it does not seem suitable to wear the costume at a reception, though guests would enjoy seeing it displayed in the reception room.

Ofttimes, when the guest list is small or distance prevents the bridegroom's people from attending the wedding, his family will have a reception for the honeymooners in their hometown. This makes his side of the family extremely happy.

It might be that the bride and bridegroom eloped or were married away from both families, in which case separate functions could be held in both their parents' homes.

BRIDE'S TABLE

It is customary to have a bride's table. The bride and bridegroom sit facing the company at the center of an oblong or semicircular table. The bride is on the bridegroom's right, the best man on her right; the honor attendant sits on the bridegroom's left; next to the maid of honor is an usher, then a brides-maid, and so on.

PARENTS' TABLE

Whether there are two separate tables for the parents and close honored guests depends, of course, on the number of people.

When all sit at one table, the arrangements are the same as with any social occasion. The bride's parents, the host and hostess, sit across from each other. The father of the bridegroom is seated on the right of the hostess and to her left is the officiant. The bridegroom's mother is on the right of the host, whose left-hand partner is the officiant's spouse. Since tables at a hotel seat from eight to ten, there is room for four more at the table. Of course, grandparents—as honored guests—would be the first choice. Other close relatives might warrant the honor if there were no grandparents or officiant present.

Some couples decide that their parents will sit with them at the bride's table. Attendants, unless there is room, sit with the rest of the company. At a long oval table, the bridal couple would sit together in the middle of one side, with the host at one end and the hostess at the other. The bridegroom's parents and the clergy and spouse are seated as explained above. Or a round table can be used with the bride and bridegroom seated facing the rest of the guests.

The seating arrangements at some ethnic weddings have the bride's family and intimates at one table, with the bridegroom's family and their honored guests at a table oposite.

Tables and chairs may be used at a buffet reception, in which case the formation is the same as with a dinner reception. However, if there is sparse random seating or only a few chairs for guests, a bride's table and a parents' table are customary.

At a less formal buffet reception the bridal couple might choose not to have a separate table but to circulate among their guests and eat at will.

The "honeymoon table" is a small round table seating only the bride and bridegroom, who have their first meal together as husband and wife. It avoids problems such as what to do with divorced parents at the bridal table, or about who sits with the bride and bridegroom. They may prefer it that way simply because most of their time will be spent circulating among the guests and with dancing.

GUEST SEATING

Ah, if you can seat all your guests so that they live happily ever afterward with the knowledge that they are special to you, you will be awarded the prize of diplomat of the year. Especially if half the guests aren't speaking to the other half.

Calm down, it is not as serious a chore as that. But a word of caution. Never try to mediate disputes by seating estranged people together. It might work out so well that you will be voted a champion in diplomacy, but it might backfire, too. Your function is a special occasion so it is best not to take a chance. Also, it is almost impossible to seat all your friends or all of one side of the family together. As long as you do not sit an adult couple at a children's table (I'm not kidding!) because you had only a certain number of tables and very few children, or because due to last-minute cancellations you had to rearrange the tables and it had nothing to do with the couple but that particular place card had fallen off the table and it was three o'clock in the morning . . . see what I mean?

Too few children? Seat them with their parents. A couple or two who do not know anyone at the wedding other than their hosts? Seat them at a table with people who are hospitable, even if you have to move one or two couples from that table who are close to the others. Your guests do not expect, nor should they expect, to be seated as if they were invited to a small dinner party in your home. Mix groups, but with discretion. A couple in their thirties should not be seated at a table with the bride's elderly great-aunts, to listen to how things were when ladies wore gloves and hats and men held doors open for them.

PLACE OR ASSIGNMENT CARDS

When you ordered the invitations and stationery you were advised, I hope, to pick up place cards (or table assignment cards), which are used at large weddings to show guests where they are supposed to sit.

As the guests enter the reception place they pick up place cards bearing their name and table number. They will find them in alphabetical order on a cloth-covered table in a convenient, unobstructed area at the beginning or end of the receiving line.

For a formal wedding, write the guests' names by hand on each card: Mr. and Mrs. Wilson; Dr. and Mrs.; Rev. and Mrs., without first names unless there is more than one couple with the same last name. One place card for a couple is appropriate, since only the table number is indicated and they will be sitting together anyway. Single people are also addressed by their surnames: Mr. Friendly, Miss Charming, or Ms. Sophisticated. Couples living together would still have individual place cards, though a joint invitation might have been sent. It is not appropriate to designate a dignitary with "the Honorable." Use the person's actual title—Governor and Mrs., for instance—or revert to Mr., Mrs., or Ms.

At smaller, more intimate gatherings, where place cards are needed, the bride and bridegroom use the names they usually call their relatives and friends, if they wish.

TABLE ASSIGNMENTS

To plan table assignments, count the acceptances, then consult the banquet manager about the number of tables needed. Now the job is ready to be completed.

Take a large sheet of paper. Draw as many circles as there are tables. Arrange the place cards into compatible groups around the circles; some tables can hold eight and others ten, as suits the table arrangements. The cards can be moved like chess pieces until the right combinations are achieved. Look on the carpet every once in a while for stray cards, please, and also count heads. Be sure to put the correct table number on each place card. You would not want an extra couple standing about wondering why there are already ten people sitting at the table they were assigned to.

Receiving Line

"*Feliciter*—may happiness await you!" was the response of ancient Romans after the wedding ceremony.

The choice of holding the receiving line right after the ceremony at the house of worship, or afterward at the reception site, is optional. This is particularly true if everyone is invited to both the ceremony and reception. If many have been invited only to the ceremony, and not to the reception afterward, they will appreciate being able to express their wishes for the couple's happy future before leaving. Then, of course, a line at the reception would not be needed. Either way it is a happy time.

Just picture it. The ceremony was perfect. The drive to the reception gave the couple a little time to be by themselves (let's pretend the driver was not there), and the photographer has taken the necessary photographs of the bridal party. Now the festivities are about to begin.

Closest to the entrance to the reception room is the bride's mother (or hostess), who receives well-wishers and presents them to the bridegroom's mother. Guests go down the line to greet the bride and the bridegroom, who briefly introduce to each other those people they may not yet have met. They should spend only a few moments; the line should move quickly.

Why do some people find receiving lines a nuisance? Why, I am asked, do I have to have a receiving line? They are so tiresome. After all, some Jewish weddings don't have receiving lines. The bride and bridegroom see to it that they visit every table and parents make their rounds also.

I know, I know (please note my reassuring tones), but if handled correctly the receiving line is practical. It is an orderly process and avoids the confusion bridal couples sometimes face when they are surrounded by guests wishing them well. The newlyweds are put at a distinct disadvantage trying to acknowledge their guests—not all of whom both will know; of course, the guests experience the same drawback. And, I venture to whisper in your ear, receiving that way relieves both guests and the bridal party of the burden of saying more than a few well-chosen words of good wishes and thank-yous.

If there are many guests at the reception, there is a way to speed up the receiving line a bit. Someone, perhaps an usher who is a relative and knows many of those present, could stand near the bride's mother. Guests give him their names and he passes the information to the hostess, who introduces them to the mother of the bridegroom, and so on down the line. Another usher could be assigned to discreetly guide people through to waiting refreshments. Sometimes there is a waiter nearby with a tray of drinks or dainty morsels of finger food to lure guests in the right direction.

If the receiving line takes place at the house of worship it is formed in the vestibule. Conversation is likely to be less inviting here, so the line moves faster.

At home, when the ceremony has taken place elsewhere, the hostess and the bridegroom's mother stand near the door while the bride and bridegroom stand together and have a word with each guest as they come near. It is a receiving line but an informal one.

Q: *Up until now I have had no objection to going through a receiving line. But now, as the bride, I am the receiver and am petrified that I won't remember anyone's name—not even my own. Any tips?*

My self-conscious friend, don't you remember movies of grand balls where the butler stands, terribly correct, calling out in a clear, resonant voice the name of each guest so that the host and hostess could be saved the embarrassment of not remembering them? How can this be faulted?

I suspect poor memory is the reason people rail against the receiving line. They prefer to avoid what might be an embarrassing performance. Try to keep your perspective and poise. Most people understand that on the most important day of your life, with all the involvement in parties and planning beforehand, you cannot be expected to recall everyone's name.

Sensible guests will introduce themselves or say something that will give you a clue as they approach you and your husband, even if they know both of you. However, you are expected to recognize your mother, father, brothers, and sisters, some relatives, and a friend or two, and it is very good form to include your mother- and father-in-law. Remember, you have been working with those names on the invitations and on table seating cards, as well as writing thank-yous, so you will not be as inept as you think.

I am sympathetic because, though I am not one for public confession, it happens to me. I have been known to cover myself by laughing about my defect. "Oh, my dears, do introduce yourselves to our friends Tina and Tom Lexius." When we entertain guests I write everyone's name down just before they arrive, if I have time—aye, and there's the rub—very often there is not time enough.

An uncle of mine by adoption—so there was no way I could have inherited his excellent memory—was in politics. He could remember the name of a person he'd met once, five years before. His method was immediately to associate the face and name with an image. It worked for him, but I think he must have had a special talent, which served him well in his professional interests.

It is true people are terribly pleased when you remember their names but most are understanding when you, like them, sometimes slip up.

Q: *Who stands in the receiving line? My future father-in-law is being difficult, saying that if the father of the bride will be in it, he is off the hook.*

I see a delighted father-in-law in your future, because it is optional for fathers of the bridal couple to stand in the receiving line. Sometimes they stand in line for a while, then mingle with the guests.

ORDER OF RECEIVING LINE

A large formal wedding usually has a long receiving line:
- Mother of the bride (or hostess)
- Father of the bridegroom (optional)
- Mother of the bridegroom
- Father of the bride (optional)

- Bride and bridegroom
- Maid of honor
- Bridesmaids

If the event is large and the line long, you might reduce the receiving line to:
- Mother of the bride
- Mother of the bridegroom
- Bride and bridegroom
- Matron or maid of honor, if related
- Fathers of the bridal couple can stand in line for a while, then mingle with guests.

At one time it was customary to have all the bridesmaids on the receiving line. The mother of the bride, as hostess, along with the bridegroom's mother, was stationed close to the entrance. But today it seems more appropriate for the mothers to take their place in the line.

The best man, ushers, junior attendants, flower girls, and ring bearers do not receive. The best man and the ushers, along with the bridesmaids—especially if they are not related to either side of the family—can circulate and join in the dancing. Thus they act as substitute hosts while keeping the line from becoming tedious and time consuming. Let's face it, receiving lines are not the reason for having large weddings—large weddings are the reason for receiving lines. I am of the don't-make-'em-too-long school.

The bride stands on the right of the bridegroom for both civilian and armed-forces weddings.

If the bride wants to she can wear gloves (if they are part of her ensemble) to receive; guests do not wear gloves.

The bride and attendants generally hold their bouquets.

The place chosen for the receiving line should not hamper the easy flow of people from the entrance to the refreshments.

Guests going through the receiving line should offer brief remarks. This is no time to ask who the newly marrieds are voting for in the next election.

Handshakes should be firm, neither wrist-breaking nor too weak.

It is the custom in some areas to have an attendant ask guests to sign the guest book, which is generally placed on a table not too far from the end of the receiving line. It becomes a memento of those who attended the reception. Only one of a married couple need sign for both: "Mr. and Mrs. Joseph Doe," or "Joseph and Virginia Doe."

The receiving line is over when all the guests have arrived and made their way down the line.

DIVORCED PARENTS IN RECEIVING LINE

When relations between divorced parents are friendly, an unmarried father might want to ask the bride's mother to receive even if he is paying for everything. Did I hear a gasp of disbelief? Shouldn't the father, as host, ask a grandmother or a female relative to stand in his stead if he does not fancy the task? Well, he and his ex-wife had that daughter together, and when the signs are compatible it should work out well. There is one important line of propriety and it is that neither parent should assume the role of host or hostess in the other's home.

I heard of a chap who gladly gave up the task of receiving to his ex-wife while he kept guests busy on the dance floor. It wasn't exactly generosity that prompted the offer. But what's the difference? The bride's mother could happily introduce people and deftly help them pass down the line, while he was free to circulate. I disagree with the school of thought that holds that divorced people, even if they are friendly, should not be in the same line. If it is simply out of the question, then the host or hostess can head the line and the other can stand farther along.

The person who stands first on the receiving line at the reception is not there because of his or her relationship to the bride. As at any social event, it is the hostess who receives. So if the bride's parents are divorced and her father and his current wife are giving the reception, both of them—or at least his wife—

should receive—as would the grandmother, if she were giving the reception.

However, when the receiving line is held in the house of worship right after the ceremony, the bride's mother heads the line no matter who is hosting the reception elsewhere. If the area is large enough, I also am in favor of fathers standing in line at that time, if they wish to and are not too busy seeing that guests go on to the reception. But sometimes the vestibule is too small to have more than the mother of the bride, the bride and bridegroom, and the mother of the bridegroom.

The general rule is that the bride's mother does not receive when someone else is hosting the reception unless invited to do so. She attends as an honored guest. If the line is held in the house of worship, then she is first in line.

At a small or home wedding ceremony, the bridal couple turn to the company after the rites are performed to receive well-wishers.

If the marriage ceremony is held in a house of worship but the reception is elsewhere, the bride's mother and the mother of the bridegroom stand at the entrance to receive. The newlyweds stand a bit farther back in the room.

SUBSTITUTE HOSTS

If the bride's mother has passed away, her father stands in the receiving line. If both are deceased, a close relative can be asked. Though it is helpful to the bridal couple to have someone stand first in line, they might feel that they can manage on their own.

DOUBLE-WEDDING RECEIVING LINE

If the brides are sisters, one receiving line is formed. There are two lines when the brides are just friends, since there are two sets of hosts and separate families involved. A double wedding of first cousins whose mothers are sisters would have two sets of hosts, but since they have the same relatives, there should be a single line.

The general guidelines are:

- Mother of the bride (or hostess) is first in line
- Father of the bride (optional)
- Older bride's mother-in-law
- Bride, who stands on the right of her husband
- Bridegroom
- Mother-in-law of younger bride
- Younger bride
- Bridegroom
- Older bride's honor attendant
- Younger bride's honor attendant

If the fathers of the bridegrooms stand in line, the father of the older bridegroom places himself on the left of his wife. The bridal couples stand next to one another. The younger bridegroom's parents stand on their son's left.

If it is decided not to include honor attendants in the line, then the bridal couples would stand next to one another and the mother-in-law of the younger bride would be last in line.

Q: *Standing near the receiving line I must have heard the bride being "congratulated" countless times. Maybe I am old-fashioned, but I thought one wished the bride happiness and congratulated the bridegroom. Am I out of step?*

I always wish both the bride and bridegroom much happiness for I, too, have accepted the implication as being impolite. I only offer congratulations when the forty-yard dash has been run or the bride has just been nominated vice president of the company for which she works. Of course, I congratulate the bridegroom all over the place.

Now, I especially avoid congratulations when, after living together for nigh on three years, both have decided that they were meant to make the ultimate "statement."

However, Webster's unabridged dictionary analyzes the word

congratulate as "wish joy." The word expresses one's own feelings of pleasure in another's good fortune. But at one time it was in poor taste to congratulate the bride, for it was taken to mean she had finally got herself a man. Why such an interpretation? Stick with "best wishes" or "have a nice life" or something to that effect.

Q: *My ex-husband is paying for the entire wedding. He and his wife are going to stand in the receiving line as host and hostess at the reception. My daughter is upset because she was told that I will not be asked to receive. Is that customary?*

This question has come up several times with divorced parents and is asked not only by the mother of the bride when the bride's father and wife are the hosts, but by the bride's father when the bride's mother and her husband are giving the reception. It hurts both, though less on the man's part since it is not a strict function of fathers to receive. The bride's mother sometimes seems more self-conscious about it. Just remember the protocol for any reception: the host and hostess greet guests along with the guests of honor, who in the case of a wedding are the bridal couple.

Tell your daughter that you understand that is the way it has to be—it is the accepted practice. Both of you should think of the other hundred and one preparations for her wedding that you will share together, and of the joy you will have helping her dress on the day. What is more, you will be the one who will be escorted to the first row to take your place of honor as mother of the bride.

To me those intimate times between a mother and daughter overshadow the brief task on the receiving line.

LADIES AND GENTLEMEN, as I have mentioned before, sometimes the tone of the voice over the phone expresses the question better than the actual words used.

Q: *I am just checking in with you on the wedding protocol of divorced parents before I start planning my wedding.*

It is a good idea.

Q: *My father is paying for the entire wedding. He wants to sit in the first pew with his wife and have my mother sit in the third. Also, he does not want her in the receiving line.*

Well, the protocol is that the mother of the bride sits in the first pew and her father and his wife sit in the third.

If the receiving line takes place in church, then the bride's mother would be the first in line to receive. However, if it is held at the reception, the host and hostess, your father and his wife, do the honors.

Do a little research in the library and quote the suggested etiquette to him. He may change his mind when he realizes that it will not show him to good advantage if he insists on usurping your mother's rightful place.

RECEIVING-LINE EXEMPTIONS

Postoperative patients or sports enthusiasts on crutches can be excused from working their way along the receiving line. They might go into the reception room to wait for a more comfortable time to say a word or two to the family.

It is particularly hard for some elderly people to wade through the receiving line; either they can forgo it or the hostess can assign an usher to take them to the front of the line to express their good wishes. The offer should be made discreetly, since it might be declined. It is up to the families to decide who will be escorted in this manner. Remember, to a twenty-year-old a graying fifty-year-old may seem ancient, nor would one want to insult a vigorous seventy-five-year-old man by treating him as if he were infirm.

Q: *I am the elderly woman who has called you many times over the past few years. I try not to be too much of a stickler for the "correct thing" but nowadays younger people don't seem to be conscious of some of the niceties that go into making life a little more gracious.*

Remember I called you when new neighbors moved in and I wanted to leave my calling card as a friendly gesture? Well, I followed your advice and took a plate of cookies, putting my calling card on top. It worked out fine.

Now I am invited to their wedding, though why they are having a big wedding when they have been living together for quite some time . . . I still can't figure that out.

As I've explained to you before, though the bride is successful in her career, she doesn't know the first thing about protocol or etiquette. She seems to use intuition, which doesn't always work. So I've been helping her with wedding arrangements and again everything is working out fine.

I've just been to the doctor and he tells me that my heart is not strong. I will be attending the wedding next week but I shall not be up to going through the receiving line, yet I don't feel comfortable about not doing so. How shall I handle it?

Mrs. Que, of course I remember you. Some of your questions are laced throughout the book I am writing on wedding etiquette. And this one about the receiving line and infirm people is most crucial.

Chances are the bridal couple will not realize you did not make the receiving line, because people become a sea of faces to them after a while. Nevertheless, you have two choices.

Just skip the receiving line and find a seat for yourself until it is over. Then you will have the strength to join in the festivities. During the reception, when the bridal couple make their rounds, you will have your moment with them.

Or, since you will be seeing the bride up until the wedding, mention in an offhand way that you are looking forward to the wedding but will not make the receiving line because you find it hard to be on your feet for long periods of time.

LADIES AND GENTLEMEN, I've always enjoyed Mrs. Que's calls. Alone, with no family, at least in the large city in which she lives, she realized that her neighborhood was changing. Younger people were moving in, and as a social being she did her best to be part of the community and apparently succeeded. She knew she had views and approaches that others were not familiar with, so she tried to understand and yet not lose her own character in the meantime.

POSTSCRIPT

Mrs. Que was kind enough to call me after the wedding, which she said was just wonderful. The bride and bridegroom, who paid for the entire wedding, stood at the entrance of the room where the ceremony was to take place, welcoming guests along with their parents. Mrs. Que was greeted with great warmth and was thanked not only by the bride but by her mother for all the guidance she had given the bride during the past few months.

Mrs. Que: I was surprised that there was no receiving line.

Small weddings really don't require a line.

Mrs. Que: Maybe not. Anyway, I really had a good time and I did wear the diamond pin on my dress as you suggested. But I did something really awful. The wine must have been strong, though I only had a little; I'm not used to it.

What happened?

Mrs. Que: The music was so lively and I was having such a lovely time. I went over to the drummer and talked to him. You know that is just not done. I feel so foolish.

Compliments are music to a performer's ears.

NO RECEIVING LINE

The couple Mrs. Que spoke about had a small wedding. They were their own hosts and apparently, since they had been living together for a while, felt that they wished to receive guests at the entrance as they arrived for the wedding ceremony. This eliminated the need for the line afterward, as all the guests were invited to the entire proceedings.

Dancing—Bouquet Toss—
Order of the Garter

DANCING

According to wedding etiquette, no one dances with the bride until she and her bridegroom have had their first dance together. But this does not mean, as some have told me, that dancing *only* takes place after the bride and bridegroom open the dancing. The party celebrating the marriage begins with the receiving line, while the dancing encourages everyone to have a good time.

At a large wedding, the music starts while the receiving line is being formed outside the reception room. For a smooth transition from the ceremony to the reception, the musicians should be able to set up early so that the strains of music float from the reception room to the receiving line.

Depending on the formality of the wedding, before a seated dinner there might be a cocktail reception where drinks are offered; some people mingle, renewing old acquaintances and touching base with family they have not seen in ages, while others like to dance. Or it might be that when the receiving line is over, guests are invited to sit at the appointed tables.

Some couples choose to open the dancing as soon as the receiving line is over. The maestro plays their favorite tune while the guests clear the floor and welcome the newly marrieds enthusiastically. As with any function, the guests' primary duty is to make the celebration a successful one by participating.

Train swept up over her left arm (she practiced earlier in front of a mirror), the bride is led by the bridegroom into the type of dance they both feel comfortable with, but one hopes that they can glide into a melody reflecting the romantic mood of the occasion, leaving the faster music until later.

The choice of when the bridal dance takes place is a personal matter, as is the order of partners who dance with the bride during this special custom. It can take place at the cocktail reception, or some prefer it after dessert has been served at a seated dinner. However, sometimes people do not feel comfortable about dancing without the bridal couple's participation, so guests do not have much of a chance to dance with the bride and bridegroom when the bridal dance takes place after the dessert.

After the bride and bridegroom have circled their way once around the dance floor for their first dance together, the *traditional* formal procedure for the bridal party to follow is:

The bride dances with her father; after a few turns her father-in-law cuts in.

Then the best man asks the bride to dance.

Meanwhile the bridegroom dances first with his mother-in-law, next with his own mother, and then with the honor attendant.

The bride's father, after dancing with his daughter, invites the bridegroom's mother to dance, while the bride's father whirls his new son-in-law's mother around.

Parents of the bridal couple dance with one another.

The head usher dances with the bride while the best man and honor attendant pair off.

Meanwhile, ushers and maids join in. At that time guests fill the dance floor.

Ushers and male guests dance once with the bride.

Perhaps the master of ceremonies can discreetly guide the change of partners and see that no one is left standing without a partner.

Naturally, divorced parents dance with their children and with their children's in-laws. But they should not be under any obligation to dance with each other if feelings are still at the awkward stage. In spite of their desire to see parents together for just this one time, children should be sensitive and allow things to happen on their own. Insisting might hurt one or both parents.

Another arrangement is:

The bride's father-in-law dances with the bride after her dance with the bridegroom.

Then the bride's father cuts in to dance with his daughter.

Meanwhile, the bridegroom dances with his mother-in-law, and then with his mother.

The father of the bridegroom and the bride's mother, along with the bride's father and the bridegroom's mother, should take their turn around the dance floor.

The best man asks the honor attendant while maids and ushers
  pair.
The best man also dances with the bride while the bridegroom
  asks the honor attendant.
Ushers should dance once with the bride, as should male guests.

Dancing can take place between courses even if the bridal
couple has not yet danced together.

The progression I like best, and which is sometimes preferred
by the couple:

While bride and bridegroom are completing their first dance, her
  parents and then the bridegroom's parents join them on the
  dance floor.
After a few steps, the father of the bride cuts in to dance with
  the bride while the bridegroom dances with his new mother-
  in-law.
The bridegroom's father swings with his wife over to the bride
  dancing with her father and cuts in; the bride's father turns
  to the bridegroom's mother to dance with her.

In some rural areas, the bridal party moves out of sight once
the receiving line is over. When guests take their places in the
dining room, there is a gentle rolling of the drum to signal the
entrance of the attendants. Couple by couple, as they are introduced by the orchestra leader, they form an aisle for the bridal
couple to move swiftly through to the bridal table while the
standing company applauds. For some this is much too theatrical
and unnecessary since the guests have already been along a receiving line and it is assumed that they know one person from
the other by then.

Whatever suits the couple's style, once the bridal dance is
over, the music takes on its own special tone, from American
swing, jazz, pop, or rock to dance rituals based on "Old World"
traditions: impressive graceful Greek male dances, lively Polish
polkas, Irish jigs, Highland flings, Virginia reels, Mexican hat
dances, or Italian tarantellas.

The hora, which is played at most Jewish weddings, is the

type of dance that allows for no wallflowers in the room, for every able body joins in. All form a gigantic circle, surrounding the happy pair, or a semicircle, so that the line, sometimes led by the bride and bridegroom, can weave its way around the dance floor while nimble feet do the traditional steps.

One custom increasing in popularity at Jewish weddings is the carrying of the bride and bridegroom on chairs. Four strong "joyful" men place the bride in a chair. Another four strong "joyful" men place the bridegroom in another chair. They lift the chairs with their precious cargo and carry them around the room. Meanwhile the music plays and the crowd cheers. With nervous grins the bride and bridegroom hold on for dear life to the sides of their chairs. One of my sources of amusing stories tells me that he played at one wedding in which the bridegroom was carried in a folding chair—the rest I leave to your imagination.

By the way, the above happens spontaneously and is hard to control once it starts. The carrying of the bridal couple generally starts during the hora and cannot be controlled by the bandleader. If the couple do not want to ride high above the company, before the wedding they should make their wishes known to the best man and their family, so the idea can be discouraged.

TOASTS

Champagne is generally the traditional drink for toasts but other liquids are also appropriate. Sometimes the bridal table is the only one that has champagne for toasting, while the company drinks wine or whatever is at hand. The bride is served first and then the rest of the table. The toast can be offered as soon as everyone is ready.

Traditionally, at a *very formal wedding* the toast is proposed when the bridal couple are seated or right after dessert and before the cake cutting. At any other type of wedding it can be given either right after the receiving line is over or before the cake cutting.

Again, traditionally, the best man proposes the first toast. The company stands and raises glasses to the newlyweds. The bridal couple remain seated and do not lift their glasses because, as at all social occasions, those being toasted never drink to themselves.

Rising to his feet, the bridegroom replies, combining a toast to his bride with thanks to both her parents and his. Sometimes fathers or mothers feel moved to follow, but often, if there was toasting at the rehearsal dinner, they made their pronouncements at that time.

THE BOUQUET TOSS
AND THE ORDER OF THE GARTER

There are certain events that some weddings incorporate but which other couples will have no part of. Guess which of these two routines souls of a shy or independent nature would find difficult.

BOUQUET TOSS

The bride tosses the bouquet and the bridegroom retrieves the garter from the bride's leg toward the closing of the wedding celebration. All single girls are encouraged to try to catch the bouquet, for rumor has it that that nimble damsel will be the next to marry.

A raised area such as a staircase or balcony is an ideal place for the bouquet toss, but most of the time it is done from the middle of the dance floor, where the bandleader can maintain contact with the festivities. The bride can either turn her back to the audience and throw the bouquet over her shoulder, or face the maidens directly, which would give her better aim.

Simple event? Seems so! But there have been occasions when the bouquet has come apart as it is tossed into the air, showering its contents on the delighted crowd; or it has been thrown so erratically that it ends up in the aisle. One place in the Washington area has a balcony just for throwing the bouquet. The bride and bridegroom stand above the crowd and all applaud the toss. However, more than one bride has turned her back on the crowd and tossed the bouquet too high, and it catches in the chandelier. The teller of these stories says that invariably a Sir Lancelot stands on a chair no wider than his frame, attempting to grab the way-ward prize while simultaneously looking up and down trying to keep his balance.

ORDER OF THE GARTER

The garter is said to be a substitute for the ribbon with which the lady presented her champion knight of King Arthur's Round Table who gallantly carried her colors into battle. The Order of the Garter was formed in England in the fourteenth century, as an honor given to distinguished noblemen, who to this day wear a heraldic garter as part of their ceremonial garb. Having said that, below please read our answer to the British Crown . . .

With the aid of the band, which plays a seductive tune, the bride sits on a chair while guests gather around. The bridegroom, on his knees, reaches for the garter, which the bride has placed just below her knee—any higher is considered provocative. Slowly, and with great deliberation, he slides the frilly blue elastic down the leg of its owner. All the bachelors gather while the bride-groom, back to the audience, tosses the garter to them. The lucky catcher, who it is said will be the next married man (sorry, chaps . . . again, 'tis written in countless books on wedding su-perstitions), is then required to put the garter on the leg of the lady who caught the bouquet—every inch above the knee equals five years of happiness for the bridal couple.

Again, simple? Seems so! However, this is the time for a treatise on the garter—a reminder of the loss of innocence—written expressly for the dear bridegroom. Since the garter is made of thin elastic, it's virtually weightless and cannot be thrown with any momentum. To give the throw more force, ball the garter so that it can carry in the air until it unfolds and lands where you wish it. Some swains, and I do not mean you, sir, throw it unenthusiastically, or before the signal from the band-leader, so that it falls limply to the ground when no one is watch-ing. Now the bridegroom has failed in this Olympian task and just won't do it again—which might be a great relief to the potential catcher, since a precocious eleven-year-old pre-damsel has caught the bridal bouquet. However, the bandleader, pho-tographer, and company are waiting for the lark to be completed, and the gentleman just has to rise to the occasion once again.

A word of caution: watch out for the newly engaged gentleman whose fiancé has caught the bouquet. I know a young man who did leapfrogs over the other contenders, for he certainly wasn't going to allow anyone else's eager young hands to put that garter on his lady love.

BIRTH CERTIFICATE, PLEASE

Q: *Is there an age limit on catching the bride's bouquet? As is customary, at a wedding I attended recently, the young ladies were gathered before the bride for the bouquet toss. A sixty-year-old widow rushed in front of them to join in the catch. Would you believe she caught it? Everyone sort of laughed, but I wonder about the appropriateness of it.*

Well, though admittedly not a girl, she was single. But it sounds to me as if Mrs. Bouquet Catcher decided on the spur of the moment to be part of the singles scene.

Appropriate? On the one hand, the bouquet toss and the garter are supposed to be fun and not taken seriously. On the other hand, the widow was at a distinct advantage over her opponents. What young girl would try to trip her for the prize? On the other hand of the other hand, age has its benefits.

Q: *But what about the twenty-year-old man who caught the garter? Though he carried it off well enough, he could not have been too happy; he had the good sense to stop at the calf of her leg.*

That was good judgment on his part, as it was when an eleven-year-old caught the bouquet and the young gentleman just put the garter around her ankle. But it is not good judgment on the part of the bandleader who depended on the young man's good sense, and who has the choice of omitting the postgarter funning when it is inappropriate. There is a thin line between fooling and foolish.

LADIES AND GENTLEMEN, after the gathering of the maidens for the tossing of the bouquet, one bandleader was heard to ask the bride whether there were any shrinking violets in the room who should be joining in the ritual. The new matron offers her mom, who, thinking to herself, "and I gave birth to this child," is caught sneaking out of the room along with two or three cousins of the unattached persuasion. Oh, well, it's all part of the game.

TAKING LEAVE

Though some bridal couples stay to the end of the festivities, they can take their leave after the bouquet-garter toss, if they wish. The bride's attendants accompany her and the bridegroom's ushers accompany him to their separate changing rooms, where the bridal couple offer their thanks for all the support given. While the attendants go back to the reception to give guests little handfuls of confetti, the bridal couple don their going-away clothes. If the newlyweds are leaving for their wedding trip straight from the reception, their parents leave the guests for a short while to bid the children a private adieu. After a signal from the best man, everyone gathers outdoors to form an aisle for the happy pair. Cheering them on to the car, the company throws rice, confetti, birdseed, or whatever the current trend. The party can continue, but chances are it has wound down by then.

Not every couple leaves their wedding reception early. Some stay and close the festivities with a final dance. The bride and her father dance and then he hands her over to the bridegroom. The music can be the same as that for the first dance. The guests form a circle and sing along, and the event closes with good-luck and happiness wishes, kisses, and hugs.

Some couples don't wish to leave the area until all out-of-town guests have left. When family and friends come from afar, or if the newlyweds live elsewhere, they might want to extend the visit another day before going on their wedding trip.

Second Wedding and Divorce

$\mathcal{Q}$uestions on second weddings and divorce overlap somewhat, so I've included both topics in this chapter. Second-wedding queries generally start with happy ones on procedure. Those on divorce are generally more complicated and often involve entire families. So, this chapter falls into two parts.

SECOND WEDDING

When a couple plan a second wedding they want to know what the guidelines are.

A bride with a conservative outlook can choose a simple wedding ceremony in a house of worship, the clergyman's office, or at home. Handwritten or telephoned invitations are issued to fifty or fewer guests, and the bridal couple have one attendant each. The bridegroom wears a business suit and the bride a street-length suit or dress. Her father, a close relative, or a friend escorts her, or she can walk alone behind her honor attendant, but generally the giving-away part of the ceremony is dispensed with. A wedding breakfast or a luncheon follows and, if desired, a gala reception takes place any time, with as many guests as desired.

However, though the couple's desire may be very simple, there are variations in approach to a second wedding that can still be within the bounds of what they consider "good taste."

Weddings have not changed much over the last hundred years. There have been variations in style but in the basic ceremony the bridal couple still exchange vows, whether they write them themselves or use the traditional wording. But what has changed is the attitude of some second-time-around brides, who want a traditional wedding including the bridal gown, headdress, and orange blossoms. A son may be ring bearer and a daughter the maid of honor. The affair from beginning to end has all the trimmings of the first time, though the bride and her future husband may foot the bill, realizing that two elaborate functions for one daughter are more than most parents can afford.

Q: *Is it incorrect for my parents to issue the invitations to my formal wedding? My friends tell me that a woman in her thirties who has been married before issues her own invitations.*

There is no reason why your parents should not do the honors.

Q: *I am helping arrange the wedding of a forty-year-old woman and a man of sixty-three—a businessman of substance and highly respected in the community. Naturally, I have tried to guide the bride about what type of function is suitable for a mature couple who have been married before. But the bride, the mother of two teenage children, is going to wear a wedding dress, and the groom will be in formal attire to go with her outfit. She insists that is what she wants and he says whatever she wants is the way it will be. They are like two young kids. I'm debating whether to continue handling the affair.*

All you can do is to remind them about the traditional wedding for a mature couple. Even if they want to have a formal wedding, I see no reason to withdraw your services. Help them have as tasteful an event as possible.

It can be so hard to meet a person one would want to marry, and most people go through a lot of loneliness before finding that special someone. When they do, happiness brims over with the wonder of it all. I can't blame them; it is like finding one's youth. As a matter of fact, I am touched by it.

LADIES AND GENTLEMEN, I think that I received the announcement of that wedding, along with a splendid photograph of the couple. But it was the bride herself who handled the details of the newspaper announcement, not the bridal consultant. The photograph was of a slim, lovely woman in her late thirties or early forties in a Victorian-style dress and picture hat. She held the arm of her husband, who was a head taller. His graying Vandyke beard and traditional formal attire lent an elegant air to the photograph. The announcement listed the participation of their children in the wedding ceremony. Could it have been so wrong, so incorrect? I don't think so.

TAKING SIDES?

Q: *As a bridal consultant I have clients who are discussing having an engagement announcement in the newspaper. The future groom, who has never been married, wants one very much. But since this is her second marriage, the bride wants to know if it would be in good taste, since at one time it was not allowed. Also, she wants her eighteen-year-old daughter to be the maid of honor, but the groom says it shows the daughter is taking sides. I am not sure how to answer that.*

Taking sides? Does the bridegroom mean the bride's daughter is taking the side of her mother against her father if she is her mother's maid of honor?

Q: *Yes, I guess so, but I am not sure.*

I see the role the bride's daughter is taking as having nothing to do with the situation outside the wedding itself. I don't see it as a rejection of her father, who could expect the same support should he marry again—for all I know, he may already have done so. She could discuss with her father whether his feelings will be hurt should she be her mother's maid of honor. What if he says yes? Then the daughter will be in an unenviable position—squarely between her mother and father. That would be unfair to her.

Remembering that this is the bridegroom's first marriage, I also suspect that there is something bothering him about having his stepdaughter in the wedding party.

The answer to the first question is that the announcement can be worded so that it reads like a forthcoming-marriage notice rather than an engagement:

Jill Candace Ode and Frederick Eldon Hampenstance are engaged to be married next September . . . [etc.]

That statement enables the bridegroom to have a notice without it being a traditional engagement announcement.

LADIES AND GENTLEMEN, the sensitive issues in a second marriage can be compounded by so many unforeseen incidents. I have not met or spoken to the bridegroom. The objection he had to his future stepdaughter's role in the wedding party did not seem to me to be his real concern. I could not ask, for instance, if he was younger than his bride and, even if he was not, I could not ask if he felt self-conscious about the fact that his bride had an eighteen-year-old daughter while he had never been married. Or maybe his family are the self-conscious ones. On page 349 I write about the husband who would not attend his stepdaughter's wedding because he did not want to set eyes on his wife's former husband—no matter how much she and her daughter urged him to attend. It turned out that it was his side of the family that was causing the tension. His son, who was being married a couple of weeks later, had asked his father not to bring his wife to his wedding because the bridegroom's mother would not attend her own son's wedding if "that woman" came, despite the fact that "that woman" had come into the picture after his marriage had failed and after the divorce.

ONCE IS ENOUGH

Q: *We had an expensive traditional wedding for our daughter the first time around. Now she is divorced, and while we are happy she is remarrying, we are not in the same financial position to do anything elaborate. What do other parents do?*

Talk to your daughter about what her expectations should be. One large wedding per child is the formula, unless money is no object. Many couples who live independent lives plan their own wedding to suit their tastes and pocketbook and issue their own invitations.

Q: *Our daughter was married at eighteen and after a few unhappy years was divorced. She has met the type of person we hoped she would meet but they want a traditional wedding. How can we convince them that it is inappropriate for a mother of a six- and a nine-year-old?*

We are also not that comfortable about the children being members of the wedding party. Were we a different brand of human being when we were young, with all sorts of conflicting feelings about our parents and divorce? Are children of this generation so advanced that they can think and feel like adults?

Well, you will get a different idea of what is done from magazines than you will from books on wedding etiquette, which are generally more conservative.

A modern second-time bride, who wants more than the conservative, simple chapel ceremony and can afford a costlier do, chooses the almost traditional type of wedding and attire to suit her age. Her father does not "give her away," and the children can participate in the ceremony. Fashion shows ankle-length gowns in off-white and various pastel shades, with headgear from picture hats to tulle attached to simple headpieces.

You will be attending the wedding of a bride and bridegroom whose event is special to them. After all, few of us view marriage as a game. Weddings are an expensive pastime. For your daughter and her husband the wedding symbolizes their special day that no other time equals—even though that road has been traveled before.

Children are less insulated today than at any time in recent history; if anything, they have to deal with problems of development and possess knowledge that in the past would have been considered way beyond a child's years.

Today's approach to these sensitive situations is to make the children part of the process so that they do not feel left out—if they can handle it. Surely you would not want them to experience their mommy or daddy coming home with a new spouse saying: "Darlings, we're married! Isn't that fun?"

Children should know how all this comes about and see the ceremony as a solemn service. There are some children, however, who just cannot take an active part in the wedding. A great deal depends on the individual child.

CHILDREN

Q: *Is it advisable for children to attend the marriage ceremony of a parent?*

Yes, if they are old enough to understand what is going on and provided they have positive feelings about the event. They can even take part in the ceremony, but if they are young, make arrangements for them to be taken home before the reception.

If the child's natural parent has died, the youngster may have a sensitive moment, so it would be a good idea to have someone standing by who is close to the child.

SECRETIVE MOTHER

Q: *I am just turning thirty and, though Catholic, was married in my husband's church in my hometown. Immediately afterward my husband and I moved to another state. It was all a terrible mistake and soon we were divorced. Now I am remarrying; my future husband and I will have a Catholic ceremony in the city in which we live. The priest has recognized the dissolution of my first marriage so we are having a marriage celebration.*

I seldom visited home though my mother did come to see me. To my surprise, I have just found out that my mother has never told her friends or relatives in her small town that I was divorced. Now she objects to having floral decorations in church and is very uptight about my choice of dress. You name it and that's what I shouldn't do.

I don't understand your mother's objection to your wedding plans; you are not being married in your hometown, so she doesn't have to offer any explanations unless you invite people she knows to the wedding. Why she was so reticent about your divorce is puzzling. It would have been better if she had announced your change of status when it happened. Surely she must have realized that you would remarry sooner or later.

As for the type of ceremony, what you wear, and so forth, these are decisions that will be influenced by the church and should be discussed with the priest. He might look upon your marriage as a first, particularly since you exchanged vows within another denomination and the marriage was dissolved through the church.

Just try to reassure your mother that it will be a wedding in the best of taste and that you and your fiancé are starting out with the same religious and philosophical beliefs.

LADIES AND GENTLEMEN, I thought her mother's behavior only happened in 1940s B movies.

SELF-CONSCIOUS RELATIVES

Q: *My sister has been married before but her fiancé has not. My mother, our other sister, and I are feeling uncomfortable about the wedding they are planning—white wedding dress and attendants. It's to be a large affair. I've discussed the propriety of it all, but she says her future husband wants a celebration and that men have a right to a traditional wedding. What is done nowadays? Surely second-time brides don't wear white?*

White would be out of style for first-time brides if you are equating white and virginity, so forget that.

Some second-time brides are conservative and dress in a more subdued manner, especially when both bride and bridegroom have been married before. By the way, did your sister have a large wedding the first time?

Q: *Yes. Now, she has asked our youngest sister to be the matron of honor, to which I have no objection since I was her matron of honor the first time. But she wants me to be a bridesmaid. How would I look in a maid's gown? I'd much rather she asked my little girl to be in the bridal party than me.*

Look at some of the styles in the bride's magazines; they are smart and not like the little-girl outfits that used to be worn. In any case, could you refuse your sister?

Q: (Silence.) *Of course not, how could I say no!*

Who is paying for the wedding?

Q: *The couple are paying for everything themselves.*

If I were you I would suggest that she not wear an abundance of sequins and pearls on lace, a long train, or a veil. The bride-groom will greet an elegant bride at the altar and you and your family will have a wonderful celebration.

GRANDPARENTS, WIDOWS, AND CHILDREN

Divorce is not the only hurtful happening with which people have to contend. Widows and widowers with children, and the children themselves, whether young or adult, have to cope with a permanent separation not of their own choosing. Trying to build a new relationship and a new life, and getting others to accept the change, can be quite tough.

Q: *I am a widow with two young children and am planning to remarry. My late husband's parents have been close to me and the children. Do I invite them to the wedding? I did not expect to feel so awkward about it and I do not want to hurt them.*

First you must decide whether you can handle having your in-laws at the wedding. Then discuss your feelings with them. After all, not only have you been a loving daughter-in-law and they loving in-laws but you share the same bereavement—though on different levels. They may not resent, and may even be happy, that you are building a new life. However I would imagine it would be painful for your in-laws to be present to witness the process.

Much depends on the type of man you are marrying. This person will have a great influence on their grandchildren. If he has parents of his own, the children's grandparents may fear they will be superseded. They will need reassurance that their grand-children will still be part of their lives, and rightly so. They may have accepted their loss, but it is still a constant source of pain. Those children are not only a joy to them but represent a sense of continuity. It will not hurt the children to have more loving people around them, but it will hurt them to be alienated from their natural grandparents, causing another painful separation.

REMARRIAGE GUIDELINES

- No announcement should be made if one or the other is still married, however thrilled the couple are with each other.
- Being married for the second time means that the first wedding ceremony was legal in the eyes of the state. Elopement is considered a legal marriage and, of course, so is a civil ceremony.
- Being free to marry means that both have gone through the process of divorce and have legal papers from the state to prove it. If an annulment took place, meaning that it is as if the first marriage never occurred, legal papers still have to be produced. Both sides should show each other these documents.
- In addition to civil divorce, some religions require a religious divorce under their auspices in order to be married again within that denomination—the Roman Catholic and the Eastern Orthodox churches, for instance. This requires advice of clergy.
- Some religions do not permit remarriage while the ex-partner is still living. They may, however, sanction what is called a service of marriage after a civil ceremony.
- According to Jewish law, which is observed by all Orthodox and most Conservative congregations, a Jewish divorce, called a "get," is required. Gets are issued by certain rabbis who have the authority to grant them. Their decisions have to be within prescribed rabbinic law. But there is one part of the divorce law that women consider unfair. A woman cannot obtain a divorce on her own behalf without her husband's permission. He can withhold the divorce until he wishes to remarry, and only then is she free to marry. The wife does not even have to be present at the divorce proceedings. Many Conservative couples include along with the ketubah (the marriage contract) the provision that should

a civil divorce occur, a Jewish divorce can be petitioned for by either party.

- Widows and widowers generally wait at least a year to remarry. My observations tell me that most people are not fortunate enough nor are they ready to seek new companionship so soon after the loss of a spouse.

  When a widow or widower remarries, his or her deceased spouse's family should be notified by letter or telephone, whether or not the family lives in the area.

- A widow generally wears her wedding ring until she remarries. A divorcée has a choice, sometimes choosing to wear the ring on her right hand; if she has children she might want to wait until they are older and then transfer the ring to her other hand.

- Even if the marriage lasted only a short time, whether because of death or divorce, the wedding presents are not returned. (See Gifts, p. 72.)

- Presents for a second marriage from those who gave the first time are not obligatory but family and friends generally send gifts.

- It is still not in good taste to write "no gifts" on invitations, so if presents are not wanted, family and friends should spread the word. Or write "no gifts, please" on a separate slip of paper and include it in the envelope.

- Traditionally, a widow uses her deceased husband's name:
                          "Mrs. James Person Ode"
  Again traditionally, should she remarry, she would assume her new husband's name.

  Today's women are more attuned to the use of their given names and their husband's surname because that is how they are known in the business world:
                          "Mrs. or Ms. Sarah Ode"
  When she remarries, her choice of name should be discussed with her new husband.

- In times past, a divorced woman used a combination of her maiden and married names:
                          "Mrs. Manning Ode"
  Today Mrs. Ex could use the designation of Mrs. or Ms., with her given name, her maiden name if she wishes, and her ex-husband's name:

"Mrs. (or Ms.) Sarah Manning Ode or Mrs. Sarah Ode" Some women, when their children are grown, take back their maiden name and drop their ex's surname altogether.

• Traditionally, a woman who has been married before does not make a formal engagement announcement in the newspaper though some publications accept one of a forthcoming marriage.

• Family and friends are apprised of the news by letter or telephone.

• Traditionally, second-wedding ceremonies are small, with only close friends and family attending. Their invitations are telephoned or handwritten.

The reception, though, can be as festive as wished and many guests can be included.

If there is going to be a large reception afterward the invitations could be printed or engraved.

The bride's parents can issue the invitations if the bride is young.

A formal invitation to the ceremony reads:

> Mr. and Mrs. James Person Ode
> request the honour of your presence
> at the marriage
> of their daughter
> Jill Candace Hampenstance
> to
> Mr. William Jones Westings
> [etc.]

If there is to be a private ceremony and a large reception:

> Mr. and Mrs. James Person Ode
> request the pleasure of your company
> at the wedding reception of their daughter
> Jill Candace
> and
> Mr. William Jones Westings
> on Thursday, January first
> at half after two o'clock
> Calvert Hotel
> Baltimore, Maryland

Note that the bride's last name is not stated and the word "and" is substituted for "to" on the fifth line.

A mature couple issue their own formal wedding invitations:

The honour of your presence
is requested
at the marriage of
Mrs. Jill Ode Hampenstance
to
Mr. William Jones Westings
[etc.]

The rest of the wording is as for any wedding invitation.

Wording for an invitation to the reception only would start with the bridal couple's names:

Jill Ode Hampenstance
and
William Jones Westings
request the pleasure of your company
at their wedding reception
on Thursday, January first
at half after two
Calvert Hotel
Baltimore, Maryland
R.S.V.P.

Informal reception invitation by bridal couple:

Jill Ode Hampenstance
and
William Jones Westings
invite you to their wedding reception
on Thursday, January first
at two o'clock
Calvert Hotel
Baltimore, Maryland
Please respond
[Address or telephone optional]

Generally, the bride's home address is given so guests can respond. However, for a couple who have been married before and have separate residences, it is wise to enclose an "at home" card to indicate where they will be living after their marriage. At-home cards are small enough to fit comfortably in the envelope along with other enclosures.

If the bride is retaining the name that she has been using since her first marriage, or if she is assuming her original maiden name, this is an excellent way of notifying everyone:

Mr. and Mrs. William Jones Westings

or

Ms. Jill Candace Ode
and
Mr. William Jones Westings
will be at home
after the first of February
11111 Permanent Drive
Baltimore, Maryland zip code

- Traditionally, second-time brides do not wear white wedding dresses or veils. The conservative bride wears off-white of any length; a head covering is optional or at the discretion of the house of worship. The bridegroom's attire follows the formality of the bride's outfit, as does the attire of the attendant(s). The modern bride who has been married before wears something that looks like a toned-down bride's dress. Shades lean to off-white and pale pastel hues. All aspects of her outfit follow the same mood.
- Should the bride think herself too mature to be escorted, she follows her attendant to the altar where her bridegroom is awaiting her. But she can be escorted by her father, her son, any male relative, or a friend. An escort is a lady's prerogative.
- Generally there is no "giving away" ceremony unless the bride is young.
- Traditionally, the bride has an honor attendant and the bridegroom is served by a best man. However, if either of the couple has children, it is becoming customary to include them in the process in some way.
- The bridal couple have the same responsibilities to their

342

attendants, who should be given small presents as well as flowers for the ceremony.

- It is not customary to have bridal showers for the second-time bride. However, if the bride's intimate friends want to "shower" her, why not?
- Prewedding introduction parties, such as dinners, are wonderful ways of celebrating the couple's newfound happiness. And if there is no time before the wedding, feting the newlyweds is always fun.
- Parents are not obligated to pay for the wedding of a second-time bride. Those costs are assumed by the couple themselves.
- Wedding cakes are always a part of any wedding reception but should be tastefully decorated.
- Toasts and music are appropriate. Well-wishers are always welcome. Music enhances both the ceremony and the reception.
- Marriage announcements are mailed as soon after the event as possible and are issued by the couple themselves or by the bride's parents. These practical announcements can be engraved or printed and are an efficient way of communicating the couple's change of status to relatives, friends, acquaintances, and business associates who were not at the ceremony.

When issued by the bride's parents, these announcements note their daughter's given name, maiden name, and married name:

Mr. and Mrs. James Person Ode
have the honour of announcing
the marriage of their daugher
Jill Ode Hampenstance
to
Mr. William Jones Westings
Thursday, the first of January
One thousand nine hundred and eighty-seven
Baltimore, Maryland

The traditional announcement for a mature widow:

Mrs. Frederick Eldon Hampenstance
and
Mr. William Jones Westings
announce their marriage
on Thursday, the first of January
One thousand nine hundred and eighty-seven
in Baltimore, Maryland

A divorced woman is free to announce her own marriage and to use the name by which she is known:

Mrs. [or Ms.] Jill Ode Hampenstance
and

A less formal announcement would read:

Jill Ode Hampenstance
and
William Jones Westings
announce their marriage
on Thursday, January 1st, 1987
in Baltimore, Maryland

A newspaper item should be sent to the wedding desk at least ten days ahead of time to be considered for publication at the first available opportunity after the wedding. It can be as complete a story as wished, but the newspaper will edit to fit space restrictions. Some newspapers do not use the designations Mr., Mrs., or Ms., and don't be surprised if, within the story, references to either party are by surname only. Others insist on mentioning whether one or both have been married before or if spouses have passed away. There should be no objection to this, especially if there are children involved. Some people, however, do not wish to be reminded of the past and others feel it has nothing to do with what is happening now.

For release after January 1st

Jill Ode Hampenstance and William Jones Westings were married in Baltimore, Maryland, on Thursday, January 1, at the Calvert Hotel in the presence of close family members, including the bride's children, Cynthia and Joan Hampenstance, and the bridegroom's son, Jonathan Westings. The Rev. Holdings True was the officiating minister. The bride, whose parents are Mr. and Mrs. James Person Ode of Washington, D.C., is a financial consultant with Safe & Safe. Westings is the son of Mr. and Mrs. Sanford Westings of Syracuse, New York. He is vice president of the engineering consulting firm Engineering Design Corporation. Mr. and Mrs. Westings' previous marriages ended in divorce. The couple resides in Baltimore.

Divorce

SENSITIVITY, INC.

Increasingly I receive questions on divorce. The children of the sixties, whose parents made divorce so popular, are now being married themselves. Wistfully, the voice of the bride agrees with me that maybe hers is not such an unusual situation—divorced parents are commonplace. But for one day in her life she would like to close her eyes and float through the wedding day as if nothing had happened. Yes, even though her parents have been divorced for years.

Divorce is a family affair that, however old they are, constantly touches the offspring—especially if there are bitter feelings on one side or both.

The difference between a holiday and a wedding is that Thanksgiving can be spent with one parent and Christmas with the other. But from the time of the engagement to the day of the wedding there are decisions to be made that involve both the bride's and the bridegroom's family. The bridal couple want both sets of parents to attend and participate according to custom.

If a divorced couple could cooperate to make events up to and including the wedding day as happy as can be for their child, this segment could just deal with questions such as who sits where in church and who sponsors the wedding. But how can two people who cannot look each other in the face overcome their animosity long enough to support their child?

Sometimes the problems that surface do not come out of old bitterness but of wedding protocol. The father may have remarried and would like his wife at his side; his former wife, the mother of his child, wants to take her "rightful" place in the proceedings.

Recently I received a telephone call from a woman whose daughter was being married. Her ex-husband had sent word through their daughter that neither of their names would appear on the wedding invitations. They would be worded:

> The honour
> of your presence is requested
> at the marriage of
> Miss Jill Candace Ode
> and
> Mr. Frederick Eldon Hampenstance

Mr. Ode told his daughter that since he was paying for the entire wedding his decision was firm. He did, however, want his daughter to let him know how his ex-wife felt about it.

Mrs. Ex was angry. She felt that wording the invitation that way would make it seem as if the bride's parents were not interested and that she had no one to sponsor her. According to custom the mother's name is generally on the wedding invitations as sponsor no matter who is paying for the wedding. That used to be true, I told her, but today it is a rule only as firm as those who are willing to abide by it.

I suggested that her ex-husband's name could be on the first line and hers below. Mrs. Ex said he simply would not hear of it. Her daughter, whose father has been married to his current wife for seven years, said that she did not want to be caught between her parents—which I interpreted to mean that she had no wish to do battle with her father. If he wants it that way, she told her mother, so be it, especially since he is footing the bill. Mrs. Ex could not possibly take on wedding expenses.

I offered a compromise. Why not suggest that he and his wife be first sponsors on the top line, with Mrs. Ex's name listed underneath? Never! was her prompt reply.

It might seem that Mr. Ode, as master of the purse strings, could issue edicts to his ex from his exalted financial position. However, it was more than likely that he was having a problem with his current wife about the wedding. It is sometimes difficult for the second wife to take a backseat when her husband's child marries. This is a part of his past she does not share. Besides, she might object to a joint invitation with only his and his ex-wife's names.

Mr. Ode also knows that Mrs. Ex would not agree to his wife's name being included on the invitations, so, being a man used to taking command, he issues his decision: no one's name, apart from the young couple's, will appear at all. Since the bride has been living on her own, the R.S.V.P.s would go to her home anyway.

I can't say that I disagree with Mr. Ex's decision. When the principals stand on their principles and no one will budge, the only thing to do is to say that this is the way it will be done.

SENSITIVITY INC.?

You better believe it! From the start of the engagement, how does one avoid the anxiety that's bound to occur, whether between divorced parents of the bridal couple or between the couple themselves?

One mother told me that she had married her current husband twenty years before, after her divorce from the father of her child. He has been as much a father to her daughter as any natural father could be, so much so that it was to him Jennifer's suitor had spoken about marriage rather than to her natural father. Her natural father has been a part of her life and has contributed some financial support, but by no means a major portion. Now, with wedding plans coming up, how will the decisions affect the feelings of the girl's father and stepfather? The mother of the bride is now besieged with questions that she doesn't want to discuss with her family until she has worked them out in her mind. Since there haven't been any unpleasant feelings so far, is it possible to avoid them now? My answer to that is that even when there are few complications, hurt feelings here and there are more than likely. How these emotions are controlled depends on the maturity of the participants.

The logistics of future in-laws meeting future in-laws presented no problem, so the first puzzle was the wording of the newspaper announcement, the first public statement involving the divorced couple. If the mother and her current husband announce the wedding alone, which she would prefer, mainly because it seems a neater statement and they are hosting the event, will the bride's father be hurt even if he is mentioned in the article? (He shouldn't be, since this is an accepted practice.) Or is it proper for the mother, her husband, her ex, and his wife to announce the wedding jointly? Suppose she, as Mrs. John Doe, and the bride's father, Mr. James Somebody, make the announcement jointly, without mention of her current husband or his current wife?

At one time, whether the bride's mother was hosting the event or not, it was deemed a chivalrous act to allow her to announce for her daughter and even to head the invitation, with or without her current husband. Now both sets of parents can announce the engagement in the newspaper if this is agreeable to all. The bride's mother and husband's name are listed first:

Mr. and Mrs. James Standish of Chevy Chase, Md., and Mr. and Mrs. John Doe of Bethesda, Md., announce the engagement of Mary Jane Doe to etc. . . .

Who expects to escort the bride? Her daughter is musing about the possibility of both her father and stepfather escorting her to the altar. Who gives the bride in marriage? These two questions are particularly delicate ones, and have been the subject of discussion over the years between the bride's mother and her stepfather when they dreamed about the children growing up and marrying . . .

There is no reason why the bride's natural father, as long as he has been part of her life, should be deprived of the honor of escorting his daughter down the aisle. The bride's mother and stepfather can give her in marriage. (This suggestion can easily be worked out when there is a "giving away," but not all denominations include this rite in the ceremony.) Her stepfather must be prepared to take a slightly lesser role in the ceremony, but if he feels secure in his place within his family he will be able to handle the disappointment with grace. The only time it would be justified for the stepfather to escort the bride would be if her father had been a distant figure in her life; how could her father turn up now expecting to be other than an invited guest?

The only way I can envision the bride's father and stepfather taking an equal part in the ceremony would be if her father escorted her and stepped back just before they reached the bridegroom, so that her stepfather could take his place at her side and hand her to her future husband. Since this suggestion is a variation in the ceremony it is essential to check with the officiant.

One young lady was absolutely panic-strucken at the thought of choosing between her father and stepfather. She wasn't keen on being escorted by both. Her fiancé came up with the solution: her natural father should escort her, while the bridegroom would ask her stepfather to be his best man. This proposal was feasible because he had no brothers. Before approaching his bride he had discussed the problem with his father, who felt it the only suggestion that would bring her stepfather into the wedding party. Lucky girl to have fallen in love with such a sensitive and understanding person who, apparently, had a fine example in his father.

Since the bride's mother and stepfather are hosting and sponsoring the event, they should be in the receiving line. Because receiving-line duties are optional for fathers, her father should not expect to be part of the line, unless he is invited, since neither he nor his wife belongs there. His wife should expect to be present as a highly respected guest and not demand any special treatment. Most important, these proposals should be made in a way that invite a positive response.

Sensitivity is also shown by many a stepmother. I have had telephone queries from women who, as hostesses at their stepdaughters' weddings, plan them from beginning to end taking extreme care not to appear as if they are usurping the bride's natural mother.

WHEN BITTERNESS REIGNS

BRIDE'S STEPMOTHER HOGS PHOTO SESSION should be the headline at one wedding.

Here is a true story: the father of the bride and his wife are paying for everything; the mother of the bride is lucky she's invited. During the picture-taking, the photographer wanted to take one of the bride's mother with the bride and bridegroom in the center and the bride's father on the other side of them. The photographer had taken similar ones with the bridegroom's parents on either side of the bridal couple and others with the stepmother, the bridal couple, and the bride's father. Mrs. Stepmother insisted she be part of the photograph in which the bride's mother appeared. When the photographer tried to explain that the bride should have a shot with her natural parents, Mrs. Stepmother would not hear of it. After all, she reasoned out loud, it was her money that was paying for the service. The bride's mother is still grieving over that one.

If you iz, then I ain't. But if you ain't, then I iz, goes the little ditty. She says to her children: if he brings his new wife then I will not attend Thanksgiving dinner (your wedding, the baby's christening, or whatever the occasion may be).

Mrs. Newlywed, whose daughter was being married, wanted to know if she should include her husband in the wedding invitations or the newspaper announcement, since they had only been married for a year and a half. I thought it should be optional, since they had only been married a short time and he had not been an influence in her daughter's life for long. It also depended on the quality of the relationship built up during that period.

Do you think he will be hurt if you do not include him? I inquired.

Not at all, was the response. On the contrary, he refuses to attend her daughter's wedding. The reason he gave was that he did not want to meet her ex-husband. Everyone, including the bride, would have liked him to come, but he simply will not change his mind. (And that, I said to myself, is the reason for the telephone call!)

Upon further discussion it emerged that her husband's ex-wife, who had not remarried, refused to come to any function if his current wife was expected. His son was getting married in a couple of months and Mr. Newlywed expected his current wife to refrain from attending.

LADIES AND GENTLEMEN, again I did not comment on what I really thought was a classic piece of manipulation. This is a way some people have learned to operate.

Instead of coming directly to the point with his second wife about the problem his son was having with his mother, the stepfather chose a roundabout way of solving a dilemma. He was denying himself the pleasure of going to his stepdaughter's wedding because his wife would not be welcome at his son's wedding.

PENDING DIVORCE

Q: *My only daughter is getting married and I am determined she will have an elegant formal wedding. However, my wife and I are in the midst of a divorce. It may be final by the time the wedding invitations are mailed. However, suppose it is not? I am in a quandary as to how to word the invitation.*

Since you cannot be sure of the timing of your divorce or of the complications that might suddenly pop up, you have a few choices. The first suggestion below is possibly the best, since it avoids any mention of divided parents at this unsettling time:

The parents of
Miss Jill Candace Ode
request the honour of your presence
at her marriage
to
Mr. Frederick Eldon Hampenstance

or

The honour of your presence
is requested
at the marriage of
Miss Jill Candace Ode
to
Mr. Frederick Eldon Hampenstance
[etc.]

Under ideal circumstances, divorced parents can issue a joint invitation. It is customary for the mother's name to appear first:

Mrs. Sarah Manning Ode

or

Mrs. Sarah Ode
and
Mr. James Person Ode
request the honour of your presence
at the marriage of their daughter
[etc.]

If both parents have remarried and are sharing the expenses, then the invitation can be a joint one:

Mr. and Mrs. George Steadfast
and
Mr. and Mrs. James Person Ode
request the honour of your presence
at the marriage of
Miss Jill Candace Ode
to
Mr. Frederick Eldon Hampenstance
[etc.]

Should only the bride's divorced mother issue the invitation:

Mrs. Sarah Manning Ode

or

Mrs. Sarah Ode
requests the honour of your presence
at the marriage of her daughter
[etc.]

Q: *I have always dreamed of the day my parents would escort me down the aisle and stand with me under the canopy for the traditional Jewish wedding ceremony. My future husband would like his parents to do the same but I feel it would be awkward, since his parents have been divorced for the last ten years. His*

*mother lives in another state; his father recently married a woman
he has been dating for the last five years, and whom my fiancé
likes. I've spoken to his mother by telephone and I detect a bit
of resentment. Keeping in mind my opening sentence, what are
our alternatives?*

Your fiancé's parents could walk on either side of him if they
could both do so willingly. But if they have not seen each other
for years and his father has remarried, I do not think anyone will
feel comfortable.

An alternative would be for the bridegroom to walk down
the aisle, or come from the side of the synagogue, with his best
man. The sequence of events would go like this: after the company
has been seated, the bridegroom's father and his wife walk down
the aisle and sit in the second or third row; his mother is escorted
by a close male relative or by the head usher to be seated in the
first row. Then the bridal procession begins.

After the bride has been escorted by her parents they take
their places under the huppah; the bridegroom's mother walks
from the first row to stand under the canopy to the right of the
best man, with the bridegroom's father on the left.

BITTER AND HOLDING

How could a couple in the throes of a divorce agree on plans
for their daughter's wedding when the only thing that could be
guaranteed was disharmony? So much so that the bridegroom's
family stepped in to take charge of the entire event, paying for
everything. Though the bridegroom told his mother that he didn't
expect his parents to undertake the expense, he was assured that
just because he was a male child didn't mean that he and his
bride should be denied a wedding. The heartbroken bride could
not understand her parents' inability to put aside their venom
for the duration. As for the bridegroom's parents, they wished
only for the bride and their son to have a special wedding day.

The bridegroom's mother expressed concern that if her future
daughter-in-law's parents were so embattled that they could not
take some joy in their daughter's happiness at finding someone
she wanted to marry, would they behave themselves at the wed-

ding, whatever the arrangements were? So, without worrying about who was to pay for what, his parents and the bridal couple went about the business of making a wedding day whose memory the couple would cherish.

There were get-acquainted meetings at the invitation of the bridegroom's family in their home. The first was with the bride's father. Her father stated frankly that he couldn't afford the wedding because the divorce had been expensive. However, he would try to help in other ways. At the subsequent meeting with the bride's mother she told them without any preamble that she would come to the wedding as a guest and that was all. Not that the bridegroom's family had asked for anything.

The main thing, decided the bridegroom's mother, was to see that the bride's parents—and the two grandmothers—were kept apart throughout the affair. Meanwhile the bride extracted a promise from both parents that they would not cause any embarrassment during the celebrations. If this promise could not be obtained it had been agreed that one parent would attend the ceremony and the other the reception.

Meanwhile, Mrs. Hostess spoke to the minister and warned the photographer and the bandleader/master of ceremonies of the serious tension between the bride's parents.

At the *rehearsal dinner*, the bridal couple was seated in the middle of one side of a long rectangular table, between the bridegroom's parents. To the right of the bridegroom's father sat the bride's mother and the maternal grandmother; to the left of his mother were the bride's father, his wife, and the bride's paternal grandmother. With such an arrangement the divorced couple did not actually have to face one another. Attendants and other guests were seated as was convenient.

At the *ceremony*, the father of the bride escorted his daughter in and then sat in the third pew; her mother sat in the first.

The *receiving line* was dispensed with. After the ceremony, the guests went to the reception room at the country club where refreshments were served accompanied by live music. Meanwhile, the bridal party took photographs in an area of the dining room. The photographer, aware of the strain, had been given a list of exactly what photographs were to be taken and with whom. That made sure that the divorced parents did not have to stand together, though enough shots were taken to satisfy everyone. Of course, there were no shots of the bridal couple with the bride's natural parents, as is customary when relationships are amicable.

For the *dinner and dancing*, the bridal party vacated the dining room while the guests were seated. Music played and the bride and bridegroom walked down an arch formed by their attendants with upraised arms, maids on one side, groomsmen on the other.

As arranged with the bandleader, who was also aware of the estrangement, there was no announcement of the traditional first dance. The bridal couple, to the welcoming applause of the entire company, moved through the arch of attendants onto the dance floor to open the festivities and have their first dance together as husband and wife. The father of the bride cut in, the bride's brother danced with his mother; the bridegroom's father danced with the bride's mother; the bride's father with the bridegroom's mother, and the bridegroom with his mother-in-law. It was all very natural and no awkwardness was apparent.

At dinner it was arranged that the bridegroom's parents, his grandparents, and the bride's father and her paternal grandparents would sit at one table. Her mother was at another table with members of her own family.

During dinner the bride and bridegroom went from table to table greeting each guest to make up for the lack of a receiving line. A toast was offered by the best man just before the cake cutting.

I understand that the divorce settlement and time have put the events into perspective and her father is now ready to assume some of the wedding expenses.

GETTING-EVEN TIME?

People call a newspaper asking all types of questions. What time is it in Timbuktu? I have an appointment in Samarra, shall I take an umbrella? What shall I do? My cat is caught in the mousetrap. So you can imagine the sorts of questions that come to the Bridal Desk, both from those who merely wish to know the correct order of things or the suitability of clothing and from those who have serious problems.

There are times when I can see clearly that what the inquirer

wants to know is how to use an important occasion to get even—
sometimes over a situation that has nothing to do with the celebration, the people hosting the event, those being honored, or
those invited. This is done without regard for the innocent. Some
people live by the adage "Don't get mad, get even," and if others
are hurt because they happen to be there, then so be it.

Vindictiveness sometimes waits years to pounce. It looks for
a time when it really counts, when it really hurts. Some use a
wedding, an anniversary, even funerals.

Q: *My father, who has now remarried, and my mother had
been separated for a few years before their divorce five years ago.
He is paying for the food at the reception and the wedding cake.
Mother simply cannot afford to participate in these expenses. My
fiancé and I are paying for everything else: church, liquor, photographs, music, and all the sundry items.*

*The receiving line is going to be in the church right after the
ceremony and not at the reception.*

*Father says that since he is paying for the wedding reception,
he has the right to insist that he and his wife, and not my mother,
sit in the first pew, and that she also should not be in the receiving
line. I am not sure how to handle the situation.*

First you must find out what is the accustomed practice. There
are wedding books in the library with guidelines on dealing with
divorced parents. Then try to approach your father on that level.
He may see how awkward his demands are.

Right now, I can tell you that it is the mother of the bride
who sits in the first row with members of her family. She is also
seated last, the signal to everyone that the ceremony is to begin.
Whether or not your father is paying for the reception, it is the
bride's father, after he has escorted his daughter to the altar, who
sits with his current wife in the third row. For your father to
insist otherwise puts everyone in a difficult position. He creates
the same impression by objecting to your mother's standing in a
receiving line that will take place in the house of worship after
the ceremony. If, however, the receiving line takes place at the
reception, he and his wife, as host and hostess, stand in the
receiving line; your mother is a guest at those festivities. Should
your father feel somewhat gentlemanly, he could invite the bride's

mother to stand in the line also, though not at his current wife's side.

Technically speaking, your father is not footing the tab for the whole reception, since you and your fiancé are paying for the music and liquor.

DIVORCED TILL DEATH DO US PART

LADIES AND GENTLEMEN, the first rule to remember is that the bride's natural parents play special roles in the marrying of their daughter. Their union might be dissolved but the child who issued from that marriage is not divorced from either parent. For one side to try to exclude the other is cruel.

I do not know the young lady's father, so she must decide whether he will withhold the support he has offered if she insists on objecting to the stand he is taking. Nor do I know if her nature is such that she can take a strong position, or whether it is feasible at this time. It depends on the arrangements with caterers and other services who require deposits; she may not be able to change her plans to suit her purse. As I have said many times before: advice is only as good as the receiver's ability to take it, and, what is more, only that person knows the full story.

Fathers are not the only culprits in the power game by any means. One young lady who is contemplating marriage mentioned it casually to her mother. The date has not yet been set and neither she nor her boyfriend is really sure they want to marry, but from that chance remark has sprung a well of bitterness. Her parents were divorced many years ago, when she was two, and her mother has been remarried for fourteen years. Her father has been part of her life and has contributed to her support. She has on occasion gone to live with him and his wife for months at a time when things weren't "going well" at home, and is employed by him in his thriving business.

"I won't have your father at the wedding," flings her acrimonious mother. "If he comes then he cannot be part of the ceremony!" The conversation continues along those lines.

They finally all decide that if the couple marry, it will be in a private ceremony. One hopes that her father will be present. If things seem too unpleasant for him, he and his wife will have a separate reception honoring the bridal couple for his side of the family and friends.

LADIES AND GENTLEMEN, please don't suppose that all severed relationships have such upsetting results. Many divorced couples, whether remarried or not, are able to come together at functions to celebrate family occasions. They participate freely and without trepidation or resentment, and do not feel a sense of estrangement at the wedding. Gracious stepmothers and even-tempered divorced parents do not titillate our sense of curiosity.

A friend of mine, who had been remarried for two years when her daughter decided to take the same path, was most anxious to have things go smoothly for the bridal couple. Though she and her husband were sponsoring the wedding entirely, her ex-husband and his wife were included in the proceedings from beginning to end. In-laws and ex-laws came together to celebrate the marriage; so much so, that during the toast to the bridal couple the father of the bride complimented his ex-wife and her husband.

. . . And so, ladies and gentlemen, the questions keep coming in; they are never quite the same as before, though the subject might be. Some are surprisingly different. It is an interesting world.

Index